CALIBAN'S SHORE

ALSO BY STEPHEN TAYLOR

The Mighty Nimrod
A Life of Frederick Courteney Selous

Shaka's Children
A History of the Zulu People

Livingstone's Tribe
A Journey from Zanzibar to the Cape

CALIBAN'S SHORE

The Wreck of the Grosvenor *and the Strange Fate of Her Survivors*

Stephen Taylor

W. W. Norton & Company
New York London

First American Edition 2004

Originally published in England under the title
The Caliban Shore: The Fate of the Grosvenor Castaways

Printed in the United States of America

Manufactuing by the Maple-Vail Book Manufacturing Group
Production manager: Anna Oler

ISBN 0-393-05805-8

W. W. Norton & Company, Inc.
500 Fifth Avenue, New York, N.Y. 10110
www.wwnorton.com

W. W. Norton & Company Ltd.
Castle House, 75/76 Wells Street, London W1T 3QT

1 2 3 4 5 6 7 8 9 0

CONTENTS

THREE

For Kikki and Princess Tree, who came along
And Tom, who yet again kept me on the straight and narrow

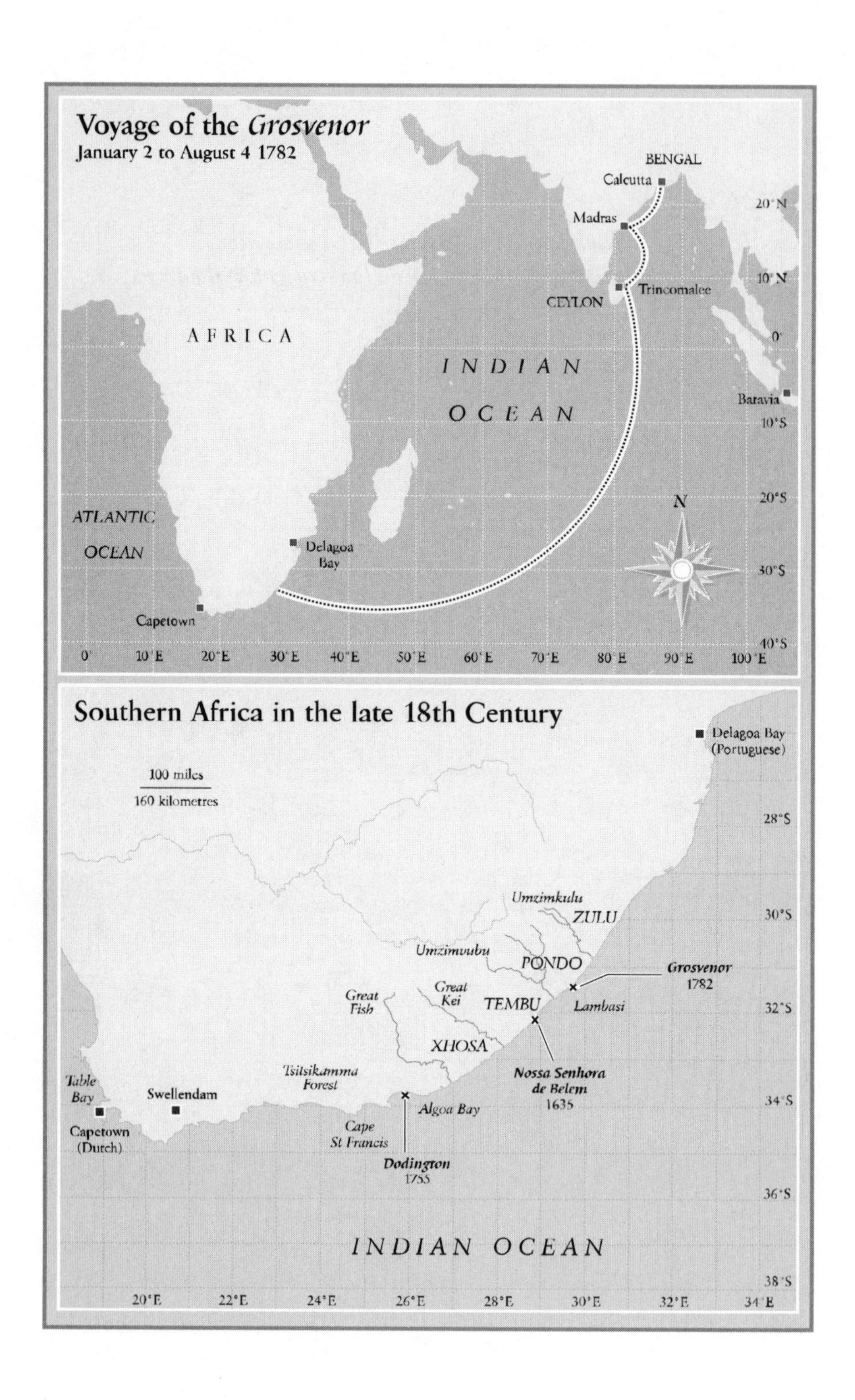

Voyage of the *Grosvenor*
January 2 to August 4 1782
BENGAL
Calcutta
Madras
Trincomalee
CEYLON
AFRICA
INDIAN
OCEAN
Batavia
ATLANTIC
OCEAN
Delagoa Bay
Capetown
N
20°N
10°N
0°
10°S
20°S
30°S
40°S
0°
10°E
20°E
30°E
40°E
50°E
60°E
70°E
80°E
90°E
100°E
Southern Africa in the late 18th Century
Delagoa Bay (Portuguese)
100 miles
160 kilometres
Umzimkulu
ZULU
Umzimvubu
PONDO
Grosvenor 1782
Lambasi
Great Fish
Great Kei
TEMBU
XHOSA
Nossa Senhora de Belem 1635
Tsitsikamma Forest
Table Bay
Swellendam
Capetown (Dutch)
Algoa Bay
Cape St Francis
Dodington 1755
INDIAN OCEAN
28°S
30°S
32°S
34°S
36°S
38°S
20°E
22°E
24°E
26°E
28°E
30°E
32°E
34°E

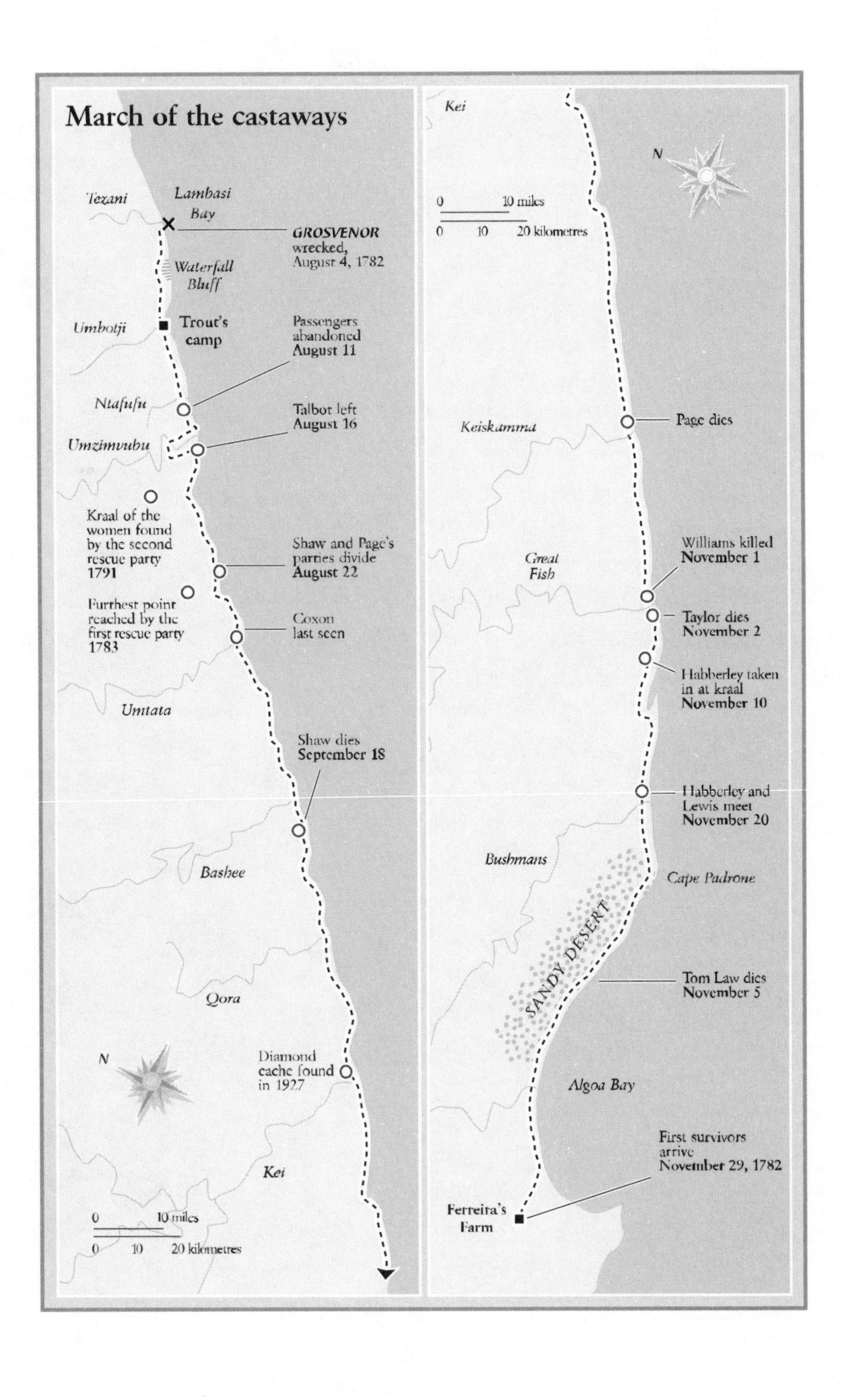
March of the castaways
Tezani
Lambasi Bay
GROSVENOR wrecked, August 4, 1782
Waterfall Bluff
Umbotji
Trout's camp
Passengers abandoned August 11
Ntafufu
Talbot left August 16
Umzimvubu
Kraal of the women found by the second rescue party 1791
Shaw and Page's parties divide August 22
Furthest point reached by the first rescue party 1783
Coxon last seen
Umtata
Shaw dies September 18
Bashee
Qora
N
Diamond cache found in 1927
Kei
0 10 miles
0 10 20 kilometres
Kei
N
0 10 miles
0 10 20 kilometres
Keiskamma
Page dies
Great Fish
Williams killed November 1
Taylor dies November 2
Habberley taken in at kraal November 10
Habberley and Lewis meet November 20
Bushmans
Cape Padrone
SANDY DESERT
Tom Law dies November 5
Algoa Bay
First survivors arrive November 29, 1782
Ferreira's Farm

PROLOGUE

The ship doubled the Cape of Good Hope on a cool July day with a brisk following wind and a film of moisture in the air that shrouded the first sight of land for seven weeks. She was an East Indiaman of 499 tons, outward bound for Madras on what promised to be the smoothest of her three voyages so far. Evan Jones, the chief mate, was moved to remark on 'a very pleasant passage' across the Atlantic and few others on board could recall so calm or swift a crossing. Only seventy-five days had passed since the Indiaman's departure from the Downs, the protected anchorage off the Kent coast, early in the spring of 1755, and she had long since left an accompanying squadron in her wake.

The weather turned almost as soon as they rounded the Cape. Jones described it as 'dirty and squally with the Wind from SSW to SSE and a very large sea' and orders were given to haul in the staysails and shorten the main in order to reduce the amount of canvas exposed to a constant gale. Captain James Samson held his course due east for the next twenty-four hours. Like any experienced skipper of an East India Company merchant vessel, he was keenly aware that he had just entered the most dangerous part of the voyage, even if he understood no better than anyone else what caused the freak conditions that made south-east Africa notorious among mariners. When, the following day, Cape Agulhas was sighted, he set a new course East-North-East. The ship was now driving directly

Indiaman in a storm between Madagascar and the Cape of Good Hope, from an etching of 1804 into the warm-water current, also called the Agulhas, which pulses invisibly along the coast.

Even with the staysails stowed and the fore topsails and the main closely reefed, the Indiaman was running along at between six and seven knots. Over the next eight days she churned headlong through squalls, until on 16 July the gale strengthened further and Captain Samson was obliged to order that still more canvas be hauled in. At noon that day they had reached a longitude of 13° 45′E of Cape Agulhas – or so Jones, the chief mate, reckoned.

At a quarter to one the following morning, a forward lookout shouted down from his post, 'Breakers ahead and to leeward!' Jones described what followed: 'The helm was immediately put a-lee; but before she came quite Head to Wind, she struck lightly and then stronger.'

William Webb, the third mate, was asleep in his cot when the first shudder went through the ship. Instantly awake, he clambered down, to feel a series of vibrations under his feet, followed by a jolt that tossed him from one end of the tiny cabin to the other. Further shocks marked his scrambled passage up the companion ladder.

By the time Webb reached the quarterdeck, all three masts were gone. In their place a mountain of canvas and rigging billowed across the deck. Water swirled at his feet and he watched in a dreamlike state as a wave broke over the side, catching up a dozen or so men in its midst and carrying them off into the darkness. Within minutes of impact with whatever she had struck, a ship as solid as the forest of oaks from which she was hewn had started to break up.

So brutally brief was the crisis that not one of the hands had an opportunity to break into the liquor barrels and drink himself into the merciful oblivion sought by seamen facing certain death. Most of them died below decks or in the cataclysmic break-up of the hull. So did the great majority of a company of Royal Artillery troops who were sharing the crew's quarters.

What saved some of the ship's officers was the location of their cabins in the stern. Jones, the chief mate, emerged from his quarters around the same time as Webb, to find the Indiaman starting to disintegrate. 'By the time I got upon deck it was falling in and other parts driving to peices [*sic*] faster than any person can imagine,' he wrote. Somewhere in the inkiness he found Captain Samson and 'asked him where he thought we were, for

I own the mainland never enter'd into my head. Nor the captain's neither, for the answer he made me was it must be some rock in the sea which never was laid down.'

Jones estimated that at one point about thirty men were clustered on the quarterdeck, but each time a wave broke it carried more of them away into eternity on a tide of foam. Samson bade him farewell, 'and said we should meet in the Next World, which words were scarce out his of his mouth, when I was wash'd off'.

Webb, meanwhile, had been clawing his way up towards the larboard side of the quarterdeck, crazily angled above the water, where he found Samson alone. The captain had a dazed appearance and managed to get out little more than that they were doomed, before the sea crashed over them. The last Webb ever saw of him was as he disappeared over the side.

No longer certain even of what portion of the ship he was on, the third mate was awaiting the inevitable when out of the darkness a voice cried, 'Land!' At first, looking over the breakers, he took the black mass ahead to be colossal seas, and had no chance to reconsider before a wave crashed over him and he lost consciousness. He awoke at daylight, numb with cold, his right arm broken, and impaled by the shoulder on a nail protruding from a beam. By pure good fortune he had been left face up in shallow water and, having thus escaped drowning, was able to disengage his shoulder from the wreckage and crawl to shore.

Out of the 270 souls who had been on the *Dodington* – for that was the East Indiaman's name – Webb was one of just twenty-three to have been spared. Others included Jones, who had also been deposited on the shore, John Collett, the second mate (but not his wife, whose body was found washed up nearby), Richard Topping, the carpenter, ten sailors and three out of the ninety-five soldiers. They found themselves stranded on an uninhabited island, barely six miles from the mainland at the eastern end of Algoa Bay. How this band of castaways endured on Bird Island for seven months while they fashioned from the wreckage a sloop that they called the *Happy Deliverance* – their adventures, quarrels and feuds, and their eventual voyage in this makeshift vessel to Madagascar and safety – is itself a great survival story.

The *Dodington* disaster echoed from London to Bengal. As well as troops for Robert Clive's latest campaign to drive the French from India, the East Indiaman had been carrying military hardware and bullion; Clive, indeed, had intended taking passage on the *Dodington* himself and had only switched to the *Stretham* at the last moment. Navigational experts were summoned to consider 'this shocking circumstance' and how to avoid any repetition of it. Already there was a strong suspicion that British maps, based on the Portuguese *Roteiro* chart drawn up almost two centuries earlier, were lethally flawed in showing the coast of south-east Africa some degrees west of its true position. Fundamentally, however, the wreck was found to have been a consequence of the 'very erroneous' reckoning of the ship's position. Whereas the chief mate Jones had calculated it as 13° 45´E of Cape Agulhas, later observations had found it to be no more than 7°E. The *Dodington* had been set on too northerly a course too early.

In 1780, Dunn's *Directory for the East Indies*, a handbook for the East India Company's mariners, drew attention to these dangers with an admonitory passage that recalled the *Dodington*'s fate: 'The loss of such a number of lives will make the skilful navigator shudder, and make him rack his invention to point out the cause of such misfortunes and contrive how to avoid the like accidents for the future,' it read. 'This unfortunate ship should be a caution for all navigators to be very cautious not to haul to the northward too soon.'

Two years after this warning, another East Indiaman was approaching south-east Africa, and she too was off course.

PART ONE

1

'A MAN OF HIGH CHARACTER'

Murshidabad, Bengal, 10 November 1781

The manner of William Hosea's departure would have befitted the Nawab himself. For eight years Hosea had been master of Bengal's richest district and all of Murshidabad was gathered on the banks of the Cossimbuzzar River for the farewell. A fleet of two-masted pinnaces and barges was drawn up to transport the viceregal party to Calcutta. Nothing about the scene indicated that he was, in fact, slinking away.

Hosea cast a last look back at his former domain: the Residence, a palace of princely magnificence fronting the river and enclosed by palms and mango groves; and the capital, stretching for five miles along the Cossimbuzzar and containing more wealthy men than London. Perhaps he paused for reflection. Here, at least, was proof of his achievements. Like Clive, he had risen from the humblest position in the East India Company's service to riches and power. Like Hastings, he had been Resident at the Durbar, the puppet-master entrusted with handling the Nawab of Bengal. Whatever lay ahead – dismissal, disgrace, even ruin – nothing could take that from him.

His wife Mary, heavily pregnant, had to be assisted down to the river and into one of the waiting vessels by a retinue of *ayahs*. The banks were lined by representatives of the Nawab in their finery, the traders and merchants who were already mourning the departure of their wealthiest customers, an army of well over a hundred servants equally lamenting their loss, and townspeople drawn to the spectacle by simple curiosity.

Street scene in Calcutta, after Thomas Daniell, 1786

Hosea had taken his leave of the Nawab with due formality. While many Englishmen were attracted by the subtlety and gracious manners of Bengal aristocrats, Hosea had never had much time for them: the Phowzdar, the Roy Royan, the Talookdars – over the years all had been treated with a brusqueness that betrayed his dislike of Orientals. Even Hosea had to acknowledge, however, that the Nawab of Bengal was a figure entitled to a certain respect. It helped that the incumbent, Mobaruk ud-Dowla, was a shadow of his formidable ancestors and accepted Hosea's authority as tax collector with placid resignation. Even their most delicate financial dealings had been untroublesome, being conducted on Hosea's rare visits to the palace as they lay on rugs, surrounded by sweetmeats, or in the gardens on quiet walks among the menagerie.

At length all was ready. The little fleet of schooner-rigged pinnaces and lumbering budgerows, bearing innumerable trunks along with tables, chests, bureaux and chairs piled atop one another, nudged out into the Cossimbuzzar for the 110-mile journey downriver to Calcutta, seat of the Company's presidency.

Despite the fanfare, William Hosea was not so much taking his leave as going like a thief in the night. None of his superiors knew of his plans, not even his benefactor and patron, Warren Hastings. It was only the previous night that Hosea had taken his closest friends into his confidence. In a letter sent ahead to Calcutta, he told Sir Robert and Lady Chambers that he and Mary would sail for England as soon as she had been delivered of the child. Lady Chambers was asked to make arrangements for a doctor to attend Mary and servants to await their arrival. The need for discretion was paramount. 'Pray keep our going home a secret for the present,' Hosea urged.

He added: 'This will be the last act of friendship you will have to perform for us in this part of the world. Our passage is taken on board the *Grosvenor*.'

Calcutta revealed itself with startling suddenness. For days the flotilla had twisted and bobbed around the interminable bends of first the Cossimbuzzar then the Hooghly, beside banks piled high with the intense green turmoil of tropical Bengal, past the site of Plassy, where Clive had won control of India. Then, around yet another bend, it leapt out of the jungle – the 'City of Palaces', the greatest metropolis in the East.

Hosea considered the splendour before him with mixed feelings. A French visitor had called it the finest colony in the world, and of that there could be little doubt. From their mooring near Chandpal Ghat on the east bank Hosea observed Fort William rising heavily ahead, a vast ramparted octagon gleaming white in the sun of the cool season. North of it, along the esplanade fronting the river, ran a line of stately neoclassical buildings from which the civic and military affairs of the East India Company were conducted. Behind this elegant façade lay the great maidan, a grassy parade ground almost two miles long and a mile deep, where Calcutta society descended by carriage in the evening for the ritual known as 'airing'. Morning dew had left the maidan as fresh and green as a garden in Surrey. Beyond it stood Chowringhee, a broad avenue teeming with carriages and palanquins and lined with the villas and mansions of the Company gentry, the *burra sahibs*.

Amid this grandeur William Hosea had landed from England, a penniless and lonely boy, seventeen years earlier; but if Calcutta represented the fulfilment of his dreams, it recalled also a darker episode in his career. The truth is, he had never felt comfortable with the place or its fashionable society, and he was uneasy again now.

The Hoseas and their eighteen-month-old daughter Frances were borne by Calcutta's most genteel model of conveyance, the palanquin – a luxuriously cushioned bed carried on bamboo poles by bearers – to Old Post Office Street and the home of Sir Robert Chambers, a rambling palace in the classic style. A judge of the Supreme Court and Hosea's confidant, Sir Robert was one of Bengal's grandest figures. In London his friends at the Literary Club included Oliver Goldsmith, Edmund Burke and Dr Johnson. As Boswell makes clear, Johnson was very fond of Chambers, although he also records how once, at a meeting in his Temple rooms, the great lexicographer was so reduced to mirth by Sir Robert's stuffiness that, on coming out on to the pavement, he had to hold on to a post 'whence he sent forth peals so loud that in the silence of the night his voice seemed to resound from Temple Bar to Fleet Ditch'. Not long afterwards, aged thirty-six, Sir Robert excited Johnson's envy by persuading Frances Wilton, 'a girl of sixteen, exquisitely beautiful . . . to take her chance with him in the East'. Behind a mask of somewhat studied eccentricity, Sir Robert played a canny hand in the political intrigues of

Calcutta. Moreover, although no more rapacious than most Company officials, he was not particularly scrupulous and narrowly escaped having to answer to Parliament for profiteering.*

Frances, his wife, was an altogether less worldly creature. The daughter of the sculptor Joseph Wilton and still in her early twenties, Fanny Chambers had a luminous beauty renowned from the Royal Academy in London, where she had modelled as Hebe for Sir Joshua Reynolds, to the corners of Bengal. She was cultivated, a good harpsichordist, and spirited yet kindly. One correspondent noted that since her arrival in 1776 she had created 'the one corner of charm and natural goodness in the hateful Calcutta of the next ten years'. She was also the best friend that Mary Hosea had known, sharing with her youth and a fondness for unmalicious gossip. Delighted at being reunited with her friend, Fanny suggested that they should go to look 'at the fashionable ladies of Calcutta who are exposing their pretty legs to view, and find fault with them'.

Hosea had more pressing concerns on his mind than pretty legs. His unexpected arrival in Calcutta could not long escape notice and the last thing he wanted was to have to explain his presence to Warren Hastings, the Governor, when he had yet to confirm the details of their passage home.

Before he set out to do so, Fanny prevailed on the Hoseas for a great service. Her eldest son Thomas, recently turned seven, had reached an age when most English children were sent home for schooling. The children of Company officials usually sailed with a servant or in the care of the ship's captain, but Mary Hosea was fond of the boy and agreed without hesitation to Fanny's request that he should accompany them on the voyage.

About fifty miles from Calcutta, at the sheltered anchorage of Kedgeree Roads, a large and grand East Indiaman lay at rest. At 741 tons, the *Grosvenor* was one of a new class of the vessels that had been carrying trade to and from the East since the royal charter granted to the merchants of London in 1600 had led to the formation of the East India Company. A three-masted square rigger, the *Grosvenor* dwarfed the company around

* As Chief Justice, Sir Robert outraged the diarist and lawyer William Hickey with his ruling in the Calcutta bazaar land case of 1793, in which he had a substantial financial interest. See Hickey (under Spencer (ed.) in 'Published sources'), vol. 4, pp. 135–9.

her, the two-masters and country ships of the coastal trade, and the smaller supply craft – budgerows, skiffs and pinnaces – swarming to and from the landings with their cargoes.

The anchorage lay on the Hooghly, midway between Calcutta and the sea, so the river served as both a door to Bengal and a channel to the other great entrepôts of Eastern trade, Canton and Bencoolen. The Hooghly defined Calcutta's character, just as the Thames did London's, though the diarist William Hickey, practising as a lawyer in Calcutta, thought the Indian river the greater:

> The noble appearance of the river, which is much wider than the Thames at London bridge, together with the amazing variety of vessels continually passing on its surface, add to the beauty of the scene . . . The different pleasure boats intermixed with mercantile vessels and ships of war render the whole a magnificent and beautiful moving picture; at once exhilarating the heart and charming the senses in this brilliant climate.

Just such a scene greeted Captain John Coxon of the *Grosvenor* as he arrived in Calcutta one day in December to discuss with William Hosea the terms of his passage. The captain of an Indiaman was a figure of substance, and as Coxon came ashore that morning in his blue-cloth coat with black-velvet collar and gold-braided sleeves, buff waistcoat, silk stockings and breeches buttoned at the calf, dress sword and cocked hat, he received his entitlement of a nine-gun salute from Fort William. He wore a wig in the style of the day and, to judge from the only portrait of him, had a youthful, even somewhat effeminate, appearance that belied his forty-two years. Perhaps he took his lodgings at one of the handsome bungalows maintained by the Company for its officers, but he could just as well have stayed with Joseph Sherburne, a retired merchant and his father-in-law. On his last voyage, Coxon had married Sherburne's daughter Harriet before carrying her off back to England.

Of his meeting with Hosea there is no record, but the outcome speaks eloquently for what passed between them. Hosea had been concerned enough beforehand, as Mary's baby, expected by mid-December, was already late and she would need at least two weeks to recover after giving birth before they could contemplate starting a journey that was an ordeal for the healthiest of women. At this stage Coxon told him that the *Grosvenor* would be sailing for Madras in less than two weeks.

Had Hosea but known it, Coxon was almost as perturbed as his would-be passenger. When the *Grosvenor* had left Plymouth on a summer's day eighteen months earlier, Coxon had had every hope that this would be his last voyage. Such were the hazards and profits of Eastern trade that most Indiamen skippers saw to it that they could retire after two or three voyages, and Coxon was captaining the *Grosvenor* on her second passage; but since being forced by bad weather to take shelter in Rio on the traversal of the Atlantic, he had been plagued by difficulties.* The outward journey had taken more than seven months, compared with the ship's maiden voyage of five. On arriving in Madras, Coxon had found the Company's forces involved in a war in which he was co-opted and his ship employed as a coastal trader, ferrying grain to British troops. For the past eleven months he had been deprived of the chance to exploit his own lucrative trade opportunities, while at the same time helplessly watching the withering of his crew. Four seamen and the surgeon's mate had died of disease and three more men had been lost to desertion; that was on top of the five who had absconded on the voyage out. To crown his woes, another eighteen men and a midshipman had been press-ganged by the Navy during a port call at Cuddalore.

The *Grosvenor* had not been a happy ship during the three years of Coxon's command, but like most East Indiamen captains he was educated and had a shrewd grasp of finances. He was also acutely conscious of social distinction and, at this point, desperate to recover his losses. As soon as he met Hosea and sensed how anxious this rich, important man was to secure an early passage from India, Coxon saw his opportunity.

Regulations laid down set fares for each category of passenger, from £50 for a cadet to £200 for an officer. As a senior official, Hosea should have paid the equivalent of a colonel's passage, or £250. These fares were more flexible on the homeward voyage, when the Company turned a blind eye to the fact that captains frequently milked, for all they were able, those officials who had made their pile and were keen to leave India rather than risk

* Outward-bound East Indiamen exploited the prevailing trades across the Atlantic, sometimes touching the east coast of South America before tacking south-east for the Cape of Good Hope.

another unhealthy season in the tropics. Even so, it was uncommon for someone in Hosea's position to pay more than £1,000 for himself and his family; but by the time he left Coxon, he had agreed to part with no less than 20,000 rupees, or more than £2,000, and a similar amount for a share of Coxon's 'privilege', the space in the Indiaman's hold that was set aside for the captain's private trade goods. In today's values, Hosea was paying Coxon more than £240,000 to get home.

The agreement had further noteworthy elements. Despite his astonishing fare, no concessions were made to Hosea's circumstances. The *Grosvenor* was to sail in a few days to Madras, where the Hoseas would have to join her after the baby's birth, making the journey down the coast in the rude quarters of a country ship. Coxon insisted, moreover, that he had other passengers waiting in Madras and could only reserve a cabin if Hosea paid £1,000 in advance. If Mary should suffer complications and be unable to travel, that would be forfeit. More than desperation, the deal suggests that Hosea had lost his nerve altogether.

Well may Coxon have rubbed his hands with satisfaction. Before sailing from Bengal he had further cause for delight.

There was a sharp social distinction between members of the colonial aristocracy like Hosea, the *burra sahibs*, and Europeans unattached to the Company, known in its ledgers as 'Persons out of the Service'. Merchants, traders and freebooters of all kinds were drawn to the East by the lure of the fortunes that could be made in a single venture. Two such men were George Taylor and John Williams.

Although both were aged about forty, they remained vigorous and hardy, bound together by family and a common sense of adventure. Williams had married Taylor's sister Sarah, and while she lived in England with their son, the two men became partners in foreign enterprise. At some stage they worked for the Company and acquired enough capital to risk a venture of their own, a trade expedition to China, which prospered sufficiently for Williams to have bought a house in the well-to-do parish of Walthamstow, north of London, decorated with objects from the East, and to have had his portrait painted by Gainsborough or one of his pupils, bewigged and surrounded by symbols of his station. Around 1779, the partners had gone back to China for one last speculative gamble.

In November 1781, while Hosea was still preparing to leave Murshidabad, they had arrived back in Calcutta from Canton with a cargo of silk and other valuables. All that remained was for them to return with their treasure to London and they would join the ranks of the flash India hands whose upstart wealth was starting to attract all the resentment that an envious upper class could direct at nouveaux riches. Tainted by trade, Williams and Taylor were the kind of parvenus who, it was sniffily said, came home to assume airs and build ostentatious villas on the tops of hills. The English had coined a new word to describe such men: they were nabobs.*

Wealth aside, nothing that is known of the pair fits Lord Macaulay's caricature of the 'savage old nabob, with an immense fortune, a tawny complexion, a bad liver and a worse heart'. From their subsequent conduct it would appear rather that they were of good heart and generous disposition, as well as being bold and determined spirits; but having risked so much, they too were anxious to leave Bengal as soon as possible to avoid jeopardising everything, their health included. This much is evident from a letter of application to the Governor General's office on 5 November 'from Messrs Williams and Taylor to solicit an order to Captain Hall to be received as passengers in the *Swallow*'. The *Swallow* was a packet, a fast-sailing vessel that carried mail, despatches and valuables between Bengal and London. Next to the application, in a red-bound ledger the size of a tombstone, is the outcome: 'Refused'.

So Williams and Taylor followed in Hosea's footsteps, beating a path to Coxon's door in search of a passage home. What they paid is not recorded, but we can be reasonably sure that, in exploiting his advantage, the captain again felt obliged to point out that he had a number of other passengers waiting in Madras. In any event, when the *Grosvenor* sailed from Kedgeree Roads a week after Christmas, the nabobs had quarters in the great cabin.

So did a young woman. While the crew had been in Calcutta the chief mate, a tough Scot named Alexander Logie, had resumed his courtship of Lydia Blechynden, a passenger on the voyage out. Lydia, an educated and handsome woman just turned twenty-three, came from a once-prosperous

* A corruption of the title Nawab.

landowning family now fallen on hard times and was on the lookout for a husband with prospects. An attractive catch herself, with a mane of red hair, Lydia saw in the *Grosvenor*'s chief mate an ambitious, resourceful man and, having spent the intervening months living in the house of William Larkins, the Accountant-General of Bengal, without receiving another – or, at least, better – offer, she accepted Logie's proposal on his reappearance. They were married on 8 December. Lydia Logie was the first of the Indiaman's trio of women passengers.

A few days after the *Grosvenor*'s departure, Mary Hosea was at last delivered of a baby girl. Charlotte was her fourth child, but the joy that greeted the birth was no less heartfelt than for her first-born. Apart from the sweetness of her nature, not a great deal is known about Mary. No details of her birth or appearance have survived, but she and Hosea had been married ten years earlier, so she was probably aged about thirty. From ordinary beginnings – her mother's letters combine palpable adoration with atrocious spelling – she had learned to hold her own in the Chambers' circle. Her correspondence indicates that she was warm and affectionate, but a terrible worrier and inclined to gossip. Life in a country station, even so grand a one as Murshidabad, had little appeal for a sociable creature like Mary, and in the echoing halls of the Residence, surrounded by servants, she frequently bewailed her loneliness. 'We live a kind of stupid life here,' she wrote to Lady Chambers, 'meet two or three times a week, and for want of conversation kill time at cards.' Her marriage appears to have been happy, however. Fond references to 'my Hosea' are counterposed with references to the scandalous affairs of others – 'How many women has that man Booth made unhappy besides ruining himself?' – and concerns for less fortunate women. Among those whom she had taken under her wing was Eliza Fay.

The indomitable Mrs Fay, one of Calcutta's most vivid personalities, prefigures the memsahibs then just starting to take their place on the stage of British India. Catty, gallant and long-suffering, Mrs Fay, in the throes of difficulties with her worthless husband, needed a protector and the Hoseas fitted the bill admirably. Mary's heart went out to her: 'How hard is the lot of that amiable girl,' she wrote to Lady Chambers. In turn, Mrs Fay confided to her sister that Mary was 'one of the most amiable women

I ever knew; it is impossible to do otherwise than love her'. Having made herself temporarily indispensable – 'I devote myself to my dear Mrs Hosea who I really think has a friendship for me' – Mrs Fay was all for taking passage on the *Grosvenor* with her. Constantly short of money, however, she was unable to afford the fares being demanded by Captain Coxon.

Mrs Fay's letters, like the equally engaging memoirs of William Hickey, record an era in transition. In what has been called 'the selfish and lascivious century', India was occupied by buccaneers, gamblers and chancers, men who had not much interest in ruling the natives but were devoted to making money from them. The East India Company, uniting such adventurers with the capital of London entrepreneurs, had become a pillar of the Hanoverian state. These days the name Honourable Company has a bleakly ironic ring, being synonymous with rapacity and corruption, and indeed there were plenty of both; but there was also an empathy with local ways – a spirit of easy-going complicity, as Jan Morris put it – that was refreshingly free of the humbug that characterised the age of imperial responsibility. Fastidious men such as Hosea were rare among a ruling caste which, in Morris's words 'responded sensually to all the gaudy seductions of the land'. White women were in short supply and taking native mistresses was the rule rather than the exception.* A contemporary source, outraged by this unconventional society, described Bengal as 'the fittest soil for lust'.

For the nabob, according to one account, the day began at about eight with the entry to his bedroom of his head bearer and manservant: 'A lady quits his side and is conducted by a private staircase out of the yard. The moment the master throws his legs out of bed the whole force is waiting to rush into his room, each making three salaams. He is dressed without any greater exertion on his own part than if he was a statue.'

The working day lasted from about ten to two, during which period married ladies played host to one another. Lunch was an epic affair, drinking, especially, being on a heroic scale: men drank madeira with the meal and followed that with between two and three bottles each of claret, chilled by being packed in a combination of chemical salts; most women managed a bottle of claret a day. Unsurprisingly, afternoons were given over to

* In 1810, there were no more than an estimated 250 white women in Bengal, among 2,000 to 3,000 men.

slumber. Towards evening, sahibs and their mems would re-emerge for an airing on the maidan. Younger blades – 'fine dashing lads' Hickey called them – drove in phaetons to the racecourse south of Fort William 'where the carriages all drew up and a general chat took place'. Formal calls at home were followed by a late supper and bed around midnight.

Signs of the leisure interests that would mark the British imperial procession around the globe were already visible. Cricket was being played, although the Calcutta Cricket Club – India's first – would not be founded for another ten years. The theatre was popular and competition between young male artists for the best parts so intense that it had given rise to duels. Francis Rundell, whose first career had been surgery, was declared the Garrick of Bengal, his Hamlet and Othello being thought especially fine.

But, like the elegant white mansions of Chowringhee whose stucco turned out on closer inspection to be cracked and peeling, the façade was misleading. There has been previous allusion here to a hateful atmosphere in Calcutta. That was, if anything, an understatement. Jealousy, malice and intrigue had infected its political affairs and poisoned its society. Among those caught up in this maelstrom was William Hosea.

If the Company's endeavours were defined by avarice, it is scarcely to be wondered at. Bengal's climate was near insufferable and quite sufficient in itself to produce pathological behaviour in the infernal months from March to June and subsequently in the rainy monsoon season, up to September. Apart from the torrid conditions, the likelihood of being carried off by disease meant that roughly four in five of those who went out to India never returned. Only men willing to stake their lives for the biggest rewards were drawn there in the first place and, given the poor chances of surviving long enough to make a fortune, it was inevitable that on top of freebooting trade methods, men should resort to any means from corruption to treachery to better their prospects.

Robert Clive had set the tone. Conqueror of Bengal and victor over his French rivals at the Battle of Plassy in 1757, Clive adopted a style both extravagant and vainglorious, part proconsul, part tycoon. When he returned to England with a fortune of around £300,000 he simultaneously awed and shocked his countrymen. The Company's directors, quick enough to seize a juicy profit for themselves, set about bringing their presumptuous servants to heel. The means was an Act creating a single governor for the three presidencies, Calcutta, Madras and Bombay, the instrument Warren Hastings, who in 1774 was charged with curbing corruption and imposing authority on the trading cliques. The task was more than even this able and comparatively honourable man could accomplish, and it would destroy him. No sooner had he been appointed than dissidents started to appear, none more dangerous than a key member of his ruling council, Philip Francis, whose hatred for Hastings was as malevolent as it was irrational.

Just what part William Hosea played in the plot against Hastings will always be something of a mystery. Like so many individuals caught up in events bigger than themselves, he tended to be carried on currents rather than to shape them. But that he was involved in trying to bring down his benefactor is clear, and the plot offers one explanation for what caused him to flee Bengal that year in blind panic.

Among the adventurers and sensualists who made their homes in India, Hosea was something of an anomaly. For much of his life he appeared uncertain whether he ought to be on his knees before fate or shaking his fist at it. Clive made the mistake of observing: 'He seems formed for war.' In fact, he was essentially a highly strung creature even after he had attained wealth and position, concealing a timorous nature with bluster. Obsequious to his superiors, he was overweening towards those of lesser rank. The great human drama of his time, the Bengal famine of 1770 in which almost half the population died – about three million people – went unremarked in his correspondence; but it is easy to be censorious, and life had not been gentle with Hosea. A wastrel father had left him to provide for his mother from his teens, a duty that he discharged conscientiously throughout his life, and beyond.

In a society oiled by patronage it was his fate to have one influential relative: Robert Orme, his uncle, was on intimate terms with Clive – indeed, wrote *A History of the Military Transactions of the British Nation in Indostan*, the work that inflated Clive's reputation as a military genius. In 1765, aged barely fifteen, Hosea took ship for India with letters of introduction, leaving his tearful mother convinced that she would never see him again. Clive gave him a commission and, by diligent toadying, he gained further powerful benefactors in General Richard Smith and Sir Thomas Rumbold, as piratical a pair of grandees as ever served the Company. When he displayed little appetite for the military, Smith arranged his transfer to the civil side, as Rumbold's assistant as Chief at Patna. A letter to Orme at this time is creepily fawning to the modern eye but was only to be expected from one in his position: 'I can never enough acknowledge the kindness of Mr Rumbold. Be assured that it shall be my constant endeavour to deserve the esteem of those by whom I am much obliged, for which you of all others is the first whose countenance I would wish to cultivate.'

His first big opportunity came in 1769 with an appointment to Calcutta. Here Warren Hastings spotted his zeal and he rose rapidly: at twenty he was made secretary to the ruling council, and before turning twenty-two he was revenue collector for Hooghly district. Having advanced thus far through assiduous humility, he was promptly seized by a disastrous bout of hubris. His letters to his superiors became patronising, then audacious. Hastings had decreed that Bengal's princely rulers were to be treated with respect, but when Hosea was told to consult an official called the Phowzdar, he bridled: 'I cannot think that because his station was once important it is any reason why it should be rendered so at this time.'

Oblivious to danger, he plunged blindly on. A letter to Hastings complained of a perceived slight by another Bengali official, the Roy Royan, and demanded: 'You will greatly oblige me with a letter to him in your own name desiring him to desist from a practice so derogatory to his station and so detrimental to the authority of mine.' Admonished by Richard Barwell, a powerful member of the council, he adopted an implicitly threatening tone, boasting of 'the confidence my superiors repose in me'. The crisis came in 1773 when he received a warning from the council which, he confided to a friend, was 'conceived in terms of such severity that next to a dismissal from the service I regard [it] as the greatest misfortune'. Panic-stricken, he returned to what he knew best: he grovelled to the council: 'I throw myself upon your generosity for an acquittal . . . your orders will be implicitly obeyed.'

His recovery was astonishing. Three months later Hastings appointed Hosea to his own former post, Resident at the Durbar of the Nawab in Murshidabad. According to the diarist Hickey, this was then 'the most lucrative office in the Company's service, the whole stipend or salary allowed by Government to the Nabob passing through such Resident's hands, in which channel a considerable portion of it always stuck to his fingers'. Why Hastings should have treated the upstart with this munificence is a mystery but, having recently taken up his challenging new post, he may have sensed the factionalism that this would create and decided to invest in the loyalty of a chastened Hosea. For the time being his protégé was properly grateful, writing: 'The continuance of your patronage will ever be my first wish and highest ambition.'

In the meantime Hosea had met Mary Brown. They were married in September 1772, and in the years they spent at the opulent but distant durbar, Hosea became a devoted husband, discovering within marriage to this soft, warm woman a measure of security. Mary gave birth to their first three children there and Hosea wrote to his uncle Orme, revelling in the role of pater familias.* We may picture them at home in Murshidabad, amid what another Resident called its 'cooing doves, whistling blackbirds and purling streams': William in powdered wig, frock coat, waistcoat, ruffles, and silver-buckled shoes; Mary all ringlets, lace and long white gown; the children at play, and the usual profligacy of servants, each with a title and a role. Hosea had succeeded beyond his own wildest dreams, a figure described by Mrs Fay as 'a man of high character and generally esteemed'. At the same time he had at last grown genuinely wealthy. Thanks to his private trade, and the benefits of handling the Nawab's transactions, he remitted to Orme's care over the years enough funds to ensure a comfortable future for the family on their return to England.

There is no indication, however, that such a move was imminent until suddenly the poison that had been seeping through the administration in the 1770s, burst like a pustule.

Philip Francis, one of three members of Hastings's ruling council, had been trying for years to undermine the Governor in secret correspondence with the Company's directors, to the extent of using forged documents. Among Francis's allies was Sir Robert Chambers who, at the end of 1779, approached his new friend William Hosea and asked him to furnish information to be used against Hastings by a parliamentary select committee.

* Two of the children had already been sent to live with Mary's mother in England. Only the third, Frances, sailed with them on the *Grosvenor*.

Sensing the strength of those mustered against his benefactor, Hosea was drawn into sending a confidential report to the plotters in London.*

The hot season of 1780 was the most brutal that anyone in Calcutta could recall and in those simmering months the feud came to a crisis. Provoked beyond endurance, Hastings contrived a duel with Francis, whom he shot and wounded. For weeks the colony remained in a state of shock. Hosea, inclined anyway to anxiety, was devastated. A bizarre letter to Fanny Chambers that could have ruptured their family friendship once and for all indicated that he might have been near a breakdown. Affronted at a perceived slight, he wrote: 'I am vastly rejoiced to find that there is no prospect of your being with us for Christmas, notwithstanding we have an Entertainment entirely on your account. If you do not bring your harpsichord you will complete my happiness. There cannot be any room for it and there is no body fond of musick in Murshidabad.'

Francis recovered from his wound sufficiently to sail for England early in 1781, where he resumed his vendetta against Hastings. Still calm did not return to India. Hastings suddenly found himself plagued by military adventures to the south by an alliance between the French and Hyder Ali, the Sultan of Mysore, who came close to overturning the British presidency at Madras.

It was during this period of continuing turmoil that Hosea had decided to leave Bengal. He may have feared that his betrayal of Hastings was about to be revealed. He may have faced exposure over some other matter, for, although not especially corrupt, he had recently engaged in a shadowy money-making enterprise in the province of Oudh. He had, moreover, just received a warning from Orme to be on his guard against the new member of the council, John Macpherson – 'He will try you,' Orme wrote. Or perhaps this rather poignant figure, neither brave nor virtuous, impossible to like but somehow not without pathos, had simply lost his nerve in the vale of intrigue into which he had blundered and wanted to remove himself and his family until the storm blew over.

Whatever his reason, it was sufficient to compel him to cast safety to the wind. Among his many fears was sea travel and he had once confided to Fanny Chambers: 'I have long since made a resolution never to leave

* The report itself has been lost. What survives is a letter from Hosea to Chambers insisting that it was for information only and 'not to be quoted'.

Bengal in an unfavourable season.' That principle was about to be abandoned.

Mary was ready to travel within three weeks of giving birth to Charlotte. There could be no question of a baby her age being subjected to the voyage to England, however, so it was decided that Charlotte would be left with Sir Robert and Fanny Chambers. This was a service in kind for Mary's agreement to take young Thomas Chambers home in her care.

Hosea, meanwhile, negotiated a passage to Madras on board a coastal ship, the *Yarmouth*, involving further expense. On 1 January 1782 he made a will disclosing an estate of more than £40,000, which although a tidy sum, equivalent to roughly £2.4 million at today's values, indicated that he was no buccaneer like Clive or Rumbold; the latter carried home the stupendous sum of £200,000. However, Hosea was also anticipating turning a large profit on a cargo of indigo for which he had paid Coxon £2,000 for part of his 'privilege'. The rest of Hosea's assets in Bengal were converted into rough diamonds worth £7,300 and £1,700 in gold and silver, which he would take on the *Grosvenor*.

By the end of January the Hoseas were ready. 'All is now bustle and preparation for their departure,' Mrs Fay wrote. She marvelled at their luggage. 'It is almost incredible what quantities of baggage people of consequence take with them,' she trilled. 'I counted twenty-nine trunks that were sent on board for Mr and Mrs H – exclusive of chests of drawers and other packages with cabin stores.'

Only now, on 29 January and at the point of no return, did Hosea write to Hastings, the man to whom he owed almost everything. Citing 'concerns of my family requiring my presence in England', he asked to be released from the Company's service. He left open the possibility of returning 'whenever the business which now calls me away can properly be dealt with'. There is no record of any reply, but Hastings retained sufficient faith in his protégé to recommend to the directors that after 'seventeen years service in several important stations', Hosea should be reappointed if he wished to return.

Three days later, the Hosea and Chambers families said their farewells. Both mothers were desolate at the moment of being parted from their children. Fanny Chambers had the comfort of a recent portrait of young Tom by the Calcutta artist John Hone, but Mary – who once insisted that to be separated from any of her children would be the death of her – had no such memento of Charlotte. Mrs Fay sympathised: 'It seemed cruel for a mother to abandon her child only twenty-five days old; but it must in all probability have fallen a sacrifice [on the voyage].'

A week later Mary wrote to Fanny from the *Yarmouth*, her head swimming from the noises of the crew and the oppressive heat: 'I had flattered myself that I should have behaved with more philosophy at the parting with my child but the moment of separation was too accute [*sic*] and I have been really ill ever since the day I left her . . . I am glad I did not see you just at the instant of my departure. We had both, my friend, more than we were able to support.' Mary was at least able to reassure her friend about Tom: 'Your beloved boy is well. I hear him say his prayers every night and his lesson every morning. He is a most amiable child and I only fear I shall love him too well.'

Even as they sailed south, Mary's own mother, Sarah Brown, was writing a letter from her modest home in Islington, full of loving excitement at the prospect of her daughter's homecoming. 'Oh my dear girl, what a happyness [*sic*] it will be to me when we once meet again,' she wrote. 'My hole [*sic*] life depends on your health and welfare. God for ever bless you my dearest and best of children.'

2

LORD MACARTNEY'S DISPLEASURE

Madras, 13 January 1782

While Hosea was still chafing against the delays to his departure from Calcutta, the *Grosvenor* dropped anchor off Madras. Captain Coxon was to take on most of his passengers here and his spirits rose. An early sailing was in prospect, for his duties to the Company's war effort had been discharged and by agreement he was to be released from any further obligation within a month.

The sooner the better, so far as Coxon was concerned. Madras was a place of evil reputation among seamen. Unlike Calcutta, it had no natural advantages as a port and although it was the oldest British settlement in India – construction of Fort St George had begun in 1640 – nothing had ever been done to endow Madras with a pier. Vessels anchored offshore so that passengers had to be ferried to and from their ships in native craft through notoriously rough surf. Spills and accidents were commonplace, but it was not just for the perils of the landing that the place was infamous. Ships anchored in Madras Roads were regularly dashed to pieces by typhoons, with grievous loss of life and cargo.

The *Grosvenor*'s cargo of rice for the garrison was offloaded without mishap, but Coxon's hopes of an early departure were disappointed. Although the captain of an independent ship, and so nominally responsible only to the owners, he was in the jurisdiction of the Company – in this instance the Madras board – and a month later he was still awaiting sailing

Lord Macartney, from a portrait by Mather Brown, 1790

orders. Like most sea captains, Coxon was impatient of outsiders who interfered with the smooth running of his ship and at this stage he rashly fired off a letter to the board, pointing out that the contract between owner and Company had expired and, 'the *Grosvenor* not yet being despatched', the Company would be held responsible for compensation. He also served notice that he would sail for England regardless at the end of thirty days.

This broadside brought a placatory reply: that authorisation to depart would be ready within ten days; but Coxon's letter had been a high-handed bluff and Lord Macartney, the local Governor, knew it. Macartney was not a good man to antagonise. An imperious patrician with powerful connections, his influence in the *Grosvenor* saga was to be potent at a number of points in the years ahead, and without exception baneful. His first intercession, evidently intended to teach Coxon a lesson, was to see to it that his departure was delayed.

Over the next two weeks cargo was ferried out to the *Grosvenor* as she lay at anchor in Madras Roads. The bulk of it was described in the official record as 'coast goods'. As well as the silk bales being transported by the nabobs Williams and Taylor, and Hosea's freight of indigo, this included textiles and sugar. A proportion would have belonged to Coxon – as captain he was entitled to carry 38 tons of goods on the homeward voyage for his own private trade – and his officers. The local value was stated as being about £60,000. Its value on being landed in England would have been around £300,000 – today about £18 million. Gold and diamonds, the transportable wealth of passengers and officers, were also being carried. Manifests show that the gold was in the form of small coins, called star pagodas, and had a total value of £65,000; the diamonds were worth £10,000 locally, considerably more in England.

On 27 February Coxon wrote again to the board, saying that the Indiaman was loaded and ready to set sail. Having been told that he would be cleared for departure by 21 February, he was becoming worried as well as frustrated. The season of a voyage was crucial to its duration and safety and the optimum time for taking advantage of the north-east monsoon – between January and February – had already passed. Unless he left within two weeks, Coxon knew, his progress would be slowed by southerly winds. From April he would run into the south-west monsoon winds, with all their delaying effect.

In response to his more emollient tone, the board issued orders 'that Captain Coxon be directed to keep the *Grosvenor* ready to proceed on the shortest notice'. But the harm had already been done. Soon afterwards news was received that a great French fleet had arrived off the coast, and all merchant departures were halted. Not for another month would the *Grosvenor* be allowed to sail.

Coxon was not the only one fulminating against the board. If one thing united those taking passage on the *Grosvenor*, it was their common desire to be quit of India. Hosea's motives were deeply hidden. Those joining the ship in Madras could be more honest about their fears: not for the first time in the city's history, a marauding army was at its gates.

Madras, founded by the British on the supposed site of St Thomas's martyrdom, was yet to be reconciled to the administrative ascendancy of Calcutta. Had not Madras, in the shape of Clive and his army, won Bengal? Neoclassical residences on the seafront testified that local traders could match their Calcutta counterparts for stylish living, and St Mary's was the oldest Anglican church in India. The traders, with their connections going back to the Company's earliest ventures among the Spice Islands, liked to refer to themselves as 'the gentlemen of The Coast', although the nature of their business with the local ruler, the Nawab of Arcot, was anything but gentlemanly.

Now though, as in Clive's time, the tenor of life was dominated by the military. A year earlier, Hyder Ali, the Sultan of Mysore, had inflicted a catastrophic defeat on British arms at the village of Pollilur, several days' march away. This astonishing reverse 'engaged the attention of the world', in the words of the Prime Minister, Lord North. More particularly, it engaged the residents of Madras, who had witnessed Hyder's cavalry thundering into the suburbs, 'surrounding many of the English gentlemen in their country houses who narrowly escaped being taken'.

Coxon found himself besieged by applicants for passage to England. Since he had named his own price to Hosea and the nabobs, the demand for space on the *Grosvenor* had, if anything, increased. Of the two other Indiamen due to sail before the end of the season, the *Rochford* was found to be leaking and declared unseaworthy, while the *Earl of Dartmouth* had yet to leave Calcutta. The opportunity for lining his purse with passage money was too good for Coxon to pass up. On her previous voyage home, the *Grosvenor* had carried thirteen passengers, which was rather more than average for an East Indiaman of her size. When she set out on her last journey, crammed into the great cabin, the roundhouse and the forward quarters were thirty-one European passengers – from officials, traders and military men, to wives, children and servants.

Among them was the singular figure of Charles Newman.

Newman was a lawyer in Calcutta, a jurist able enough for his colleague and near-contemporary William Hickey to note that he had 'made a fine fortune by his profession'. He was a dandy, with a fondness for silver possessions bearing his monogrammed initials, whether his personal cutlery, the buckles of his shoes, or the buttons on a green broadcloth coat that he wore on his appearances in court. Aged in his mid-thirties, with a wife and child, he was also close to Hastings. In the intrigues that divided the Company's affairs, Newman was among the few whom the Governor could unequivocally call 'my own agents'.

He had come to prominence in the most sensational scandal in Bengal's history. Three years earlier, on the night of 8 December, 1778, no less a figure than Hastings's old enemy Philip Francis had been apprehended with a bamboo ladder outside the house of George Grand, a lowly Company writer. Grand was not at home, but his wife, by consensus Calcutta's greatest beauty, was in an upper room. The former Mademoiselle Noel Catherine Werlee, not yet aged twenty, was a creature as exotic as she was ravishing, with what one scribe was moved to describe as 'the stature of a nymph, a complexion of unequalled delicacy, and auburn hair of the most luxuriant profusion.' There was a hint of the Orient to her features, which enraptured the French; Napoleon callied her 'Anglaise ou Indienne'. The Bengal artist Zoffany celebrated her in paint, and Francis was far from being her most prominent lover. Grand, however, who had wed her before she was fifteen, was sufficiently outraged to take the issue to the Supreme Court, claiming the fantastic sum of 1,600,000 rupees (£160,000) from Francis for having deprived him of the 'solace, affection, comfort and counsel' of his wife.

Newman had acted for the injured husband in a case that transfixed Calcutta for months. In forensic manner he had led Grand's servants through their evidence: the *kitmugar*, who had found the ladder against the window of Mrs Grand's bedroom; the *jemadar*, who had seen Francis coming out of the house and detained him; and the *bowanny*, who had told of Mrs Grand trying to order Francis's release (to which the *jemadar* had replied: 'I will not hear you, you may go to your room.'). Newman had extracted testimony to show how Francis had first blustered – 'Do you not know me? I am the Burra Sahib' – then tried to bribe his way out of the situation – 'I will give you money. I will make you great men' – before fleeing.

It says something for Newman's powers that he persuaded a three-man Bench to accept the word of native witnesses rather than the most powerful man in Bengal after Hastings, despite the intercession of Sir Robert Chambers. Although the judges assessed the figure placed by Grand on his wife's virtue as a touch on the high side, he was awarded 50,000 rupees (£5,000) against Francis. One of the three dissented, Chambers finding that adultery by his crony was not proven. The Calcutta chronicler H. E. Busteed noted laconically: 'Without in the smallest degree insinuating that the Chambers dissent was influenced by [non-legal] considerations, it may be pointed out that long before the trial he and Francis were the closest official allies, if indeed not something more.'

Francis then rather undermined his friend's judgment by installing Mrs Grand as his mistress, but the arrangement did not last. After Grand divorced her, she found another protector before sailing for Europe, where she continued to dazzle powerful men and eventually sealed a heartwarmingly improbable career by becoming the wife of the French statesman Prince Talleyrand.

Newman's ability, and no doubt his humiliation of Francis, had meanwhile caught the attention of Hastings, who started to assign him delicate diplomatic tasks. One such mission had now brought him to Madras.

For years concerns had been growing at the Company's headquarters in Leadenhall Street about business practices in the southern presidency that went beyond mere peculation and profiteering. The Madras gentry were bound so deeply to the Nawab of Arcot by a mutually dependent system of loans and patronage that their interests no longer converged with those of the Company. This buccaneering clique, known as the 'Arcot Interest', had undoubtedly encouraged the Nawab to plunder neighbouring rulers, but were also suspected of selling intelligence about British military deployments to the French settlement at Pondicherry. Worst of all, the Arcot Interest was reputed to own a vessel named the *Elizabeth*, which was sailing under French colours while engaging in piracy against British shipping off the eastern, or Coromandel, coast. The main suspect was none other than Sir Thomas Rumbold, Hosea's old patron, who had recently retired as Governor of Madras and returned to England with a fortune breathtaking even by the standards of the Orient. Suspicion had also fallen, however, on his successor, Macartney.

Newman arrived from Calcutta in November 1781 with orders to collect evidence against Rumbold and other Company servants who, in the words of the directors, 'are supposed to have unwarrantably acquired large sums of money contrary to law and their own solemn engagements'. Hastings's private instructions were for Newman to get to the bottom of the Arcot Interest's treachery.

At first Macartney made a show of cooperation. Newman was invited up to Fort St George to meet the Madras board, who 'handsomely flattered me with assurances of every assistance in their power'; but his questioning of officials was met with blanket professions of ignorance. He tried to speak to Macartney's *durbash*, his interpreter and go-between in dealings with the Nawab, but the *durbash* fobbed him off. Rumbold's former *durbash* was equally obstructive. When Newman appealed to Macartney, he was told that the Governor had not 'weight sufficient to prevail on [the interpreters] to give evidence'.

Newman's suspicions grew when he attended a session of the board at which a letter from the Nawab was read out in which he too declined to assist the investigation, and the board hailed him 'for refusing to turn informer'. With growing exasperation, Newman tried to appeal over Macartney's head. He issued a public notice, asking for information about fifteen named Madras citizens said to have received from the Nawab sums of between £10,000 and £40,000 'for bringing about the Revolution of 1776'.* In this astonishing episode, Lord Pigot, an earlier Governor appointed by the Company to deal with the Arcot Interest, was arrested by his councillors and died suddenly in their custody. That outrage had never been punished but, on hearing about Newman's public notice, Macartney objected that it was irrelevant to his investigation.

* The fifteen so named included not only Rumbold, but Sir Edward Hughes, the admiral commanding the Royal Navy squadron on the Coromandel coast.

Newman was ill with a fever, he was being kept at arm's length by Madras society, and he was a long way from his family in Calcutta. His attempts to obtain information were being frustrated at every turn. At some point, however, he started to receive information. On 1 February he wrote to Macartney; referring to the pirate ship operating under French colours, he said it was 'notoriously spoken of in the settlement as true . . . that the *Elizabeth* did belong to one of the gentlemen of this place'. He had found, nevertheless, that 'the spirit is so much against enquiries that those few who could and would give information on the subject dare not stand forth because they would be condemned by the settlement at large.'

This bombshell elicited a reply from the board's secretary that took issue with 'the general style of your letter, as well as some particular passages' and objected to 'a strong disposition in you to lay at their door the ill success of the enquiries committed by the Directors to your charge'. Newman replied on 13 March; with declamatory flourishes that would have graced his old courtroom, he declared that he would not accept 'blame which I conceive to rest with you [Macartney]'. He scorned the board's claim to have done all in its power to get to the bottom of the scandals:

> I can not, nor will others who know what the influence of a Governor is in India over *durbashes*, join in the Idea that the Board [is unable] to prevail upon them to give evidence.

Challenged to prove a conspiracy, he drew himself up: 'Do the Board seriously expect that I should comply with this requisition? May not [this] form a part of that evidence which is to be transmitted only to the Secret Committee of the Hon'ble Company? And might not the discovery be making those persons from whom I derive my knowledge [into] victims?'

This hint that he had come upon damning evidence seems at last to have caused a flicker of panic in Madras. The board's final letter to him before it cut all communication denounced his manner as 'disrespectful and improper' and vowed to make representations to the Secret Committee, trusting that it would receive 'that justice which has been in vain expected from Mr Newman'.

Now Newman determined on action. There could be no question of returning to Calcutta. He would sail for England to lay his evidence before the directors. So he called on the captain of the sole Indiaman in port,

John Coxon, and impressed on him the urgency of his mission; and further space was found in the *Grosvenor*'s crowded passenger quarters.

Macartney had at last tired of toying with Coxon. On 27 March orders were issued for the *Grosvenor* to join a Royal Navy squadron recently arrived in Madras and to sail under its protection towards Ceylon. There she was to await the *Earl of Dartmouth* or, failing her arrival, to proceed home a single ship. Macartney would later claim that he had delayed the *Grosvenor* in order to provide her with a naval escort. However, it was an explanation he never saw fit to give to Coxon, who could be forgiven for concluding that the Governor had kept him out of spite. Determined that his treatment would not go without response, Coxon presented himself that same day before Stephen Popham, a notary public, and issued a sworn statement, relating his trials at the hands of Macartney, deploring the 'great risque' to his ship and cargo caused by his departure so late in the season and 'in justification of himself . . . protesting against the said Right Hon'ble the President and Council of Fort St George for having delayed him'.

So it was that, with barely a day's notice, Coxon's passengers mustered on the beach to be rowed out to the *Grosvenor*, joining the two already on board, Taylor and Williams. The most striking thing about them was the number of uniforms on display, not just maritime but army, French as well as British. They came, borne by palanquins and carriages, to the shingle beach where journeys to and from Madras invariably ended and began. Lesser figures came on foot, perhaps with a *wallah* holding an umbrella to shield them from the sun. The winds carrying the monsoon rain had blown themselves out and the light on a clear blue sea must have dazzled the eyes. At the water's edge, teams of Tamil oarsmen, stripped to the waist, stood by their *massoolahs*, surfboats made of wood and coir, for the hair-raising dash through the breakers out to where the *Grosvenor* lay in that shimmering sea. Solid and proud, she suffered nothing by comparison with the men-of-war, frigates and ships of the line, of the Royal Navy squadron commanded by Admiral Sir Edward Hughes, which was massed some distance off.

The senior Army officer among the *Grosvenor*'s passengers was Colonel Edward James of the Madras Artillery, accompanied by his wife

Sophia. The couple were probably in their mid-forties, having wed in 1763 when James was still a captain. He had left no glittering mark on the events of his time, but had been a witness to both triumph and disaster. He was probably at the capture of the French garrison at Pondicherry in 1761. He had been among the officers led a merry dance by Hyder Ali and, having risen to command the Madras Artillery, he had doubtless been at the Pollilur debacle, which saw the virtual annihilation of the Madras Army, including the deaths of sixty out of eighty-six British officers and more than 2,000 men. That catastrophe had caused not a few hearts to quail and, while there is no evidence that Colonel James had lost his nerve, he may well have thought it time to leave the field to younger men.

Of his wife Sophia we know only her maiden name, which was Crockett, and the fact that she was married at the garrison church of St Mary's within Fort St George. The name Crockett was not uncommon in Madras, so the likelihood is that Sophia was the daughter of a local official or trader, rather than being one of that rather sad band of young women deemed unmarriageable at home and so sent to India to acquire a husband. The colonel's servant was a soldier named William Ellis, while Sophia had an *ayah*.

A second officer of the demoralised Madras Artillery was also returning home. Of Captain Walterhouse Adair, however, nothing at all is known.

In contrast to these redcoats, we are on firmer ground with the two men in blue army uniforms. Colonel Charles d'Espinette and Captain Jean de L'Isle were prisoners, French officers of the Pondicherry regiment who had been assigned to help Hyder harass the British. Colonel d'Espinette was aged fifty-four, Captain de L'Isle – a short, ruddy man – twenty-seven. The details of their capture are not known, but they were being repatriated in a prisoner exchange. As officers they were treated as gentlemen – d'Espinette retained his servant, a man named Rousseau – although obliged to share a cabin with one another.

Five more British soldiers were returning home after their discharge, one of whom is of special interest to the *Grosvenor* story. John Bryan, aged in his thirties, had served in the Madras Army for about ten years. Such a career lent him an automatic distinction, for if there were few more desperate services for a poor young Englishman to enter than the Company's forces, there had been no more deadly theatre of operations for British soldiery in recent times than Mysore. Bryan had survived a brutal disciplinary regime, tropical disease and the Pollilur disaster, in which hundreds of his comrades had died and thousands more been taken captive and forced to defect. He was, in short, a remarkably lucky man, a resourceful one, or both. Having escaped India, he was heading home with a shrewd instinct for danger, a small amount of capital, and practical smithing skills acquired in the Army. As troopers, Bryan and his four fellows would have messed with the sailors on the gun deck.

Among the other passengers we should take note of the half-dozen youngsters, and in particular one Thomas Law. Aged about seven at the start of the voyage, Thomas was identified by the sailors as 'a young gentleman' and 'the son of a gentleman of quality who was very rich'. What makes this opinion additionally interesting in our race-obsessed age is that no mention was made of the fact that Thomas was Anglo-Indian. His father, also Thomas, was indeed 'a gentleman of quality', the son of a Bishop of Carlisle, who had arrived in Bengal as a clerk at the age of fourteen and formed a relationship with an Indian woman. He was barely sixteen when she gave birth to their son. Young Master Law, as he was called by the sailors, was being sent home with a servant to school.

Robert Saunders was also the son of a Company official and aged about six. Having no servant, he was travelling in the care of Captain Coxon. The two young female passengers, Mary Wilmot and Eleanor Dennis, were aged seven and three. They too were on their way to be educated in England.

As they came on board, the officers and crew surely cast a speculative eye from the quarterdeck and rigging over those for whose welfare they were about to become responsible. They would have expected to spend the next six to eight months, depending on the ease of the passage, in close proximity to these strangers.

That evening, as the passengers took their first meal together in the cuddy, the main topic of conversation was the unknown fate of the *Grosvenor*'s most distinguished couple and their alluringly empty cabin. In his four years as a captain, Coxon had never carried so prominent a personage as the Resident of Murshidabad, but his regret at losing the cachet that the Hoseas would have brought to his table, as well as the outstanding half of their £2,000 passage money, may have been tempered by the opportunity of auctioning the cabin space among the other well-heeled passengers.

The news arrived soon after dinner, as the passengers were about to take a turn on the quarterdeck: a country ship named the *Yarmouth*, carrying William Hosea and his entourage, had just dropped anchor in Madras Roads.

Hosea had given up hope a number of times. With the north-east monsoon behind them the journey to Madras would have taken a few days. Instead, the *Yarmouth* had been labouring for more than a month against the countervailing south-west monsoon, following a course that described a wide arc out into the Bay of Bengal and approached Madras from the south. Captain Richardson made the best use he could of the currents, but Hosea had thought the prospect of arriving before the *Grosvenor* sailed all but gone.

In the last week of March, six weeks after leaving Calcutta, the *Yarmouth*'s lookout had sighted land and the following day they had arrived at Pondicherry, where a French frigate and two smaller vessels lay at anchor. Although no more than the skipper of a country ship, Richardson was turned into a fire-eater by the sight of an enemy. Mary Hosea, the children and another woman passenger, were sent down to the ship's magazine, a hell-hole where the temperature was well over 120°F, while the *Yarmouth* ran alongside the frigate, forcing her to strike her colours, then set fire to her. The British crew cheered while a thousand Frenchmen could only look on vainly from the shore.

Mary was still almost prostrate with exhaustion and fear from her ordeal in the magazine when the *Yarmouth* slipped into Madras Roads at about 8 p.m. on 29 March. Their joy at finding the *Grosvenor* still at anchor was soon alloyed by news that she was about to sail with the Royal Navy. Two hours later, Coxon came on board and, after confirming that he was under orders to join the fleet, gave them advice that was bizarrely misleading. As Hosea related it to Sir Robert Chambers in his final letter, Coxon told him that his cabin was ready and that 'he had resisted many solicitations' from others seeking its comforts. He then went on to say that 'there were doubts of the fleet sailing in the morning'.

Reassured that he had a day or so to transfer his party and their mountains of baggage to the *Grosvenor*, Hosea sent Mary to bed, ordered transport boats to come to the *Yarmouth* at daybreak, and issued instructions that he was to be awakened at 4 a.m. He then lay down to get a few hours' sleep himself. Barely had he put his head down than the officer of the watch roused him, at 2 a.m., and told him that the fleet was under way.

The *Yarmouth*'s crew threw themselves into the task of bringing up the trunks and furniture and loading the ship's boat to be rowed across to the *Grosvenor* with Hosea. Having deposited one load, he returned with the Indiaman's boat for another. Already, however, 'the fleet was at a considerable distance, and I thought it best to despatch Mrs H and the children under the care of Richardson in his boat, desiring him to send it back instantly. My poor Girl was by this time so ill that she went into the boat more dead than alive.'

Even as the two boats started back for the *Grosvenor*, however, Hosea realised that distance was rapidly opening up between the *Yarmouth* and the fleet and if he waited for the rowing boats to return, he would never catch up. A native *masoolah* was summoned and loaded 'with everything that I could perceive of most consequence'. Hosea was about to be subjected to the standard trick in trade of the Madras boatmen, an edge-of-the-seat process of bargaining and renegotiation as the craft tossed around in the sea:

> I gave them money and promised large rewards. They put off and imagine my mortification when I found myself obliged to return, the boat being [so] overloaded that they refused to go without I would lighten her. I scarcely knew what to sacrifice & when it was finished it was broad day & the fleet four leagues from the land & every moment lessening to my view.

On the *Grosvenor*, meanwhile, Mary, seeing the land falling towards the horizon, became convinced that her husband was being left behind. She assailed Coxon – 'she raved, she entreated, she threaten'd'. Coxon shortened the *Grosvenor*'s sails to slow her speed, only to receive a signal from Admiral Hughes ordering him to catch up.

So valiantly did the *musoolah* rowers exert themselves that Hosea had reached a rear ship, the *Rodney*. 'Giddy, stupid, almost insensible of everything that had happened,' as he put it, he was taken to the captain's bed while the ship crowded sail to catch the *Grosvenor*. Mary was inconsolable, now certain that Hosea had been abandoned, until . . .

I reached the *Grosvenor* about eleven & flew to the best of women who, overcome by the variety of conflicting passions, fainted in my arms.

While it took Mary a few days to recover from this traumatic episode, Hosea's sense of relief was palpable. His spirits were not even dampened by discovery that among their possessions left on the *Yarmouth* were the foodstuffs they had brought to relieve the dull fare of an Indiaman table, including their own livestock and wines. His books – 'a choice collection for the voyage' – had sadly also been lost, along with all young Tom Chambers's clothing. Still Hosea's mood remained buoyant. Their fellow passengers on the *Grosvenor* seemed as congenial a group as might have been hoped for: he mentioned in particular Colonel and Mrs James and the nabobs Williams and Taylor. Lydia Logie, the new wife of the chief mate, was 'the finest lady'. He had reassuring news too about the Chambers's son: 'There are a great number of children in the ship & Tom is very happy & a great favourite with everybody. He has a most excellent Temper & is very easily managed.'

Well might Hosea have reflected that the upheaval had been worth it in the end. All the anxieties of Bengal were behind them and they were bound for England, home and comfort. The teenage boy who had left seventeen years earlier with nothing was returning, a man of substance and family, in pomp.

3

ISLAND OF OAK

At sea, north of Ceylon, 9 April 1782

The *Grosvenor* whispered along almost due south through the Bay of Bengal under full sail. In that mighty company there were twelve ships running close to the Coromandel Coast towards Ceylon, men-of-war sailing in a line bow to stern with the solitary Indiaman, but apart from the cries of the crews in the rigging and the crack of canvas as topgallants were unfurled, there was only the hiss of their passage through the sea, the slap of water against oak bows.

The *Grosvenor* was a compact version of the great warships, the sixty-four-gun ships of the line in the Royal Navy squadron commanded by Admiral Hughes. Her apple-cheeked hull was built to carry cargo, her quarters were designed for comfort, and in these respects she was representative of the finest merchantmen of her day. A new class of even larger East Indiamen was about to be launched, raising the standard tonnage from 800 to around 1200, but for her time the *Grosvenor* was an owner's ideal, capable of transporting 750,000lb of tea across the world and accommodating her passengers in conditions that were the closest thing to luxury travel offered by the age.

At the same time she could give a good account of herself against a foe. She was pierced for twenty-six cannon. The gun deck – 5ft 10in below the main deck, sufficient for a tall man of that era to stand upright – carried ten nine-pounders on each side, while the quarterdeck, where officers and

Ships off Fort William, engraving 1736

passengers promenaded, had three six-pound cannon on either side. The *Grosvenor* sufficiently resembled a frigate of the Royal Navy to have intimidated the pirates then preying on merchant shipping in the Bay of Bengal. Her crew were trained for naval warfare, and her magazine bristled with the tools of battle: boarding pikes, muskets, bayonets, pistols, cutlasses, muskets and hand grenades, as well as thirty rounds for each cannon and around fifty barrels of powder.*

She had been built by the firm of Wells at Barnard's Wharf, one of the larger shipyards at Rotherhithe, on the section of the Thames just east of the Tower of London that loops south in a large 'U' around the Isle of Dogs – a bleak, foul-smelling stretch of water about four miles in extent that launched one of the greatest maritime fleets in history. She was the second East Indiaman of that name, the first having returned in 1768 on the last of her scheduled four voyages, the average service life of an Indiaman. Both were seemingly named after Richard, the first Earl Grosvenor, a Cheshire landowner who had made a significant financial investment in them. At 741 tons, the second *Grosvenor* was completed in 1777, her hull being 138ft 10in long and 35ft 3in at its broadest point. (A new seventy-four-gun ship of the line, the battleship of the day, was about 165ft long and 45ft in the beam.) Her hold had a depth of 14ft 3in. A single oak around a hundred years old was required for every ton of the completed vessel, so roughly 740 mature trees from the clay soil of Sussex had gone into her construction. It is barely to be wondered at that oak had become a strategic resource of the highest priority and a source of constant friction between the Company and the Navy.

Mere statistics do nothing to convey the mysterious grace of the three-masted square-rigger, the pulse-quickening beauty of an object caught between the elements of air and water, part of each yet not fully of either. Fanciful it may be, but there was something about an Indiaman under a full press of sail that might be compared with a giant seabird skimming across the sea. Each vessel was founded upon a keel of elm, then built up in layer upon layer of oak, interlarded with decks of spruce sanded with

* In armaments and dimensions, the *Grosvenor* was not unlike the frigate, HMS *Surprise*. This twenty-four-gun sixth-rate, French-made but captured by the Royal Navy in 1796 and in service until 1802, was salvaged from history by Patrick O'Brian in his maritime novels and relaunched as Jack Aubrey's best-loved ship.

holystones to a skinlike smoothness underfoot. The shipwrights who made them were craftsmen rather than technicians, as dependent on eye and instinct as they were on any construction plan, selecting timber for a curve or shape that suited the overall scheme of things, much as a chair-maker would have done, so that each completed ship, while one of a type, was also sui generis, a unique organic island of wood, held together by the finest Spanish iron and borne on clouds of canvas.

Each had her own disposition. No less than the man who commanded her, and to just as enduring effect, a ship acquired a reputation among seamen for her temper – her speed, comforts and sailing abilities, as well as that indefinable accretion of myth and folklore among an intensely superstitious fraternity that made her known in the taverns as a happy or an unhappy place in which to serve.

The *Grosvenor*'s maiden voyage had started from Plymouth in February 1778 and ended back at the Downs in November 1779. Her performance with a following wind had been first-class, a constant rate of six or seven knots, and she had been obliged to shorten sail or her companions, the *Osterley* and the *Hillsborough*, would have been left in her wake. Still, the officers thought her performance could be improved when sailing to the windward and she had been returned to the shipyard for corrective trimming, an adjustment of ballast in her hold to lower her by the head.

Proud as he was of his ship, Coxon was none the less delighted to have so formidable an escort. The arrival of the French fleet in the Bay of Bengal had cast a new shadow over his prospects and despite lingering resentment at his treatment by Macartney, he must have realised that he was fortunate to be in company with Admiral Hughes's squadron. The French fleet was commanded by Pierre André, Bailli de Suffren-Saint-Tropez, who, for all the grandiloquence of his name, was a brilliant and gallant admiral. He had been sent to India after France's entry into the War of American Independence to bring Hughes's squadron to battle, while at the same time French land forces were aiding Hyder Ali. Suffren had a distinct edge in ships and manpower over the Royal Navy fleet, and within a week of sailing from Madras, Coxon discovered just how lucky he had been.

*

Escorting the *Grosvenor* was the least of Hughes's concerns. Between Hyder on land and Suffren at sea, British enterprise in India was in jeopardy; but it was at sea – the means of supplying and sustaining land forces – that the balance of power lay. When Holland had entered the war as France's ally the previous year, Hughes had bombarded the Dutch garrison at Trincomalee on the island of Ceylon into surrender and installed a British command. His task now was to land reinforcements and for the time being it was a priority to avoid the French.

Unknown to Hughes, his foe was cruising in the same south-easterly direction. Three times Suffren crossed his wake before the moment near midnight on 8 April when a French lookout spotted the British squadron's lights, off the north-east coast of Ceylon. Suffren changed course to close with them.

The following day Hosea sat down in his cabin and started a letter to Sir Robert Chambers in a tone of almost boyish excitement:

> Here we are after innumerable escapes in the latitude of 9´ about a degree to the Eastward of the Island of Ceylon, surrounded on all sides by the French fleet, which it will be impossible to get clear of without a Battle. They seem resolved that the admiral shall not make good the landing of the troops for the garrison. We must fight our way thro' them to make good our object.

In their first encounter, the Battle of Sadras two months earlier, Hughes had been lucky to escape without suffering a major defeat. Numerically the Royal Navy fleet was almost a match for the French, but Suffren's copper-bottomed French ships were faster and more manoeuvrable. At the same time, although brave and able, Hughes was no Nelson. He was, moreover, at an acute disadvantage in manpower: every one of his ships had been affected by scurvy or fever. The men who had been pressed from the *Grosvenor* and other Indiamen at Cuddalore months before had barely affected the rate of attrition. Hughes raged helplessly that his vessels were 'more like hospital ships than men-of-war'.

With a following wind he tried to outrun the French, who lay about fifteen miles off. For two days the wind continued to favour him and the fleet reached the latitude of Trincomalee ahead of its pursuers. Soon after noon on 11 April, the squadron bore up and set studding sails to change direction, aiming to cut the French line. Just then the favourable wind dropped, and instead of being able to tack south-west for the port, they drifted past it.

As dawn came up, the squadron found itself about thirty miles south of Trincomalee – with the French fleet drawn up and barring the way. With no option but to fight, Hughes issued the order to beat to quarters. Although the *Grosvenor* had kept up with her escort throughout, it appears that Coxon drew off as the naval crews took up battle stations. So far as is known, the *Grosvenor* took no part in the action.

It was some hours before the fleets formed up in line and the first thunderous volley of the Battle of Providien was not fired until around noon. Hughes's flagship, HMS *Superb*, a seventy-four-gun third-rate, was soon in the thick of things against Suffren's *Orient*, another seventy-four. Along the line of battle eleven English ships were engaged against twelve French, but at the heart of the affray *Superb* and the seventy-gun *Monmouth* were under a sustained concentration of fire from three of the enemy. For the first two hours they passed broadside on, pouring volley after volley into one another.

Superb's decks were thick with smoke, illuminated by the red flash of continuous cannon fire and awash with the blood of fifty-eight dead and dismembered men. At least double that number were wounded. On the *Monmouth*, the devastation was even greater. Her foremast and mizzenmast had been shot away and thus disabled she limped towards the rear of the line, only to be raked by successive broadsides from seven passing French ships. Her decks, too, ran red – forty-six of her men had been killed and more than a hundred wounded.

The battle was followed with fascination and pride from the decks of the *Grosvenor*. Amid the swirling smoke and the acrid bite of powder on the nostrils, one young crewman, William Habberley, recalling his former shipmates pressed in Cuddalore and now manning Navy carronades, cheered at the courage of the *Monmouth*. Habberley, a lad brought up in London's docklands and barely out of his teens, thrilled to see how the man-of-war's captain, his flag shot to pieces 'and the ship greatly damaged . . . nevertheless nailed the colours to the stump of the mizzenmast and defended the ship till the action closed'.

By four in the afternoon the ponderous lines of warships remained intact but had drifted dangerously close to the coast, when Hughes showed his fighting qualities, wearing round in perfect order to engage the French on the port tack. Now *Orient* lost her foremast in a crash of rigging and sails, forcing Suffren to transfer his flag to *Ajax*. Another French seventy-four, *Brillant*, was also damaged, and although none of Suffren's ships was crippled to the same extent as *Monmouth*, when the dark started to close in at about six, casualties and damage were spread evenly between the two fleets. The English had 137 killed and 430 wounded, the French 139 dead and 351 wounded. Hughes, surveying his battered fleet, wrote: 'Nor had any one ship of the squadron escaped without great injury in her hull and masts, and all were much torn in their sails and rigging.'

Providien was the bloodiest of the five battles fought between the French and English fleets in the East Indies in 1782–3, a precursor of the epic contests to come in European waters, but as indecisive as the other four. For the next few days, while bodies wrapped in shrouds were dropped over the side and running repairs were made to shattered ships and wounded men, the two fleets eyed each other warily over a distance of about five miles, like bloodied and exhausted warriors. Finally, on 19 April, Suffren raised sail and advanced to within two miles, making every show of launching another attack; but when Hughes held his line the French broke off and tacked to the north. For another three days the squadron remained at anchor before *Monmouth* was sufficiently restored to proceed with the rest, limping into the lovely harbour of Trincomalee on 22 April.

For Coxon the most immediate consequence of the battle was further to strain the capacity of the *Grosvenor*'s quarters, for it brought on board yet another passenger.

Captain George Talbot, RN had been a senior member of Hughes's command, the captain of the sixty-four-gun HMS *Worcester*. But he joined the *Grosvenor* under a cloud. Hughes had made it known that at the battles of Sadras and Providien, 'several of his captains had failed him badly'. Without mentioning names, the admiral complained: 'One is a dotard, no longer of any use. Another goes into action passably but has much deteriorated. Five others have behaved very indifferently.' The *Worcester* had been hindmost in Hughes's order of battle, and the fact that Talbot was leaving the campaign at this stage strongly suggests that he was the 'dotard' deemed of no further use. Hughes acknowledged, however, that there was 'no case for a court-martial', and there may have been personal differences between the two, for in the months ahead Talbot would show no lack of spirit. He came on board with a suite, a small retinue that included a coxswain, Isaac Blair, and a youth referred to on the passenger list, intriguingly but opaquely, as 'Captain Talbot's young lad'. As the boy was unnamed, he was probably either Indian or Anglo-Indian, and a servant.

Their arrival did nothing to ease the discomfort below decks, and while there is no evidence that having Talbot on board undermined Coxon's authority, it is reasonable to suggest that it may have introduced a certain tension into the great cabin. Although there was a general social equivalence between Navy and Indiamen captains, the former tended to look down on their counterparts as having lost caste through trading. As one naval man put it: 'The habit of buying and selling goods must have a tendency to detach an officer's thought from those high and delicate refinements which constitute the distinction between the art of war and the art of gain.' For Coxon, who had previously demonstrated touchiness in matters of his authority, and harboured well-founded fears about his comparative lack of experience, these were deep waters.

John Coxon came from the social dormitory of the Indies trade, a middle class that, in the words of one authority, 'was gradually gaining a secondary gentility towards the end of the 18th century'. To William Hosea, who described him as 'a plain man', he was clearly not quite a gentleman, but to judge from his surviving correspondence and logbook, he was educated and had an ordered mind. Nevertheless, his rise to command had been distinctly unconventional.

Officers learned the sea the hard way – mostly from boyhood, usually after a spell as midshipman, a junior petty officer. Coxon came to the sea comparatively late and his first voyage in an Indiaman, the *Pacific*, in 1764, was not as a seaman at all but as the ship's purser. He was aged about twenty-four at the time, a delicate-looking young man, responsible for finance and accounting. In this, and his shrewd exploitation of money-making opportunity, he showed a flair that was for mercantile rather than maritime affairs. Certainly nothing in his previous experience of the sea prepared him adequately for the sudden rise to officer rank that followed. For his second Indiaman passage he was made up to fourth mate before going directly to the rank of chief mate.

All this was thoroughly irregular. Coxon had escaped not only the usual rigorous apprenticeship in the shrouds, but also bypassed the ranks of third and second mate which, it was stipulated, candidates for command should hold for probationary voyages before promotion to chief mate. As so often in the murky world of the Company's affairs, such rapid progress hinted at powerful patronage if nothing else. Coxon's next step up, to the command of the *Grosvenor*, would have required something more: money.

The Company liked to make the claim that its captains were the finest navigators in the world. In reality, as C. Northcote Parkinson observed in his classic study, *Trade in the Eastern Seas*, they were nothing of the kind. Navigational pioneering was done by Navy men; Indiamen captains kept to a beaten track in which there was generally no need for brilliance. But the rewards for competence could be spectacular. A captain's salary did little more than keep him in madeira and provide for his family at home. His prospects lay rather in the opportunity for private trade – space in the hold for 55 tons of goods on the way out, 38 tons coming home – and all that he could wring out of his passengers for their accommodation. This pragmatic compromise with its skippers evolved from the Company's inability to prevent them from trading in the exotic rarities that it sought to monopolise. In the earliest days of the spice trade, when a pennyworth of nutmeg was worth £2 10s in London, private speculation by seamen who, quite naturally, sought proper recompense for their perilous existences had threatened that monopoly, and regulation of the practice now allocated space not just to the captain, but his senior officers too. Although profit margins had come down, captains still expected to make enough in two or three voyages to retire in the style of the nabobs they transported.

Coxon's will was to disclose an estate of a modest £4,120, which suggests that his previous voyage as captain had been no more a commercial success than it had been harmonious. However, that makes no allowance for his investments, in acquiring both the command of the *Grosvenor* and her cargo for the second voyage. These would only have borne fruit on his return to Britain, where the £8,000 estimated value of his private goods in the hold would have translated into almost £50,000, or about £3 million today. His sale of passages and cargo space had already earned another

£10,000 with a further significant consideration to come from the successor whom he would nominate. All in all, Coxon stood to benefit handsomely from what he intended to be his last voyage before returning to Bengal, where he would set up as a merchant on an estate he had just acquired from his father-in-law, Joseph Sherburne. Perhaps Coxon felt that he was not suited to the sea. Before taking leave of his wife Harriet and baby son Joseph, he had presented her with a miniature painting of himself in the recently introduced uniform of an Indiaman captain. Despite the gold braid and wig, it is not the portrait of an authoritative man; even aged forty, he appears almost too slight and youthful for command and there is a hint of softness, a pudginess about the chin.

It would have been extraordinary had there not been deficiencies in Coxon's seamanship, and he had become dependent on two strong subordinates. Neither was his social equal but each had a depth of experience that he lacked. It was not, on the evidence, a healthy association – at least insofar as the running of a happy, efficient ship was concerned.

Coxon had first encountered Alexander Logie in the old *Grosvenor* in 1770. In contrast to his captain, Logie had come up the hard way, going to sea at the age of fourteen as an apprentice in a coastal vessel, then as a seaman to the West Indies before making his first voyage to India as a midshipman in the old *Grosvenor*, when Coxon was fourth mate. Logie had then gained experience as an officer on two further passages to the Caribbean before returning to serve under Coxon. Henceforth they were a team. Although Logie sailed once more across the Atlantic, he had tied his fortunes to Coxon's star.

The second of Coxon's trusted henchmen was also of modest background and had come up almost exactly the same way as Logie. Thomas Beale had gone to sea as a boy and joined the old *Grosvenor* aged seventeen as an ordinary seaman when Coxon, then about thirty, had been chief mate, and Logie, twenty-one, a midshipman. By their next voyage – with Coxon still as chief mate and Logie fourth mate – Beale had risen to midshipman. When Coxon had been approved as captain and proudly taken command of the new *Grosvenor* on her maiden voyage in 1777, Logie and Beale had followed him, as third and fourth mates respectively.

The log for the outward journey gave little hint of incipient trouble. Each day's entry began with the weather, a record of the distance covered, an observation of latitude and an estimate of the infinitely more vexed question of longitude.* Even quite mundane events were recorded: 'a.m. Washed the gundeck and swabbed with vinegar. p.m. Exercised the great guns.' 'Found several spare sails with rat holes in them.' When tragedy or indiscipline occurred they were no more than were to be expected on board: 'At 6 a.m. John McDonach one of the Company's recruits fell over board and was drowned.' 'Punished George Taylor with a dozen lashes for cutting William Muir across his arm with a knife.'

But as the months went by and the strains of the journey started to tell on officers and men, human drama emerges in terse entries that hint at more complex events. The desertions began as soon as they landed in India:

July 21 – Ran from the ship in the night five seamen.
August 9 – Having liberty to go on shore, four men did not return.
August 17 – Having liberty to go ashore, eight men did not return.
August 30 – Run from the ship in the night with the Jolly Boat, two men.

Desertion was common enough when men had been so long at sea, and was not in itself a sign of a troubled ship. Lascars – Indian sailors from the eastern Muslim states – could usually be found as replacements and on this occasion at least three of the deserters returned. In all, however, the *Grosvenor* lost sixteen men through desertion and another ten to death by disease.

Even more serious were the signs of disciplinary problems that surfaced as she was preparing to depart for home. On 29 October, Coxon recorded: 'Punish'd Edward Matthews quartermaster with a dozen lashes for insolent and Mutinous behaviour, and six lashes for refusing to do his duty.' After they sailed, matters came to a head.

The *Grosvenor*'s chief mate then was David Drummond. He too had sailed with Coxon before, but whereas Logie and Beale had benefited from his patronage, Drummond had once been his superior. Ten years earlier, Coxon had been fourth mate to Drummond's third mate. In those

* Latitude – position north or south of the Equator – was readily calculable from a noon sun sight. Longitude – position east or west of a home port – was far more difficult to establish and for centuries was generally calculated by 'dead reckoning', various crude means of estimating a ship's speed. Innumerable vessels were lost through navigational error before John Harrison's chronometers, which kept accurate time differentials between ship and port, enabled captains to determine their whereabouts accurately.

close quarters, grudges and enmities were easily conceived and if Coxon suffered at Drummond's hands it would have been natural for him to take revenge when the opportunity arose. Equally if, as it appears, the team of Coxon, Logie and Beale had become a clique, they might simply have excluded Drummond, then turned on him.

The entry for the log of 15 February reads: 'In the evening, suspended Mr Drummond from his station as Chief Mate for neglect of Duty.' When the *Grosvenor* reached St Helena a month later, Drummond was still suspended. He immediately appealed to the island's Governor and Council to be reinstated, protesting his innocence. While Drummond was admonished, it was the lightest rap on the knuckles, for his application was successful. Coxon wrote in the log: 'I was desir'd to attend the Council, and after they had inquir'd into the merits of the case, Mr Drummond was reprimanded by them for his behaviour. They at the same time recommended his making a proper acknowledgment of his fault before them, to restore him to his Station, which he readily complied with, and promis'd better Behaviour in future.'

Drummond would pose Coxon no further difficulties, but discord persisted. The ship was off Ireland when the captain had two men clapped in irons, 'Robert Newstead, seaman, for attempting to run from the ship and Alexis Adamson, quartermaster, for Mutinous behaviour.' They remained in irons for ten days, an unusually harsh punishment, at which point the log records:

> Punished Adamson with two dozen lashes for Mutiny and refusing to do his duty & afterwards confined him in irons again. Newstead being sensible of his behaviour in attempting to run from the ship and making proper confession, released him.

If Newstead was apologetic, he was not contrite. Nine days later, he was among twelve men who deserted as soon as the ship reached Dublin.

When the *Grosvenor* left again for India, not a single foremastman remained of those who had been on her maiden voyage. Just seven men stayed with Coxon: his servant, four petty officers, and Logie and Beale. As chief mate, Logie was now set to reap the rewards of his loyalty, for Coxon was leaving the sea and a ship's owners usually accepted a captain's choice of successor.

Promoted to third mate, Beale too was keen to exploit the benefits of his rank. On the outward voyage, he accepted £50 each from two young cadets to mess in his quarters, and then failed to meet his side of the bargain. When they objected, he abused and lorded it over them in the mess – to the point that they made an official complaint on landing. Beale, it would seem, was a fairly typical sea bully. Worse, however, he was an arrogant dolt.

The *Grosvenor* spent almost two months in Trincomalee, awaiting other arrivals. Indiamen usually sailed in company, both to assist one another in adversity, and to enable captains to consult one another on navigational questions at a time when the science was still at a fairly rudimentary stage. Coxon had good reasons for not wishing to voyage alone into what were, for him, uncharted waters and, faced with taking the route across the Indian Ocean known as the Outer Passage, he delayed his departure, hoping for another stray Indiaman at the end of the sailing season.

Trincomalee was one of the world's great natural harbours, with sheltered sandy bays on either side of a peninsula, at the end of which Fort Frederick stood hundreds of feet above the sea at the edge of a cliff top. As the days went by, and still the *Grosvenor* remained at anchor, passengers had the chance to seek rooms in the fort, although many visitors found Trincomalee's mosquitoes intolerable and preferred to stay on board ship. There was also an opportunity for walks, for fishing, and for a break from the fare served up by Coxon's Portuguese cook, Antonio da Cruza. Among the local delicacies were a rich soup made from monitor lizards and roasted wild pig; but while the passengers enjoyed a respite from shipboard life, no such option was available to those with whom they were to share the voyage ahead. The crew spent those eight weeks in searing heat, broiling miserably in their hammocks.

Along with thirty-five passengers, the ship had a crew of 105. Of that number sixty-five were the foremastmen who scrambled up ratlines into the rigging, hauled themselves along yardarms to spread sails and performed other gravity-defying duties for £1 3s a month in the case of seamen rated ordinary, rising to £1 11s on being rated able. An able seaman walked down the gangplank after an eighteen-month voyage with a little over £20 in his pocket, before heading to the nearest tavern.

They came from the bottom rung of a society as unequal as any of its time: on the one hand, a privileged few able to enjoy what London offered Casanova: 'a magnificent debauch – sup, bathe and sleep with a fashionable courtesan' for six guineas; on the other, an underclass drawn from all the poverty and brutishness depicted by Hogarth. Life in the gin-soaked lanes off the Thames was particularly nasty and short; while life expectancy across the country was thirty-seven years, in London it was in the mid-twenties. Justice for miscreants was summary and savage; *peine forte et dure* – crushing to death – had been abolished less than ten years earlier, and public executions were still a popular spectacle.*

For young men entirely without prospects or education, the sea may have offered an escape from this world – that is if they could stay alive long enough to learn the ropes, avoid the ravages of scurvy and fever which took off on average 10 per cent of crews on voyages to the East, and then find themselves lucky enough to be serving under a fair and competent skipper, not on some hell afloat. Nevertheless, the life expectancy of the English seaman was probably no more than that of the poorest Londoner.

Sailors had long been identified as a community apart, with a distinctive dress that marked them almost like some odd religious sect. Habitués of waterfronts around the British Isles, they dwelt at land's edge even when not actually at sea, and, like all outsiders, were regarded with a certain wariness. By the end of the eighteenth century, however, England was established as a great seafaring power and her seamen had been taken to the nation's heart by a popular culture that mythologised their mystique. Arne's 'Rule, Britannia' set the tone in 1740, but it was words by David Garrick and the music of William Boyce for a pantomime featuring the ballad 'Heart of Oak' that created an enduring image of the jolly tar as a seeker of honour and glory on the high seas, a world in which none were so free as the sons of the waves. The Viennese master Joseph Haydn, on a sojourn in London, set a breezy hornpipe to an English lyric celebrating the sailor, 'High on the giddy bending mast, fearless of the rushing blast'.

* Just two days before the *Grosvenor* sailed from England, London was convulsed by the Gordon Riots, seven days of all-out anarchy – the storming of prisons, attacks on the Bank of England – that only ended when soldiers opened fire on the mob, killing 285 people. Afterwards thirty of the ringleaders were hanged at Tyburn.

Most popular of these idealised period pieces, however, was Charles Dibdin's lament for a dead shipmate.

> Here, a sheer hulk, lies poor Tom Bowling,
> The darling of our crew;
> No more he'll hear the tempest howling,
> For death has broached him to.
> His form was of the manliest beauty,
> His heart was kind and soft.
> Faithful below, Tom did his duty
> And now he's gone aloft.

An officer of the times offered a harder-edged but more persuasive view: 'The multitude of these men are wholly illiterate, their ideas [as] wild, confused and indeterminate as the elements; their dispositions naturally generous, though turbulent. Fearless, or rather thoughtless of consequences, they will run every risk to satisfy the caprice of the moment.'

Improvident, reckless, dissolute, but brave and dependable . . . the qualities of the tar have acquired the ring of a stereotype. Still, they echo what we know of an exceptionally close-knit and interdependent society. Sailors trusted their shipmates and obeyed their commanders, not only because of the severity of the regime, but because it was the best way to survive. Allowing for a tendency to romanticise him, the English seaman was a doughty fellow – at least in his own environment; and if there were plenty of toughs and desperadoes, along with a few pessimistic 'croakers' and the occasional solitary mystic, there were also enough men who could be counted as worthy companions of Tom Bowling.

It would be a mistake, however, to see the community below decks as homogeneous. Among the *Grosvenor*'s foremast men we find Scots and Irishmen, and no fewer than seven Italians. There were Catholics and Protestants, fourteen Johns, seven Thomases, five Williams and four Jameses. A handful might be taken as broadly representative.

Thomas Lewis and John Warmington were experienced hands who had set topgallant sails from the Sargasso Sea to the Sunda Straits. Neither would still have been thought of as young in seamen's terms – Warmington had recently turned twenty-nine – and years in the rigging had left them as weathered as the canvas they hauled and hoisted. They nevertheless retained the wiry fitness of youth. Lewis hailed from Belfast, Warmington from a village near Newquay, in Cornwall, that had produced generations of seafarers. The Warmington clan had another, darker association with the sea. A generation before John's birth, the Warmingtons had been involved in wrecking at the coastal town of Perranporth; this practice, which generally involved plundering wrecked ships, rather than actually luring them onto the rocks as folklore would have it, had resulted in a number of Warmingtons being summoned to a manorial court, although they had evidently argued their case sufficiently stoutly to have escaped the assizes. John himself may have been ready by now to quit the sea, for shortly before sailing in the *Grosvenor* he had married a village girl, Elizabeth Roberts. He and Lewis were rated able and were able to sign their names in the ship's impress book in which receipt of their wages was recorded.

John Hynes was an Irishman, born in Limerick, and had never been to sea before joining the *Grosvenor* in Dublin near the end of her previous voyage, when the crew had been so depleted by desertions that Coxon had been forced to take on unskilled men to get her back to the Downs. Hynes had gained sufficient experience to be rated ordinary.

Three youngsters are of particular interest. Even by the standards of the age Robert Price was young when he went to sea, being about eleven when Coxon took him on as his servant on the outward voyage. In addition, Price helped to serve meals in the cuddy and carried out some of the seaman's simpler duties. He was now aged about thirteen, a bright and lively boy. Barney Leary was also in his teens, a lad of no education and little intelligence, but great physical strength. Of all the seamen on board, he was the only one rated a landman, a complete neophyte.

By comparison, William Habberley was an old hand, although only twenty-one. Born into a once-prosperous family a short distance from the taverns and slums of London's docklands, he had been apprenticed, in 1778 while still in his teens, to a seasoned mariner, William Shaw, with whom he made his first voyage to the West Indies. Two years later Shaw joined the *Grosvenor* as second mate and took Habberley with him as his servant and as a seaman, rated ordinary. Unusually for one of his calling, Habberley was sufficiently educated to be able to write – his prose was rough but exemplified the vigour with which he did everything – and this, along with his tutelage under Shaw, indicates that he would have qualified in time for officer rank.

Captains waged a constant struggle to recruit even inexperienced hands and cast a wide net among the nationalities not only of Europe but also of Asia. Sailors from the ports of what is now Italy were especially welcome on English vessels, being unaligned in the conflicts of Europe; of the seven on the *Grosvenor* little is known besides their names, but two were to play notable parts in her story. Francisco di Lasso was from Genoa, Francisco Feancon, known as Bianco, from Venice.

The impressing of *Grosvenor* sailors in India explained the presence on board in significant numbers of another group, one often overlooked. Few Indiamen were able to start the homeward voyage without lascars, Muslim sailors who were recruited to make up the numbers of those lost to disease, desertion and the press gangs, and who made just the single journey before being shipped back to India as passengers. They did not have a high reputation among captains, being regarded as unreliable in bad weather and, unsurprisingly, prone to die in severe cold; it was barely to be wondered at either that they showed little inclination to risk their lives against England's foes in battle, for which they earned a reputation for cowardice. Of the *Grosvenor*'s sixty-five foremastmen, twenty-five were lascars. Although these bearded and turbaned figures were a constant visible presence on deck and in the rigging, their names are not recorded in the ship's impress book.

Evidence of integration is mixed. Although the lascars abominated the whoring and drunkenness of European seamen, they frequently joined in the gaiety of Saturday 'grog nights' on board, when songs were sung and hornpipes danced. Certainly there was no room for segregation on the gun deck, where the crew lived in the space forward of the mizzenmast. They messed in groups of five between the great guns, at tables that were stowed away between meals, and slept in hammocks slung fore to aft so closely that they brushed against one another with the ship's movement.

All these men with the exception of Hynes were making their first voyage in the *Grosvenor*. For performing their day-to-day duties they were divided into two watches, starboard and larboard, and came under one of two officers – Logie, the chief mate, or William Shaw, the new second mate. In the divisions that were to affect the ship's company, Shaw stands out as a catalyst.

From the little that is known of him, William Shaw was an unlikely candidate for the role of a Fletcher Christian. Like Logie, he had learned his craft from the bottom, but there similarities ceased. Logie was a rough Scot, while Shaw, according to Habberley, whose description is the only one we have, was 'an amiable man of delicate constitution'. His seamanship, however, was proven. Still aged only thirty-one, Shaw had served in every capacity and alone of Coxon's officers had commanded his own ship. He made his first voyage to India as a boy of fourteen when he was identified as a potential officer and made a midshipman in the *Bute* before being approved as fourth mate in the *Prime*. These three passages east were followed by four across the Atlantic, the last one to Grenada as captain of the *Duchess of Devonshire*. It was then that young William Habberley came under his wing.

When the second mate and his lad came on board the *Grosvenor* they were, like all the deckhands, newcomers to an established hierarchy. Below the triumvirate of Coxon, Logie and Beale, came a tier of petty officers. Coxon's old hands included Robert Rea, the bosun, a sergeant-major figure in charge of deck activities, John Hunter, the gunner, and John Edkins who, as caulker, was responsible for keeping the ship watertight.

It would have been only natural for a certain rivalry to have arisen between Logie and Shaw. Both were experienced men of similar age, and they were required to work closely as officers of their respective watches; that Shaw had already been a captain added spice to the relationship. Evidence that this gave rise to disciplinary problems while they were at sea is scant and circumstantial. What can be said is that Shaw inspired loyalty in the men and when the time for a choice came, the common seamen demonstrated a preference for his leadership over that of the triumvirate.

For the duration of their stay in Trincomalee, Coxon was preoccupied by matters other than harmony among his officers. Day after day he scanned the horizon for sight of one vessel in particular: the *Earl of Dartmouth* was originally to have accompanied the *Grosvenor* from Madras but had failed to arrive in time. There was now little likelihood that she would pass this way, but Coxon held on as long as he dared. He could, in fact, have waited until doomsday, for the *Earl of Dartmouth* was at the bottom of the Bay of Bengal.

As the weeks passed, it would have been surprising if the passengers had not grown restive. No one sailed on an Indiaman with any pleasurable anticipation and the perception of later generations that sea travel could be stylish, enjoyable, and even sybaritic, was unimaginable. It was, quite simply, an ordeal – 'the mere anticipation a kind of terrible nightmare', as one contemporary source put it. Adding to the strain was the fact that conditions inimical to social harmony were being shared among persons of consequence. Men and women accustomed to having their own way, to spacious and luxurious surroundings and the attention of armies of servants, found themselves facing a voyage together of perhaps six months in an area rather smaller than a decent-sized drawing room. On the *Grosvenor* this area was being shared by eighteen privileged passengers, for the majority of whom the sole escape was a cabin in which there was barely space for a cot. The other sixteen, the discharged soldiers and servants, were given hammocks among the crew; some secluded quarter in the bowels of the ship was found for the *ayahs*.

The potential for discord was recognised by the Company, which had drawn up regulations for conduct at sea, which were issued to passengers and read in part:

> The diversity of characters and dispositions which must meet on ship-board makes some restraint upon all necessary; and any one offending against good manners, or known usages and customs, will, on representation to the Court [of Directors] be severely noticed.

The gentlefolk kept to the aft. The largest living space was on the quarterdeck, starting with the roundhouse at the rear. This low but spacious and bright area, about thirty feet long, included the captain's and officers' cabins and a stateroom lit by a gallery of six windows set into the curved stern. Immediately forward of the roundhouse was the cuddy, where meals were taken and which gave on to an open stretch of quarterdeck, extending about forty feet forward to the mainmast, used for promenading and 'airing'. Immediately below the roundhouse, on the gun deck, was the great cabin, an area about thirty-five feet by thirty, which was subdivided at the start of a voyage into individual cabins relative to the rank of passengers and the passage money they had paid. Sufficient space had still to be left for a general living area enclosed in the aft by a stern gallery of eight windows. The only other space for the passengers' use was the poop – the rear upper deck, perhaps thirty feet long – although this was a little exposed in all but the calmest conditions.

William Hosea was undoubtedly feeling the strain. It was fully seven months since he and Mary had left their home in Bengal so abruptly, no doubt believing that with good fortune they would by now be back in England. That desperate race to join the ship in Madras must have seemed almost a lifetime ago, and now that he had regained his composure, Hosea was not impressed with his quarters.

For an outlay of £2,000 he would have been expecting the entire great cabin to be at his disposal. As it was, he and Mary with Frances and Tom Chambers had been allocated part of the roundhouse, with room just for their cots, a pair of chairs, a washstand and writing desk. A bookcase was superfluous, since his books, along with bedlinen and provisions, had been abandoned on the *Yarmouth*. Sweltering in the cabin, Hosea wrote fretfully, and a little testily, to Chambers: 'We have no news of our dear Charlotte, which has not a little added to the many uneasinesses we have experienced lately. The heat is intolerable – the sun is vertical & being at anchor, no wind can reach our cabin.' Mary tried to be uncomplaining but found the whole business a trial: 'May the Almighty give my little woman strength to bustle thro' all her fatigues and difficulties. I can at all times depend on her spirits of resolution.'

With space so short, the great cabin had been partitioned with sheets of canvas into four doubles and a single. Colonel and Mrs James and the traders Williams and Taylor occupied the two most spacious doubles. Talbot may well have been less happy at having to share a smaller cabin with the Army captain, Adair, for quite apart from the question of space, a Navy captain was equivalent in Army terms to a colonel. The paroled French prisoners were also mixing messes, Colonel d'Espinette being quartered with his junior, Lieutenant de L'Isle. Where space was found for poor Charles Newman is not clear. Each of them had room for just a 'sea-couch', a cot with drawers underneath that served as a lounger during the day, and perhaps a washstand.

The passenger best provided for was Lydia Logie, cosily set up with her husband, the chief mate, in his cabin, typically 'a neat well-furnished little room' about twelve feet by ten, with the services of her maid; but the four unaccompanied children, Thomas Law and Robert Saunders, and Eleanor Dennis and Mary Wilmot, were in two tiny partitions.

By the middle of June even Coxon's patience was exhausted. No other Indiaman was likely to appear so late in the season. Sailings from Bengal would not recommence with any frequency before August and to wait until then would have been almost unthinkable.

Admiral Hughes, his duty to the garrison discharged, sailed on 14 June. In the months ahead, he was to fight three more indecisive battles with Suffren, but the French challenge to British ascendancy in India was effectively over. Hyder Ali's death before the end of the year ended the threat to Madras.

On the eve of the Navy's departure, Coxon raised anchor. As the *Grosvenor* slipped out of harbour with 140 souls on board, the crew clambered into the crosstrees and unfurled her topgallants. As the island receded and the Indian Ocean opened out broad to the horizon, they raised a cheer. At last they were sailing home.

Below, the passengers were gathered on the quarterdeck, watching the land slide away, Hosea with his secrets and Newman with his confidences, the former foes James and d'Espinette with old campaigns to talk over, and the merchants Taylor and Williams with their fortunes securely baled up in the hold and their dreams of palaces in the shires.

There, too, Mary Hosea, torn with longing for the baby she had left behind. Taking a last opportunity to write to Fanny Chambers before they sailed, she concluded with a prayer and a plea: 'God bless you. Kiss my infant a thousand times for me.'

4

A LIGHT IN THE DARK

At sea, Indian Ocean, 13 June–3 August 1782

Lord Macaulay thought there no place so propitious as an Indiaman for the formation either of close friendships or deadly enmities. A voyage over several months in so confined a space tested the tolerance of everyone. Quite often, it exposed the true character of individuals as only extremity can:

> Any thing is welcome which may break that long monotony, a sail, a shark, an albatross, a man overboard. Most passengers find some resource in eating twice as many meals as on land. But the great devices for killing time are quarrelling and flirting. The facilities for both these exciting pursuits are great. The inmates of the ship are thrown together far more than in any country-seat or boarding-house. None can escape the rest except by imprisoning himself in a cell in which he can hardly turn. All food, all exercise, is taken in company. Ceremony is to a great extent banished. It is every day in the power of a mischievous person to inflict innumerable annoyances; it is every day in the power of an amiable person to confer little services. It not seldom happens that serious distress and danger call forth in genuine beauty and deformity heroic virtues and abject vices which, in the ordinary intercourse of good society, might remain during many years unknown even to intimate associates.

The *Clyde* Indiaman off Natal, engraving 1826

The *Grosvenor* was at sea for fifty-two days after sailing from Trincomalee. Little detail of that time survives. We know, however, that the passengers were without the usual diversions of sailing in company: the banter hurled between vessels; the sense of association with others, however remote. Their isolation went deeper. No vessel bound for the Indies hove in sight, bringing news shouted across the water of affairs that might keep the company in conversation for days. Before their departure, all the talk had been of the momentous events in North America after Cornwallis's surrender at Yorktown eight months earlier, but of subsequent events they heard nothing. They did spot one ship early on, a fast-sailing packet that soon overtook the *Grosvenor*. It was the *Swallow* and the merchants Taylor and Williams, who had applied unsuccessfully for passage on her, may have watched ruefully as she scudded by and dropped over the horizon. After that the days slipped imperceptibly one into another, the Indiaman swaying and creaking along under her press of canvas, a solitary speck in that immensity of blue.

Even in the Company era, British India was obsessed with caste, and Coxon ordered his dinner table in the cuddy along lines of precedence. Some captains went in horror of women's company, but Coxon was no rough sea dog and Mary Hosea, as wife of the Resident at Murshidabad, was placed at his right hand at the centre of the table, with Sophia James at his left. William Hosea naturally took his place on the right, but there may have been some dispute over who ranked next, Colonel James or Captain Talbot who, notwithstanding the circumstances of his arrival, had a real eminence on any English vessel.

Deciding who stood elsewhere in the pecking order raised other tricky questions. What about the nabobs Williams and Taylor, who had paid handsomely for their passages and had a right to expect a certain deference? And where did the dandy Charles Newman, whose concern for appearances was manifest, rank beside them? The fact that he had so antagonised the Madras Council might have counted in his favour with Coxon, who had his own reasons for detesting those honourable gentlemen; but how did he stand with Colonel James, with his impeccable Madras connections? It was in the manner he handled such delicate points of etiquette that a captain could ordain whether a voyage proceeded in relative harmony or gave rise to such friction as had led to duels.

Among the ladies, quarrels and intrigues were no less common. Of Sophia James's disposition nothing is known. Mary Hosea, sweet-tempered and affectionate – 'it is impossible to do otherwise than love her', thought her friend Mrs Fay – was unlikely to make enemies; but it is entirely possible that Lydia Logie, handsome, red-headed and garrulous, became a trial to those confined closely with her. On short acquaintance Hosea had written forebodingly that, although the chief mate's wife was the finest lady, she 'really speaks prodigiously'.

Sexual politics on board can be glimpsed in a letter written by Mary Hosea's friend, Eliza Fay, who was taking passage on another Indiaman at around the same time.

> The woman, of whom I entertained some suspicion from the first, is I am credibly informed, one of the very lowest creatures taken off the streets in London; she is so perfectly depraved in disposition, that her supreme delight consists in rendering everybody about her miserable . . . I have been repeatedly compelled (for the Honour of the Sex) to censure her swearing, and indecent behaviour . . .
>
> The gentlemen were in general too fond of the bottle to pay us the least attention; after tea we were never asked to cut in at cards, though they played every evening.

If the fact that all three ladies on the *Grosvenor* were married meant there were fewer opportunities than usual for flirting, the conditions for quarrelling could hardly have been bettered, and once the cold suspicion that served the English abroad on initial acquaintance had relaxed into amity or hardened into hostility, coalitions started to form of more or less like-minded individuals.

Hosea and Newman were already acquainted. They were on different sides in the Hastings feud and, while there is no reason to suppose that Newman was aware of Hosea's treachery, there was some awkwardness between them. A year earlier Hosea, dealing with a Bengali official in typically high-handed fashion, had dismissed a powerful *zemindar*, or tax collector. The man had hired a lawyer and launched a Supreme Court suit against Hosea and the Company. Asked by Hastings for his legal opinion, Newman had reported that there was little doubt the *zemindar* would win and recommended that to save embarrassment to the Company, he be paid his costs and damages. In the end, the discomfiture was Hosea's. He and Newman would have weeks to discuss the finer points of the Hastings regime.

Whereas Newman and Hosea were Company men, trustful of convention and authority, Taylor and Williams had savoured the fruits of individual enterprise. As adventurers, they had more in common with the military men and may have found a fellow spirit in Talbot, who was fond of the gentlemanly pleasures of cards and madeira. How inter-service rivalry manifested itself between Talbot and his Army peer James in those close quarters is not known. There is a possibility, however, that they discovered a mutual fate as ageing rejects; Talbot had, in effect, been sacked from the Navy and James, whatever his virtues, had not enjoyed a notably distinguished record.

Apart from the confinement, the deadly boredom and the constant lurching motion – in bad weather even mundane tasks were impossible, and it became a question of holding fast to avoid injury – what most people remembered of an Indiaman voyage were the sounds and smells:

> . . . the cries of the sailors; the creaking of the ship's sides; the wind in the rigging; the lapping of water; it is universal, ceaseless. And then there are the appalling odours from which there is no escape, that detestable tar, the emanations from that odious galley.

The cries of command and the thud of activity on deck from 5 a.m. ensured an early rise. Breakfast might be followed by a promenade before the first challenge of the day: how to deal with the yawning empty morning. The worthy took up self-improving studies – languages and history were popular – and Hosea, who had planned his reading so diligently, must constantly have lamented the loss of his books. Time hung heavily, and great was the opportunity for the squabbling and backbiting that drove some delicate souls to the hermitage of the cabin. Dinner at two lasted well into the afternoon, with the natural consequence of sleep or gossip. More turns around the quarterdeck were followed by tea at six. By seven the men had settled to whist, which consumed the evening until a light supper of cheese and biscuits at nine, with perhaps a few more hands of cards before a general retirement.

Dinner, announced by a drumbeat, was an almost ceremonial affair, providing a fleeting reminder of life as it ought to be and reassurance that the rituals governing social order were still in place. Men as well as women frequently acquired an entirely new wardrobe before a voyage – William Hickey spent the fantastic sum of £2,000 on clothing and cabin furniture for his journey home in 1794 – and both sexes dressed as if for an event at Government House in Calcutta: the gentlemen in wigs, jackets, breeches and stockings; the ladies, lace and silks crowned with elaborate coiffures, and Coxon presiding with self-conscious dignity in full fig along with the first and second mates. Forward, in steerage, the third mate Beale and his juniors were also in full uniform at a lesser court. Toasts were standard: to absent friends, to good weather and 'To a happy Sight of the next Land'.

The courses were served by the ship's steward, a burly, warm-hearted man named Henry Lillburne, helped by Coxon's servant, the thirteen-year-old Robert Price. Lillburne had a way with youngsters and kept a paternal eye on Price. He had also taken under his wing the seven-year-old Thomas Law who, although accompanied by a servant, had suffered from homesickness since saying farewell to his father in Calcutta. The little Anglo-Indian boy sought Lillburne out, receiving the odd titbit from the pantry as well as a kindly word.

At least to start with, the table fairly groaned with food – 'a rude kind of plenty', one source called it – even if the fare was hardly up to the standard that Bengal society was used to. 'Ill-concocted soups, queer-looking ragouts and jelly the colour of salt water,' sniffed one lady.* The hold contained 40 tons of salted meat, including beef, pork, bacon and tongue, 15 tons of potatoes, 6 tons of flour, 2 tons of cheese, 4 tons of groceries, five barrels of herring, and six chests of oranges and lemons.

Live provisions also came from the bowels of the ship, parts of which resembled a farmyard. The *Grosvenor* was unusual in not having a cow – Hosea bemoaned a lack of milk – but carried all the other livestock that turned the fore lower deck on most Indiamen into a crowded manger: pigs, sheep and goats snuffled and bleated shoulder to shoulder in piles of increasingly malodorous hay. The poop was even noisier, being stacked with coops of chickens and ducks, which set up a clamour that carried to the

* The British in India were renowned for their appetites. Mrs Fay, no mean trencher woman herself, gives as a typical menu for dinner in Calcutta: 'A soup, a roast fowl, curry and rice, a mutton pie, a fore quarter of lamb, rice pudding, tarts, very good cheese, fresh churned butter, fine bread, excellent madeira.'

roundhouse below. So notorious was the noise of poultry that when, as often happened, the coops were swept away in a storm, the blow of their loss to the table was considerably softened by the peace of silence overhead.

Nor were the passengers stinted on drink. There were 2,700 gallons of wine and 500 gallons of spirit for the captain's table, as well as 7,000 gallons of beer and 1,000 of rum for the sailors' grog. Nevertheless, the captain was under instructions to set his passengers 'an example of sobriety and decorum, as he values the pleasure of the Court'. In these respects, Coxon was a model commander.

The social focus was the cuddy, a space on the quarterdeck that served as dining room and all-purpose living area, whether for cards or for those occasions given over to spontaneous entertainments, dances or musical performances. A woman passenger wrote of one such occasion during a heavy swell off the Cape:

> All the furniture being removed out of the cuddy, I led off; but had only gone down one couple, when a tremendous lee lurch put us all in confusion. I declined standing up again, but the rest in three or four hours, tumbled about in the prettiest manner, and when no longer able to dance, made themselves amends by singing.

Privacy was the most elusive pleasure. Some passengers virtually took to their cots for the voyage, discovering that reading in bed could be 'a most delectable recreation'. Oil lamps or candles provided light, but because of the fear of fire all flames had to be extinguished in cabins by 10 p.m. It was then, in the late hours, that a solitary spirit might find balm in an hour alone on the quarterdeck, amid the slap of water and billowing sails in all that inky blackness.

Plainly these conditions were not conducive to conjugal relations, let alone honeymoons. During the *Grosvenor*'s voyage, however, it became evident that the marriage consummated in the chief mate's little cabin had borne fruit. As Lydia Logie was seen taking her exercise, the crew marked the steady swelling that had begun beneath her gown.

For the remainder of June and through July, the *Grosvenor* tacked across the Indian Ocean, following the route known as the Outer Passage, which ran east of the Maldives chain, swept in a great arc over the empty vastness at the very heart of the ocean, and passed east of Mauritius and south of the huge island of Madagascar. They were sailing directly against the prevailing monsoon, which came from the south-west and therefore dictated that they should bear south to latitude of about 35°s, then tack north-west until they encountered the coast of Africa, where they would pick up the Agulhas current to help them around the Cape of Good Hope. In a bad day of squalls, they might make only 30 nautical miles, but with a fresh wind they could cover 160 miles.

Although no record exists of the voyage, the logs of two other Indiamen on the same course at almost precisely the same time illustrate conditions at sea. Their parallel dramas cast light, moreover, on what was a fateful season in the Indian Ocean.

Days before the *Grosvenor* left Trincomalee, the *Chapman* and the *Earl of Dartmouth* sailed from Madras. Two weeks later, as they were tacking round the island of Cap Nicobar, northernmost of the Nicobar chain due east of Ceylon, the *Earl of Dartmouth* went on to the rocks and was dismasted. The log of the *Chapman*, which went to the rescue, records: 'Most of the passengers and crew were sav'd', although adding, 'the people in general were much wounded by the rocks'. Some were taken on by the *Chapman*, which sailed on without hint of trouble for four weeks; log entries indicate squalls with gales and occasional bright patches. The first death, of a caulker's mate, came on 4 August. Two weeks later a passenger died, followed by a succession of crewmen and more passengers. A baffled Captain Walker responded to the unseen hand carrying off his people by ordering that the decks be washed daily, but there was no interruption. Over the next ten weeks a ghostly procession of names stalks through the log so that by the time they reached St Helena, no fewer than thirty-one bodies had been slipped over the *Chapman's* side after a short prayer. No cause for this disaster is hinted at, although in all probability it was scurvy, aggravated by overcrowded conditions.

Meanwhile the 729-ton *Valentine* was closely following the *Grosvenor*'s course. Among those on board was Mary Hosea's old friend, Eliza Fay, who had hoped to sail on the *Grosvenor* but had been unable to afford the rates being levied by Coxon, and had then missed the *Earl of Dartmouth* – 'she too is absolutely *crowded* with passengers'. As it was, in her straitened circumstances, Mrs Fay was forced into quarters that she found a trial:

'A more uncomfortable passage can hardly be imagined. The port of my cabin being kept shut, and the door opening into the steerage, I had neither light nor air but from a scuttle. Half the space was occupied by a great gun.'

She was no happier with the *Valentine*'s captain, John Lewis, 'a very tyrant' who made his dislike for women clear – 'I cannot *abide* ladies,' he told the astonished Mrs Fay ('So much for this gentleman's *respect* and politeness!') – and did his best to drive them from the cuddy – 'He swore so dreadfully, making use of such vulgar oaths and expressions that Mrs Tottingham withdrew intirely from the table.'

Whatever his manners, Lewis kept a meticulous log in a copperplate hand that shows throughout their course southwards conditions were cloudy and overcast, with frequent squalls and rain. He made regular observations of their latitude, the ship's position relative to the Equator, but so far as the far more awkward question of longitude was concerned – their position relative to the Greenwich meridian – the log is silent. The revolution in navigation created twenty years earlier by John Harrison's timepieces and other chronometers remained beyond the reach of most mariners, who resorted to a variety of methods of estimation, each one as fallible as the next. Still, Lewis had reached the southernmost point of latitude that would take him past the Cape and had a fine following wind when he posted a lookout to watch for land on 17 July. For another ten days they made progress westwards, when Mrs Fay wrote: 'He declared that we had rounded the Cape of Good Hope.'

Lewis's consternation can be imagined when, on 31 July, he took his bearings:

> Longitude observed at 51 minutes after 9am, 33° 51´E, to my utter astonishment.

Far from having passed the Cape, they were still in the Indian Ocean. Lewis tacked north-west and maintained a watch through day and night. On 6 August they sighted land.

Mrs Fay had a fit of the vapours: '. . . the *East* coast of Africa; so near, that before we tacked *flies* were seen on the shore – had this happened during the night, nothing could have saved us from shipwreck. Can I sufficiently bless Providence for this escape?'

On reaching St Helena, Lewis tried to redeem himself by giving 'a grand entertainment on the *Valentine*'. Two days later the *Chapman* arrived, 'in a most dreadful state', with news of the *Earl of Dartmouth* wreck. Once again Mrs Fay thanked Providence, for this was 'the *very ship* I was, as I *then* thought, so *unfortunate* in *missing*'.

Of the *Grosvenor*, however, there was no news. It would be months before Mrs Fay heard that Providence, so kind to her, had not favoured her friend Mary Hosea.

All through July the *Grosvenor* ploughed south through squalls and rain, propelled by the kind of winds that all captains hoped for, ranging from steady breezes to strong trades. Having no previous experience of the Outer Passage, Coxon must have been delighted with their progress as he reached the southern extremity of his course around 24 July and tacked westwards towards Africa.

The first crisis came on 27 July when the *Grosvenor* ran into what Alexander Dalrymple, who conducted the subsequent inquiry, called 'a hard gale'. For weeks the weather had been overcast, but now there was a gathering of black clouds that closed in as high seas bore down on the ship, so that she began to lurch and plunge. Rain sheeted in, the sky became momentarily dazzling with lightning, and thunder pealed across that black ocean from one side to the other like some invisible wave of doom. At such times passengers tended to retreat – some, who wished to nurse their dread alone, to the privacy of the cabin, some to the cuddy where, holding fast to chairs cleated to the deck, they might fill their glasses and make as good a show of sang-froid as they could. Of those on board the *Grosvenor*, the former category was most likely to have included the Hoseas, the latter Captain Talbot and the nabobs.

Sometime during the night of 27 July the storm blew itself out, and when the passengers emerged on deck in the morning, damp and bedraggled – for inevitably during a storm the sea washed through the ports – it was to a calm, if grey sea. Dread was replaced by euphoria and, as people will who have shared a crisis, they congratulated one another on their deliverance. Later that day a two-masted brig was spotted to the west, and although it was out of hailing distance, the sight of another vessel – the first in more than six weeks – served as a further reassurance, for it confirmed that in their endless, empty world they were not, after all, alone.

Not even intelligence that the mainmast, already weakened when they left Ceylon, had been badly sprung during the storm could dampen the mood of high spirits. All that day the hands worked to 'fish' it, reinforcing the fracture with roped splints. To further ease strain on the mast, the top-gallant section was taken down. Henceforth, the mainmast was double-reefed and the *Grosvenor* was, in effect, under reduced sail.

Coxon resumed taking observations. His previous voyages in the favoured season had been via the Inner Passage, which ran south-west through the Maldives and on, west of Madagascar, running close to the African coast through the Mozambique Channel. Using the Outer Passage, far out in the Indian Ocean, set a more severe priority on the calculation of longitude in order to judge when the coast of Africa was being approached. What method Coxon used – lunar observation or dead reckoning – is not known. It was, in any event, to prove as fallible as that employed on the *Valentine*.

Still the outcome might have been different if Alexander Logie had been at his post. In those final days, however, the chief mate – Coxon's means of contact with the crew as well the navigator on whom he depended – had fallen severely ill and was confined to his cabin. His place as officer of the starboard watch had been taken by the oafish third mate Thomas Beale.

On the evening of 3 August they made merry. It was a Saturday – grog night, when an additional ration of rum and water was dispensed among the crew – and William Habberley recalled that the men 'drank jovially to our absent friends'. Land was approaching and, having been away for two years, Habberley noted how the prospect of news from home put the mess in an especially cheery humour.

In the cuddy, Coxon was also in expansive mood as he held forth. They were fairly slipping along with the following easterly now and as Lillburne and Price served supper that night the youth heard Coxon say that he expected to sight land in a couple of days. That would be Natalia, the south-east coast of Africa, so named by Vasco da Gama on doubling the Cape of Good Hope in 1497 and spotting land on Christmas Day. From there they would follow a course south-west around the Cape to the Atlantic.

It was much regretted that, being at war with the Dutch, they could not call at Table Bay. The little settlement, founded 130 years earlier to victual shipping bound for the Indies, had a reputation as the tavern of the seas, a hospitable berth notable for a flat-topped mountain that was the most striking topographical feature many travellers could recall. It was also a welcome source of fresh produce and a wine called constantia that naval men like Talbot could testify was extremely quaffable. However, like other Indiamen that year, the *Grosvenor* would have to sail straight on for another three weeks or so to St Helena.

Despite this doleful intelligence, there was reason to celebrate. They were near the halfway stage, had come through all that the weather could throw at them, and those who knew St Helena said it was almost like an English port – cottages with sash windows, green hills and valleys, and fresh food. As the decanter circulated, Coxon had his own reason for a little inward pleasure, and even an additional glass of madeira. It was his son Joseph's third birthday.

Up on the quarterdeck, Thomas Lewis, the Welshman, was at the helm. The night was pitch-black, with hard squalls blowing from the south-west. At some stage before midnight, Coxon came on deck and was heard by Lewis to say that he estimated they were about 300 miles from land.

The coast of south-east Africa was notorious for its treachery. What caused the violent storms that had driven dozens of Portuguese, Dutch and English vessels ashore, or the rogue waves that had simply swallowed unknown others, remained a mystery to those who used these waters; the science of hydrography had yet to establish that when a fast-moving warm current such as the Agulhas, which courses beside south-east Africa, encounters low-pressure systems arriving from Antarctica, the meteorological consequences will be comparable with pouring icy water into a vat of hot oil. But if the cause was unknown, the dangers were not. Coxon had reached a stage in the voyage that called for especial caution. The loss of the *Dodington* was in living memory, and the standing order arising from it could not have been clearer. Dunn's *Directory* spelled it out:

> The loss of such a number of lives will make the skilful navigator shudder, and make him rack his invention to . . . contrive how to avoid the like accidents in future.

Shaw took over as officer of the watch at midnight. Among those on the new watch, with the seamen who had been exuberantly swilling their grog, was Habberley. Whatever he had drunk, the young Londoner was keen and alert. He was in the first flush of his manhood, resourceful, intelligent, and exhilarated by the exotic world that had been revealed to him since leaving home as Shaw's apprentice. Coming on deck, Habberley noted that the earlier fine, fresh gale had greatly increased in the first watch, to the point that the mainsail had been hauled in, to avoid strain on the sprung mainmast, and even the foremast sails were close-reefed. Over the next hour the wind veered to the south-west and with the sea running high and furious, Habberley and the rest of the hands were ordered into the crosstrees to take in the topsails, leaving the *Grosvenor* under just the main foremast sail and the mizzen staysail.

While engaged in these manoeuvres, Habberley spotted two large lights, high and slightly north of their course, west by north-west. He reported immediately to Shaw. For a while the lights became visible from the deck, then disappeared. A few theories were exchanged. Habberley ventured that the lights had appeared to be spreading, as though across a landscape, but the consensus was that they were a phenomenon of the air, 'something similar to the Northern Lights'.

The lights reappeared. Studying them before they vanished again, Habberley formed the opinion that they were on land and came from 'fires kindled by natives some distance [away]'. The reason the lights kept disappearing was that they were still far off and land formations such as hills were intruding on the line of sight. This was not a phenomenon of the air at all: the *Grosvenor* had arrived at Africa.

Habberley was no more than an ordinary seaman, and Shaw's servant to boot, but they had been together for four years and were on terms close enough for the apprentice to press his opinion, and for the second mate to accept it. Shaw issued orders to change course, bringing the *Grosvenor* around with the wind abaft. At this stage Coxon, who was in his cabin but sensed that they had put about, came up. The captain did not budge from his judgment that they were nowhere near land. He countermanded Shaw and 'gave orders to let the ship remain with her head to the west'.

The watch was changed at 4 a.m. Beale now came on deck as the officer in charge. Shaw told him of the lights and 'cautioned him to keep a good look out'. From the third mate's actions it is evident that he treated this admonition with contempt.

It was about two hours since the first alarm and the lights had vanished again; but all that had happened was that they had again passed behind some feature of the land. The *Grosvenor* was still on a converging course with the coastline.

Soon afterwards Lewis, who had stayed with the watch and was now at the top of the foremast, came swinging down the ratlines in a rush. He told his shipmates that he had seen a great mass of land on the starboard side. They peered into the murk, across foaming crests. Some wanted to see the looming blackness as merely another squall rolling in from the north-west; but Habberley, who had also remained up, was no longer in any doubt, and he and Lewis together persuaded a quartermaster, William Mixon, of their peril.

Mixon ran aft to where Beale stood on the quarterdeck, declaring that he had seen land under their lee bow. Its distance was unclear but immediate action was imperative.

Beale scoffed. What went through his mind in these moments can only be imagined, but it is obvious that he would have nothing to do with any action that vindicated the second mate's opinion. He fulminated against Shaw. All this talk of lights and land had queered the hands. Shaw had panicked. Shaw was not a member of the inner circle. Coxon said that they were 300 miles from Africa and that was an end of it. As two of the seamen later told the inquiry:

> Mr Beale said that he, Mixon, certainly was mistaken, and took no further notice of it, not even so much as to go to the opposite side of the deck to examine it.

According to another of the hands:

> Instead of paying any attention to their information, Mr Beale only laughed at their want of knowledge, and gave not the least credit to their conjecture.

Mixon knew by now just how close they were to catastrophe. He dared to defy Beale and went to Coxon's cabin. This time the captain responded. He came up on deck and ordered the helm to be put about to the opposite tack. The boatswain piped for all hands. Already roused by the clamour, they were on deck in moments, being urged into the rigging to hoist more sail as they valued their lives.

That desperate race lasted just a few minutes. They were executing a manoeuvre that required the ship to describe an arc taking her directly towards the land before she could come about with the wind behind, enabling her to accelerate away into open sea. With the land to the lee, everything now depended on whether they had enough leeway.

They had worn round, bringing the wind on the starboard side, when out of the inky bank all around a foaming swirl came up on the port bow.

When the *Grosvenor* struck, just after 4.30 a.m., it was not with a shudder, but with a shock of such force that Habberley, who had been watching proceedings in a sort of trance, expected the masts to snap like sticks, and was bemused to note they were still standing. In that instant the men, who had just been engaged in revelry, stood looking at one another, and for a frozen moment each recognised in the other a dead man.

5

'NOTHING BUT CONFUSION AND DISMAY'

29°54′E. 31°23′S, 4 August 1782

All anyone knew was that they had struck hard. Just what they had struck – a rock, a reef, an island – was anyone's guess. It was dark, with rain sheeting across the deck as that first wave of dread passed through the ship.

The first reaction on deck was panic. 'Nothing but confusion and dismay prevailed,' Habberley recalled, 'no one knowing what to do for the best, but running distractedly about the vessel imploring the Almighty to deliver them.'

From ladders and companionways other sailors and passengers came pouring on deck. They were greeted by an overwhelming spectacle. Claps of thunder broke above the ship and the sea swirled around darkly like a malevolent spectre. As the Irishman Hynes related, perhaps with a touch of poetic licence: 'Despair was painted on every countenance. Mothers were crying and lamenting over their children; husbands over both.'

Gradually it became clear that they had not struck some isolated rock in the middle of the ocean, for through the dark the outlines of a looming land mass could be made out. All might not be lost. At the same time the horror on the women's faces forced the sailors to take a grip of themselves, and Coxon did his best to restore order. Shouting above the clamour of the storm, he 'assured the passengers that he was not without hope of being able to save them all; and therefore begged them to be composed'.

Wreck of the Grosvenor, East Indiaman, detail from the painting by Robert Smirke, 1784

Habberley and most of the hands were unconvinced. The *Grosvenor* was stuck on what appeared to be an outcrop of the main land mass, but they saw no prospect of the great majority of people reaching it alive, 'the ocean running mountains high, so that had we attempted to get the boats out we could not have survived one minute'. In raw, gangling prose, he conjured up a terrifying image of the scene:

> Our situation was most dreadful, excessive darkness being added to the violent squalls of wind and rain, accompanied with lightning, the surf breaking over the ship and rolling round us with a most terrible noise, the great surges dashing her against the rocks, which in the dark appeared so steep that should any of us have ventured to have reached them and succeeded we were then fearful of the impracticableness of our climbing them.

But as minutes passed and the hint of daylight appeared on the horizon, and as the ship remained above water and their position showed no sign of deteriorating further, a measure of calm settled on the mob milling about the deck. At about 5.30 a.m. the wind shifted from the south-east to the north-west, so that it was coming off the land, and Coxon started to discuss with Logie, roused from his sickbed, and Shaw the prospects of getting the ship afloat again. The word from the hold was that she had not yet taken on much water, and Coxon announced that if they could get her off the rocks and keep her afloat until daylight, they might be able to run her ashore in a safer spot. She was broadside on to the shore as the hands set to, adjusting the sails to carry her off.

No sooner had her bow twisted loose than her mortal wound was exposed. The rock had acted like a plug staunching a haemorrhage; with the plug removed she was doomed. The stern remained fast, but water poured in at the head and within ten minutes was up to the gun deck.

Had she drifted off at this stage, she would have filled rapidly and sunk like a stone taking everyone on board with her. Just as they had previously strained every muscle to get her off, now all efforts were directed to keeping her stable on the rocks. To lower her sails as quickly as possible, the hands ran forward with axes, hacking away at the mainmast until it crashed over the side and was swept on to the rocks in a heaving mountain of canvas and spray. Then the foremast was cut down; it would not clear the side, threatening to pull her about with the force of the current dragging on the canvas, but she stayed fast by the stern. Again a kind of equilibrium had been reached. Even so, they had only bought time – a few hours at most.

In the growing light of day they were at last able to take their bearings and, again, these offered some small measure of relief. This was no island: with a spyglass on the distant land Coxon could see huts and a mass of dark figures assembling on the shore. Habberley estimated that the reef on which the *Grosvenor* was stranded was about two cables' length, or 400 yards, from land. His memory or judgment must have played him false, for a study of the scene today indicates that she could have been no more than 100 yards from land. The shoreline was a low mass of rock extending for hundreds of yards in either direction; around that craggy line a cauldron of white surf boiled and seethed. Yet just beyond it a high ridge rose in grassy tranquillity. They were no great distance from safety. The agonising question was how it might be attained.

Two light craft might be able to take them off in stages. The jolly boat, about twelve feet in length, was manoeuvred on deck, but the dying *Grosvenor* was low down by the head with waves breaking over her side, and in a surge of foam the boat was swept up the quarterdeck and smashed against the wheel and roundhouse door. That left the yawl, a sailing boat large enough to carry about twenty people at a time. It was hoisted over the side, and was immediately dashed to pieces.

Marooned as they were, the first sign now appeared of what would become a pattern of behaviour, with crewmen, mostly young and fit, trying to fashion their own means of survival, and passengers, exposed and vulnerable, seeking to purchase theirs. Robert Rea, who as bosun was the ship's top seaman, a non-commissioned officer responsible for enforcing discipline and liaison between crew and quarterdeck, organised some of the men to start building a raft. Meanwhile, as Habberley related:

> The captain and passengers offered great rewards to anyone who would swim to the shore with the end of a line. After much persuasion, two Italians of the names of Pandolpho and Barchini said they would.

The two men stripped down and were lowered over the stern to the water with lines clenched in their teeth. From the side the entire company watched in taut silence as they battled through the surf towards the shore about fifty yards distant. The two heads could be made out in the churning surf. Barchini was almost at the rocks when he was picked up by a wave and hurled against that black mass with sickening force. For a moment he lay there, splayed across the rock, then was dragged back into the water and was seen no more. Joseph Barchini was the first of those on the *Grosvenor* to die.

Pandolpho too was hurled close to the rocks, but was then pulled back by an eddy, and in that moment seized his opportunity to swim in the last few yards and clamber on land. A cheer went up from the *Grosvenor*. It was by no means clear how they might use it, but they had a lifeline.

About three hours had passed since the Indiaman had run aground and the wind off the shore had eased. Three lascars now also plunged into the water and succeeded in reaching the shore. Once again the ship fell silent as it was seen that the dark figures originally spotted through the spyglass had come down to the water's edge; but although the seamen, 'were immediately surrounded by the natives', Habberley wrote, they were not molested by them. Instead, the figures, clearly tribesmen of some sort, turned their attention to the mast and rigging washed on to the rocks.

With the lines carried by Pandolpho and the lascars, a hawser was dragged to the shore, fastened to a rock and winched taut to the mizzenmast. Then, using a metal eye threaded on to the hawser, a deck grating was rigged to form a platform that could be hauled by rope between the ship and the shore. The device appears to have been the idea of Isaac Blair, Captain Talbot's coxswain and himself a Navy man, who made a successul test run to the shore with a load of essentials. Again a cheer went up and there was some talk of bringing up the women and children to carry them to safety; but just the one journey was made before disaster struck. The rope to haul the platform back to the ship was allowed to fall slack and it became caught in the rocks; an attempt to jerk it free only succeeded in breaking it.

The first signs of a breakdown in discipline occurred at about 11 a.m. At least a dozen men broke ranks and swarmed on to the hawser, starting to haul themselves along it. Their weight caused it to sag in the middle so that breaking waves washed them off. Nine men drowned or were dashed to their deaths, including John Woodward, a quartermaster. This loss of discipline left the hawser trailing in the surf and in effect took the platform out of commission. No further use was made of it.

A few others swam on after falling off the hawser, among them Francisco di Lasso from Genoa, and Robert Price, the captain's servant. Di Lasso managed to clamber to safety, but the boy was hurled head first against the rocks. Had di Lasso not seized him by the hair and pulled him out, he would have drowned. As it was, his head poured blood from a terrible wound and he was left senseless. Price was to carry a livid scar across his forehead for the rest of his days, but the incident created a lasting bond between man and boy, one that kept them together through all the trials of the months ahead.

Back on the ship, panic again took hold. As Habberley put it:

> The greatest part . . . gave themselves up for lost while others . . . went about the vessel plundering and breaking everything open and in a most beastly manner getting intoxicated. Two were supposed to be drowned in the lazaretto, where the liquors are kept.

Habberley and the other sources are silent on the whereabouts of the passengers at this time, or just what Captain Coxon and his officers were doing; but it is indicative of Coxon's blindness to his true situation that he had the idea of firing the *Grosvenor*'s cannons. This common signal for ships in distress off the British coast was unlikely to have any effect in the middle of nowhere off Africa. More crucially, when the gunner went below to the powder room and found it almost full of water, nothing was done to remove the small remaining quantity of powder from the magazine. Otherwise, Coxon is significant by his absence from the accounts of critical events. Beale was spoken of, darkly, as the architect of their fate – 'everybody considered Mr Beale highly blamable', wrote Habberley – but he too goes unmentioned for any activity during the wreck.

Nothing is heard of Hosea either, from the time that he joined Coxon in offering a reward to the sailor who reached land with a line. However, either Hosea or Coxon – probably the latter – had the presence of mind to go to the place of safekeeping in the captain's cabin where small items of value were being kept and remove the packages of diamonds. By far the largest of these was Hosea's and contained the stones valued at about £7,000 in which he had invested to carry some of his capital back to

England. Gems would have other purposes, if they managed to reach the land.

At some stage as well, the women, children and most of the male passengers – although not Captain Talbot, who remained on deck – were moved to the roundhouse in the stern. It appears that they had enough time to choose a few items of clothing and personal possessions. They may have been told to be ready to quit the ship at a moment's notice, but in the state of utter disorder that now prevailed there is no certainty that they were offered any advice at all.

William Hickey, who experienced peril at sea more than once, left a vivid description of a group of Indiaman passengers in similar circumstances:

> The door into the great cabin was soon torn off, exposing to our view the foaming surges through the great cabin's stern windows . . . At this awful hour did it occur to me what I had somewhere read, that death by shipwreck is the most terrible of deaths . . . In a storm at sea, in a miserable cabin on a filthy wet bed where it is as impossible to think as to breathe freely, the fatigue, the motion, the want of rest and food, give a kind of hysteric sensibility to the [human] frame, which makes it alive to the slightest danger.
>
> If we look round at the miserable group that surround us, no eye beams comfort, no tongue speaks consolation, and when we throw our imagination beyond – to the death-like darkness, the howling blast, the raging and merciless element – surely, surely it is the most terrible of deaths!

Among the few who had kept his head was the bosun Robert Rea, who continued supervising those making a raft. At about noon it was ready, and was cast over the side attached to a hawser. Five men clambered aboard. Most of the others gathered at the side, some with little bundles of their possessions, watching as the raft was tossed about and as those on board, their faces ghastly with fear, were soaked in the surf breaking over it. At this sight the rest lost heart, according to Habberley: 'No more would venture, but declared they would sooner stay and perish with the ship, it being no better than certain death to go on the raft.'

That judgment was immediately and savagely vindicated. Borne along on a powerful wave, the raft was smashed to pieces like the jolly boat and the yawl before it, this time against the rocks. Four of the five – including a midshipman named William Milbourn and the poulterer Christopher Shear – were killed. Thus ended the last organised rescue attempt.

Amid the terror and despair, individuals were able to recall afterwards glimpses of surreal events on shore. The half-dozen or so seamen who had gained safety were pulling dead and injured shipmates from the water; and the dark figures who had come down from the ridge during the morning were now gathered there in great numbers. They were paying the sailors scant attention and had started a series of bonfires into which they were feeding the foremast and other flotsam from the ship.

It was not long after midday, and the *Grosvenor* was in her death throes. Still impaled on the reef by her stern, her head down and almost filled with water, she was sliding over on to her beam ends when, with a series of thunderous cracks, the great oak timbers of her hull started to break up. In a final clap, she came apart in the middle, at the main hatchway.

There were still about 120 people on board. About a hundred of them were left on the stern half, including the passengers. Also on the stern was Habberley:

> The sea having nothing [to stop it] rushed so violently into the roundhouse as obliged us to immediately get the ladies out at the starboard quarter gallery and place them on the quarter of the ship.

The passengers were to remain on this rear gallery, while the crew clung to the poop deck above. Although water was pouring in, the stern was still borne up on the reef and showed no immediate sign of sinking. Floating free, the fore half was brought round on the current, so the bow came up by the stern. Among those stranded there on the foc's'le was Captain Talbot. In this moment of direst peril, the weather eased and the tide turned, and at this fortuitous coincidence the danger of the two halves being carried along and smashed against the reef receded.

Now, though, there was no more talk among the sailors of how the women and children might be saved. In a chilling summary of this new crisis, Hynes related: 'All hands began now to do the best they could for themselves.'

Habberley tried to put it in less stark terms: 'We expected now the part of the wreck we were on to go instantly to pieces, when we should be all entangled together amongst the fragments of the wreck, and those who could swim would stand no better chance than those who could not; therefore determined me to try the hawser and, if washed off, to trust to my swimming as I could swim expertly.'

Shaw, the second mate and his mentor, also decided to leave the ship and take his chance in the waves. So did Jeremiah Evans, an old hand who had seen the four corners of the Earth but never experienced anything like this before. The three of them stripped down to their trousers. At this point Coxon reappeared and, according to Habberley, tried to dissuade them from climbing on to the hawser, 'representing to us the almost impossibility of our getting on shore by that means, so much of the hawser hanging in the water and the surf incessantly breaking over it'. What Habberley reported as suasion by Coxon was more probably an order to stop his second mate from leaving the ship, but the captain's authority was already compromised and he was ignored.

A number of other men were already grappling and dragging themselves along the hawser. Buffeted and repeatedly engulfed by the sea, Habberley inched painfully towards land; it was about a quarter of an hour before he dropped to the water at the edge of the rocks and was pulled by willing hands to safety. Evans followed, though both had to go to Shaw's assistance, at further personal risk to themselves, or he would have been drowned.

Exactly how the miracle occurred is hard to say, for the sources are confused and conflicting. Alexander Dalrymple took evidence from a number of survivors but made little attempt to answer the question, seeing it perhaps as having little bearing on the final outcome. Nevertheless, a miracle it was, in which tide, wind and fortune all coincided to bring deliverance.

Plainly the gale had blown itself out by mid-afternoon and the malevolent force of the sea been dissipated. It was at that point that the timbers of the stern finally started to give out. There must still have been about eighty people in the stern, gathered on the poop and at the rear gallery, when the deck splintered and the stern split in two. Somehow, almost everyone scrambled on to the larger section, the starboard quarter, as it lifted clear of the reef and, in that moment, floated again.

At around the same time the wind, which had been blowing off the land, turned about. The starboard quarter – seething with bedraggled men, women and children, the grandees rubbing shoulders with tars for the first time, the ladies with their *ayahs* – started to drift towards the shore. Seeing this, and noting that the hawser was still attached to that section of the ship, those already on land started to haul on it. Slowly at first but steadily it came on, and as it did, those stranded on that battered little island saw their approaching salvation. With growing excitement the men pulling on the hawser realised that they could manoeuvre the hulk into a sheltered inlet among the rocks. As it came in, men splashed into the shallows and hands reached up to help down the women and children while those who were able clambered down themselves and felt the first shocking sensation of solid ground underfoot.

Other parts of the wreck followed, borne on the wind and the tide. The forward half, which had split from the stern hours earlier, came in almost intact, bringing with it Captain Talbot. Others came clinging to flotsam, not a few of them bruised and wounded by timber. One by one they emerged, to join the growing number gathered on a rock shelf that surrounded the cove and sloped up towards the grassy ridge.

That there is no record of the emotions registered in that moment of deliverance is hardly surprising. An entire day had passed since the first impact, and if there was one prevailing sense it was sheer and utter exhaustion. But the sensation simply of being on land must have added to another sense: that of disorientation. They had been at sea for almost two months, and through the waves of fatigue came sensations of dizziness and weakness in the knees. Many would have lain or sat down among the rocks to steady themselves.

The casualties were mainly those who had struck out from the ship in trying to save themselves, and included fourteen members of the crew. Two men who went into the lazaretto and drank themselves into oblivion were never seen again. A melancholy fate had befallen the little Anglo-Indian boy who had come on board as a member of Captain Talbot's suite and who was not seen after the ship struck; but he was the only missing passenger among the thirty-five who had sailed from Trincomalee. Of the crew of 105 that set out, ninety-one had landed alive – severely injured in some cases, sick also, but nevertheless alive. The women and children were without injury, the families intact.

Exhaustion, and perhaps euphoria as well then. Something else too: a sense of dreamlike strangeness. For in the gathering gloom of that first evening in Africa, among the fires burning at the edge of the Indian Ocean, they found themselves in the midst of the dark figures who had gathered on the rock shelf, and whom they now saw were half-naked tribesmen. The two groups surveyed one another with mutual incomprehension: on the one hand, the dishevelled castaways; on the other, black warriors with high conical hairstyles and daubed with red mud.

PART TWO

6

THE CALIBAN SHORE

Lambasi, Pondoland, 4–5 August 1782

Among the paintings inspired by the *Grosvenor* story is an oil by the English artist George Morland entitled *African Hospitality*. A florid piece of Enlightenment romanticism, it depicts the immediate aftermath of the wreck. The distressed Hosea family are at the centre of the tableau, against the backdrop of a lightning-pierced sky and the dying Indiaman. William, dishevelled and apprehensive, kneels supplicant-like before a half-naked warrior. Mary, all ringlets and disarrayed muslin gown, clutches baby Frances while reclining exhausted in the arms of a black Mother Earth figure. The warrior's burly physique and weapons – a spear and an anachronistic quiver of arrows – assert his dominance, but his open hands, gesturing to a shelter, offer no threat, only compassion. The sturdy matriarch, surrounded by infants, meanwhile shows by her embrace a readiness to enfold these new babes. Elsewhere, Africans are carrying sailors ashore, succouring them with food and drink. The tempest from which they have emerged is contrasted with the idyll to which it has brought them. All will be well for the castaways, the image says; they have fallen among noble savages.

Morland was the most gifted English artist of his day, a prodigy held to be the natural successor to Reynolds and Gainsborough, and the painting, from 1790, captures the moment in which a crusade was born. Reckless, dissolute, a drunkard, and frequently in debtors' prison, Morland had made his name with sentimentalised scenes of rustic

African Hospitality, detail of engraving by John Smith, 1791
from the painting by George Morland

English life before being recruited by the embryonic Emancipation movement to produce *African Hospitality* and its companion piece, *The Slave Trade*, a scene of white seamen brutalising an African family. The artist's challenge to contemporary wisdom – the paradoxical representation of beastliness in Europeans and humanity among Africans – was brave and visionary, and the success of *African Hospitality*, exhibited at the Society of Artists, may have surprised Morland himself. He cannot be blamed for the doggerel that appears beneath an early edition of the mezzotint reproduction:

> Dauntless they plunge amidst the vengeful waves
> And snatch from death the lovely sinking fair.
> Their friendly efforts, lo! Each Briton saves!
> Perhaps their future tyrant now they spare.

The picture retains a sense of wonderment, capturing as it does the instant in which two alien cultures met, and contrasting to startling effect the helplessness of the white gentlefolk, tossed up like Shakespeare's mariners in *The Tempest* on an inaccessible shore, with the self-assurance of the semi-naked blacks. And if the overall effect is somewhat cloying, it is still an intriguing counterpoint to the subsequent Victorian portrayal of Africans as wide-eyed berserkers, the heathen foes of Empire. All the same, it is hard to look at *African Hospitality* without wondering how Morland came by his concept of these events, and what the castaways would have made of it.

With black sea pounding around them that first evening, passengers and crew sprawled in loose-knit groups at the water's edge. It was just twelve hours and a lifetime since the first juddering impact. They were drenched and cold, and most were too exhausted to move, too stunned by the enormity of what had befallen them to take it in. Some wandered about, disorientated or distracted. Others lay, seemingly lifeless or clutching injuries from their battering in the water. But few could take their eyes from the scene before them.

Half-naked figures flitted amid the flames of half a dozen fires flickering along the rocks. The apparitions went about their work with silent intensity, absorbed by a single task. Heedless of the aliens tossed up in their midst, they were feeding wooden wreckage into the flames in order to extract the metal fittings. They were dark, almost black in complexion. One sailor noted, 'They went quite naked except a slight covering round the loins,' although another saw that in addition, some men wore cloaks made of cattle hide which hung from shoulder to knee. 'Robust and well proportioned', they wore their hair piled on their heads in hollowed cones. One of them, coming upon a sea chest, smashed it to pieces to extract the brass nails, which he stuck into his hair as ornaments.

To some of the Europeans' treasures they were entirely indifferent. While the nabobs' bales of silk drifted in on the tide, the natives paused merely to cut open one or two with assegais and inspect the contents before returning to the fires. More wood was tossed on to the flames and, as each piece was consumed, an iron ring here or a few steel bolts there were extracted from the embers, dipped hissing into a pool, and added to a growing pile of metal oddments.

For an hour or so after the last of the survivors came safely ashore, the two groups remained in this state of utterly disconnected proximity. Then, quite suddenly as the light faded, the tribesmen gathered up their booty and, without a backward glance, disappeared over a grassy ridge into the darkening hinterland.

Among the seamen, initial relief that the cloaked warriors evidently intended them no harm was soon replaced by a sense of bewilderment. There was something unnerving about the systematic way the men had gone about stripping metal from wreckage, almost a familiarity with the process, like carrion-eaters knowing how to get at the choicest bits of a giant carcass. Then there was the curious indifference of the natives to their plight. The seaman William Habberley, for one, found it unsettling . . .

> . . . our dreadful situation not apparently affecting them, as they never offered us any assistance.

Now, though, in the gathering gloom, the castaways were alone with the snap of the fires and the crash of the sea. Where the tide swirled around an inlet, the *Grosvenor*'s forecastle and stern reared high and black against the dying light, a grotesque spectre of the grand Indiaman. This sight of what had been their home for these past months brought home a renewed sense of shock and loss.

Gradually the seamen were roused to action by some of the objects washed up. Geese and chickens lay lifeless in sodden heaps on the rocks. A few creatures from the ship's menagerie had escaped alive, including some pigs, which could be heard grunting at the sea's edge. A sudden hunger awoke, for no one had eaten that day. Fires were stoked and, while women and children gathered around for warmth, the men collected the dead fowl and roasted them. Just twenty-four hours earlier, diners in the cuddy had been replete with supper and madeira, and men in the mess jolly with grog and song, drinking to absent friends. But that night, 4 August, after months together at sea, they ate as a company for the first time.

Convention was restored after the meal. The seamen moved a short distance off, leaving the passengers and officers to a kind of privacy. Soon afterwards it began to rain and they were reunited in a common state of damp misery, broken by the cries of the injured and the mutterings of those in the grip of a waking nightmare. All through the night men and women dozed off and awoke, feeling at first a vague unease but also half-expecting to feel the familiar rocking of the ship. Their systems habituated to the motion, some actually felt themselves to be still at sea, and in their semi-conscious state had a moment of relief as the wreck became, briefly, just a terrible dream. Then they came fully awake, to find with sickening terror that they were, indeed, cast away in Africa.

Dawn came up on the morning of 5 August on a world turned upside down. Like any ship's company, those on board the *Grosvenor* had sailed with an apprehension of danger. What they had feared was shipwreck and death. Shipwreck and survival was not a possibility that anyone had much considered. In the event, the great majority had survived. Seamen and passengers had, of course, escaped shipwrecks together before; but never had a company from so broad a spectrum of British society found itself so distant from the old certainties, or so ignorant of the shore on which they were lost.

Some of the demons of the night, at least, had disappeared. The spectral figures were nowhere to be seen and the men were able to study at leisure the shore on which they had foundered. In her death throes, the *Grosvenor* had been drawn into an inlet composed of a low shelf of flat rock that narrowed from a width of about fifty yards and rose in tiers to a grassy ridge. What was described by some of the men as a 'steep, almost perpendicular' cliff and represented as such in paintings of the wreck was, in fact, a tier of rock on the south side of the inlet rising to a height of about 30 feet above sea level. The south-west wind that had brought them to grief churned up the sea boiling around the inlet and, as the Indiaman was smashed to smaller and smaller pieces, those watching from the shore had cause to reflect again on their astonishing escape.

Venturing up on to the ridge during the morning, the men found it barren of trees or any other sign of life as it rose gently inland. The coastline that stretched away on either side was rocky but also seemingly devoid of significant features. On closer inspection, however, a bay to the south of the inlet concealed a large tidal pool separated from the sea by a wide sandbar.

The bay, known as Lambasi by the natives from time immemorial, was about a mile broad, with the pool at its centre. But for their circumstances, the place might have struck the men with its loveliness. Surrounded by beach, forest and rock faces, the pool was fed by a stream and a river, the Tezani, which came down from a distant ridge of hills and threaded its way through a valley surrounded by sheer walls of black sandstone to a height of about 80 feet, sprouting wild banana and flowering protea trees. The scene was a microcosm of what lay beyond: a gentle green pastoral, a scene to gladden any eye, concealing something altogether more primordial.

A semblance of shipboard discipline was re-established. Shaw and Beale mustered the men for roll-call, and an inventory was taken of the fifteen dead. Along with Captain Talbot's lad, they included nine foremastmen, John Woodward, the quartermaster, William Milbourn, a midshipman, Simon Griffiths, bosun's mate, and Christopher Shear, poulterer. Among the injured was Coxon's servant, Robert Price, still insensible after being dashed against the rocks. Many others had gashes and fractures. Logie, the chief mate, roused from his sickbed during the wreck, had lapsed again into feverish unconsciousness. With neither instruments nor remedies, there was little that the surgeon Nixon could do for any of them.

There were 125 castaways in all. The ninety-one seamen included the captain and five officers, eight servants, twenty petty officers and artisans, thirty foremastmen and twenty-five lascars. Among the thirty-four passengers, eighteen fell into the category of gentry, eleven were servants and five discharged soldiers.

We get glimpses of them that first morning. Despite the panic of the wreck there had been enough time to dress and collect a few valued possessions, and Charles Newman had on the green broadcloth coat with silver monogrammed buttons that he had used to wear to the Bengal Supreme Court. In the gold-braided jackets of a colonel and a Navy captain respectively, Edward James and George Talbot cut equally incongruous figures in these new surroundings. The traders George Taylor and John Williams, as well as donning their breeches and coats, had managed to scoop up a number of valuables, gold chains and watches; these offered little comfort as they looked down on the bay from a grassy ridge to see the silk bales that represented their fortunes, the product of years of endeavour, drifting limply at the sea's edge like jellyfish.

Lydia Logie, her mane of red hair hanging dishevelled around her shoulders, wearing the gown she had slipped into after the ship had struck, watched over her sick husband. Married just eight months, now visibly pregnant, Lydia had ventured around the world to meet her mate, only to have the prize of their new life snatched away. Logie, the strong, reassuring figure of the *Grosvenor*'s quarterdeck, appeared now shockingly vulnerable, bathed in the sweats of dysentery, the seamen's 'bloody flux'.

A few yards off, William and Mary Hosea clung to each other and their child Frances. Hosea had with him his valuable package of diamonds, so not everything had been lost; but the couple had been reduced to a pitiful state. As we have seen, Mary's letters are suggestive not of a doughty memsahib but rather a sweet, considerate woman, inclined to fret about her family and her health. From the outset, she had been full of worries about the voyage. On the eve of their departure her friend Eliza Fay wrote: 'Her anxiety [is] great.' Mary had died of fear more than once during the previous twenty-four hours and, having spent a night out in the open, was now shivering in her still-damp gown, trying to comprehend what sort of a place it was that they had come to. Utterly traumatised by the succession of disasters that had befallen them, she must have felt they had become the playthings of a malevolent spirit. Hosea himself, agonising at the recollection of how close they had come to missing their passage on the *Grosvenor*, was additionally burdened by the fact that they had succeeded only because of his obstinate determination to be quit of India.

Their fate now rested in the hands of one man. John Coxon, however, had problems of his own. His ship and his cargo were lost; it was his negligence that had helped to bring them to this place; and his most trusted and able officer was sick and possibly dying. Coxon's record offered little to encourage a belief that he was the man to guide his charges to safety, and from the outset he seems to have been overwhelmed by that responsibility.

When a troublesome seaman was purposely marooned, he was not left without resources. Alexander Selkirk, history's best-known castaway, was landed on Juan Fernandez island in 1704 with a pistol, gunpowder, a hatchet, a knife, some provisions, a pot in which to boil them, a Bible, bedding, navigational instruments and charts. He survived for four years and four months before being rescued. Another seaman, accused of sodomy and abandoned on Ascension in 1721, had in addition a fowling piece, a tent, buckets and a water cask. He fared less well and was found some years later, a skeleton beside a diary that petered out in mid-prayer. Thanks partly to the circumstances of the wreck, but also to events in the immediate aftermath, the *Grosvenor* castaways were not nearly so well endowed.

The crew spent the morning of 5 August foraging at the water's edge. Debris was strewn among the rocks and a wave of flotsam bobbed in on the tide. Shoes were quickly collected, for many of the men had lost theirs in the wreck; but according to Dalrymple's report there were many other useful objects as well:

> Plenty of timber from the wreck and the booms and sails were cast ashore, sufficient to have built and fitted several vessels; nor were tools, as adzes, &c. wanting.

Two sails were recovered, including the mizzen topsail still attached to the yardarm. They were carried the few hundred yards down to the tidal pool, where the stream provided fresh water for drinking and bathing, and rigged as tents, one for the women and children, the other for food and essentials. The men set up their own camp further upstream. Drenched bales were broken out and soon the grassy verge was festooned with tents of bright silk.

Meanwhile Habberley and another group of men found: 'A pipe of wine, a barrel of arrack and a cask of flour with a tub of beef and pork, which were all carefully conveyed to the tent and taken care of under the captain's directions.'

If their immediate needs were met, their situation was nonetheless dire. They were lost on a shore known to none, halfway between England and India, and hundreds of miles – quite how many would be a matter of much conjecture – from the nearest European settlement, without charts or navigational aids. Coxon knew that the Portuguese were at Delagoa Bay to the north and the Dutch at the Cape to the south, but the two were separated by well over a thousand miles and he was far from clear about his position in relation to either. Rescue by another ship had to be discounted, as no vessels landed between these ports except in emergency. That left two possibilities for deliverance. The most straightforward was an overland march to the nearest Portuguese or Dutch outpost. The second was to deploy the skills of the artisan crew – carpenters, caulkers and coopers – to build another vessel. Although a challenging task, it would not be the first time this had been done by seafarers wrecked in southern Africa.*

In any assessment of their plight, one factor stood out: the castaways were quite without firepower. In their haste to abandon ship, Coxon and the officers had failed to ensure the salvage of either charge or ball; the *Grosvenor*'s

* After the East Indiaman *Dodington* sank off Algoa Bay in 1755, the survivors used her timbers to build a small vessel, which they called the *Happy Deliverance* and sailed to Delagoa Bay.

entire load of gunpowder was at the bottom of the sea. Their pistols and muskets might as well have been there too. Whether for defence against human or animal assailants, or for hunting, the firearms were useless.

They were not long in being confronted with their vulnerability. That same morning the natives returned.

The official inquiry into the *Grosvenor* disaster, commissioned by the directors of the East India Company, was conducted by Alexander Dalrymple, the Company's hydrographer and the man responsible for its seafaring operations. His findings, published in August 1783 and based on his interrogation of survivors, are brief and dispassionate. One sentence, however, stands out for its pithy eloquence:

> In great part, their calamities seem to have arisen from want of management with the natives.

Dalrymple was no deskbound bureaucrat. In his youth, he served the Company as a minor official in Madras in the 1750s before sailing to the Malay peninsula and discovering a passion for cartography and navigation. From 1762 he made a series of voyages to the Indonesian archipelago and China, and ten years later published accounts of his travels. However, it was his interest in the great geographical issues of the South Pacific that made his reputation and saw his elevation to the position of hydrographer. A disputatious and cantankerous Scot, Dalrymple was a figure formidable enough to have crossed swords with the hero of the age, the navigator James Cook, over the existence of *Terra Australis Incognita*, the Great Southern Continent.* When he sat down to take evidence from the *Grosvenor* survivors at the Company's Leadenhall Street headquarters in the summer of 1783, he had Cook's fate clearly in mind.

Cook's voyages between 1768 and 1780 established him as an explorer in the heroic tradition of Da Gama and Magellan. Not only did he add

* Dalrymple produced a widely accepted chart in 1769, locating *Terra Australis Incognita* in the South Pacific, a vast land mass south of the Indies and west of the Americas, and then denounced Cook for failing to substantiate this contention by venturing further south after his epic circumnavigation of New Zealand. Cook held that there was no such land mass and obtained his revenge by demonstrating as much on his next voyage.

immeasurably to geographical and maritime knowledge, but he brought home the image of an enchanted world – of sun-kissed Pacific archipelagos, lovely in aspect, abundant in the fruits of nature and, above all, lavish in hospitality. Cook had seemed to establish an understanding with the islanders, seeing them as noble in their nakedness and simplicity, and winning their trust. One of his protégés, a Society Islander named Omai, was lionised in London, being taught etiquette by Joseph Banks, introduced to King George, painted by Reynolds and generally made a fuss of. Between Cook and his French contemporary, Louis de Bougainville, who was captivated by Tahiti, the fashionable salons of London and Paris were flushed with enthusiasm for the philosophy of Rousseau and the purity of the noble savage.*

Then, in January 1780, Britain was stunned by news that Cook was dead, stabbed and beaten to death in a skirmish with his beloved Pacific islanders. The *London Gazette* reported that the cause of this affray 'with a numerous and tumultuous Body of the Natives' was their thievish activities. There were dark hints of cannibalism.

The murder of the great mariner made a profound impression on its time. To a nation invested with a growing sense of its own righteousness and power, it seemed that Cook's reward for trusting and befriending the natives had been treachery: in the end, it turned out, the noble savage was just a savage after all.

If the islanders of far-flung archipelagos were seen by the English public as brutes, another race occupied an even lower place in the scales of humanity: the dark, semi-naked inhabitants of Africa. Partly this was based on ignorance. Of the region south of the Sahara little more was known than had been postulated by Ptolemy 1,600 years earlier in a map showing the Nile taking its rise in two great lakes watered by the *Lunae Montes*, the Mountains of the Moon; even now maps of the African interior were embroidered with fantastical creatures and freakish humans, and

* Cook was remarkably perceptive about the impact of Europeans on indigenous peoples, writing: 'We debauch their Morals already too prone to vice and we interduce among them wants and perhaps diseases which they never before knew and which serves only to disturb that happy tranquillity they and their fore Fathers had injoy'd. If any one denies the truth of this assertion let him tell me what the Natives of the whole extent of America have gained by the commerce they have had with Europeans.'

when, in 1790, James Bruce published an account of his journey to the source of the Blue Nile, he was dismissed as a fantasist. However, a second factor underpinned a common belief that the natives of Africa were not quite human.

The British slave trade started on a small scale in the 1560s. Opinions of the coastal people of West Africa were never high. 'The Negroes [are] a people of beastly living, without a God, lawe, religion, or common wealth,' wrote an early English visitor. But as the trade gathered pace, it fed yet darker perceptions of Africans. By the late eighteenth century, Edward Long, a historian, could describe Africa as 'that parent of everything that is monstrous in nature', and its inhabitants as 'libidinous and shameless as monkies'. Visitors to the kingdom of Dahomey vied with one another in depicting the savagery of the regime. One, Archibald Dalzel, wrote of the king's palace ornamented with human heads and bestrewn with bodies, and went so far as to claim that removing poor wretches from these circumstances to the plantations of Jamaica and Virginia was an act of compassion. By the time of the *Grosvenor*'s last voyage, more than two million West Africans, an annual average of 20,095, had suffered the questionable mercy of the Atlantic slavers. That same year one of the most notorious episodes in the history of the trade occurred: Luke Collingwood, captain of the Liverpool ship *Zong*, cast into the sea 131 ailing slaves whom he suspected might not survive the voyage to Jamaica, in order to collect the insurance.

Intellectuals – writers in particular – contested the notion of a beastly savage with an equally ethnocentric if more benign alternative. While George Morland depicted Africans as noble on canvas, William Blake and Robert Burns did so in words, the latter in verse, penned in Scotland, celebrating a supposedly idyllic life 'in sweet Senegal'. Of how Africans actually lived or thought there was little knowledge and even less understanding; but often there was sympathy. Samuel Johnson's friend Hester Thrale thought interracial mixing was 'preparing us for the moment when we shall be made one fold under one Shepherd'. Daniel Defoe, one of the earliest opponents of slavery, may be said to have created the literary prototype for the noble savage in the form of Crusoe's Man Friday, while Johnson challenged the slave trade in typically ebullient fashion, startling the men of Oxford with a toast,

'To the next insurrection of the Negroes in the West Indies.'*

It would be facile to claim that the racial debate going on among European polemicists had any effect on the crew of the *Grosvenor*. Among ordinary seamen the issues of class and hierarchy were more relevant, and the survivors' accounts of the people they encountered are marked by bewilderment rather than hostility. Nor is there any information to suggest that Captain Coxon shared the view of another Indiaman captain who wrote of the natives at the Cape of Good Hope that 'of all people they are the most bestial and sordid. They are the very reverse of human kind . . . as squalid in their bodies as they are mean and degenerate in their understandings.' But attitudes among some of the castaways, a dread of this shore and its inhabitants, undoubtedly had a bearing on what passed after the wreck. Dalrymple's judgment that there was a 'want of management with the natives' was, if anything, an understatement.

In accounting for what followed it may also be relevant to note that the news of Captain Cook's death had reached England just four months before the *Grosvenor* sailed for India. Coxon's conduct after the wreck bears all the marks of one acting in the shadow of the illustrious mariner's fate.

There was no immediate hint of trouble on the natives' return. Indeed, the dark figures approached in a way that signalled peaceful intentions. This time they were accompanied by their womenfolk, who remained some distance off with the warriors' spears and shields. As before, it was clear that their sole interest was metal from the wreck.

At first the seamen took the natives' presence in their stride. There was at least one amicable exchange. Two men, John Warmington and Barney Leary, related that when the tribesmen came among them, they 'pointed [to the north-east] and said something, which they imagined was to tell them there was a bay that way'. The natives were gesturing towards Delagoa Bay, and indicating that yonder the castaways could expect help from others of their own tribe.

While struck by the novelty of the natives' appearance – 'woolly-headed and quite black', noted another foremastman, John Hynes, who had never

* Johnson had a black servant, Francis Barber, a freed Jamaican slave whom he treated as a nephew, encouraging his education and providing for him in his will. Barber later became a teacher and married an Englishwoman.

left his Irish homeland before the start of the voyage – the sailors were initially content enough to let them share in the bounty of the wreck. It was not long, however, before scavenging became more like high-handedness. 'They seemed to consider everything as belonging to them,' Habberley complained.

More important than the attitude of the seamen was the alarm and dread that the natives' return had excited among the passengers. Hynes noted that when the blacks 'began to carry off whatever seemed to strike their fancy', it

> excited in the minds of our people, particularly the women, a thousand apprehensions for their personal safety.

It is not hard to identify those most likely to have been affected. Nothing in Mary Hosea's life had prepared her for these horrors. She may have travelled across the world, but as a Calcutta lady her experience of dark peoples was limited to *ayahs*, *chowkidars*, *kitmugars*, *jemadars*, and other servant *wallahs*. Living in India may even have made her more disposed to anxiety, for it inculcated a conviction that the forces at work beyond Company settlements needed to be kept at bay. Her resources were now exhausted.

To Mary's condition was added her husband's attitude to people of dark race. William Hosea had little enough time for cultivated Bengali nobles, and none at all for the lowly of any other race. His response on being advised once that 200 sepoys – Indian troops in the Company's service – were being cared for as invalids in Madras was chillingly redolent of the *Zong*'s captain. 'This is certainly a very melancholy circumstance & might be easily remedied by throwing them all into the sea,' he wrote. Highly strung and nervous, Hosea was not a man likely to behave rationally on finding himself at the mercy of those he saw as inferior.

At some point during the day, Coxon had talks in the makeshift canvas tent with his officers and the senior passengers, including Hosea. Whatever the nature of the discussions, they did nothing to resolve a delicate situation. After the miracle of their deliverance from the sea, a jarring pattern of events resumed.

It was clear that survival would depend on the passive cooperation, if not the direct assistance, of the local people. It was also obvious that the natives would seize on useful objects from the wreck, and that this foraging would have to be balanced against the castaways' own needs. The ship's company was quite formidable in number and certainly not defenceless, for although without guns they had at least half a dozen cutlasses. An opportunity existed for some firm-handed gesture of friendship, leading to barter. Africans had been trading food with seafarers for generations. Yet no attempt at communication was made at all. Instead, the situation was allowed to drift through the afternoon, to the point that the sailors felt they were without leadership, and the natives were given too broad a licence to plunder goods that were essential to the castaways themselves.

Coxon was understandably concerned about the possibility of trouble between the sailors and the natives, and had given orders that the men were not to offer any kind of resistance unless attacked. But while it was important to avoid provocation, it was vital to demonstrate that they were not afraid. In those critical early days, the captain adopted a tactic of ignoring the Africans entirely, evidently in the hope that they would simply go away. Whether he was persuaded of this approach by Hosea, whose opinions as the senior civilian had acquired a new influence now that they were back on land, or had decided on it himself, is not possible to say. It was, in any event, a terrible mistake.

One incident defined a pattern. Habberley was with a group of men scouring the rocks when they came upon copper saucepans and carpenter's tools. These precious finds were being carried back to the camp when the seamen were surrounded by warriors

> who endeavoured to wrest them from us, but being loath to part with such conveniences, we held them fast and would not suffer them to take the same. They then immediately had recourse to their arms and appeared determined to have them.

The confrontation was resolved by Shaw, who told the men to surrender the items. They obeyed reluctantly, Habberley related, 'not out of any fear of the natives or their arms, but out of respect for Mr Shaw'. The incident signalled that the sailors were anxious to avoid confrontation. That impression might have been balanced by a subsequent demonstration of firmness, but it was not. Thereafter, Habberley wrote, they were obliged to conceal 'everything we found made of metal . . . otherwise [the natives] would not let us have them'.

As well as trying to ignore the natives, Coxon seemed reluctant to engage with his own men, for no attempt was made to communicate with them either. Tension rose through the afternoon. In the absence of leadership, men were starting to ask who was in charge now that they were no longer at sea. Habberley noted: 'Many sailors and lascars, thinking all command at an end, were beginning to be very disorderly.'

Some hands found a barrel of arrack and got drunk. By this time Habberley believed that there really was a danger that the unruly and increasingly frustrated men might provoke the natives and bring down an attack on them all. Only now did Coxon make an appearance, moving among the men with Shaw to calm them and 'prevent tumults'.

The moment of danger passed and, as the sun went down, the natives again went off into the dark; but the sudden ugly turn of mood may have been seen as a portent. A few sailors were heard muttering about leaving. Lascars, too, were talking of striking out on their own; it could have been argued by the Indian sailors that they had a better chance of survival among another dark-skinned people than if they stayed with the Europeans.

One seaman caught the mood. Joshua Glover, a foremastman of unknown background and age, turned his back on his shipmates and, when the natives disappeared with their booty that evening, he went with them. The consensus among the company, according to Habberley, was that Glover was a loon, 'disturbed in his mind'. Events were to show that he was nothing of the sort.

An uneasy quiet descended on the camp. A ration of arrack was distributed among the men, along with flour and portions of salt pork and beef. The flour they mixed with water to bake into cakes that were eaten with the cured meat. Afterwards the seamen were divided into watches, and at the end of that first full day in Africa, guards were set 'to prevent the natives from plundering or sacrificing us'.

7

PONDO'S PEOPLE

'There used to be a folktale. The old women of former times would say, "There are white people who wear clothes. They will one day come to this country." Our forefathers would ask, "Where will they come from?" The answer was, "They are on the other side of the sea." Our people would query this, saying, "How could they cross the sea?" But, indeed, there came white people who wore clothes.'

Lugubu ka Mangaliso, Nguni chief, 1916

Even today the coast where the *Grosvenor* was lost is a space of great emptiness and profound silences. Its boundaries are difficult to define because it is as much an area of consciousness as it is a geographic location. To start with, though, it can be reached by driving southwest from the South African port city of Durban for about ninety miles to the little seaside town of Port Edward. From there one proceeds on foot – a few miles to the Umtamvuna River, then across it to where a band of unbroken beach begins and stretches for miles ahead into a hazy mist of pale blue. It is here that the emptiness begins and where one can mark the beginning of the Wild Coast.

The far limit can be roughly defined at the point where the Kei River debouches into the Indian Ocean, so its extent is not great. Of South Africa's 1,749-mile shoreline, the Wild Coast accounts for only 180 miles

Amapondo by William Taylor

or so. Yet this stretch encompasses an old world, an elemental place that even now has the power to delight, to enlighten and to disturb. It is untouched by modern roads, largely beyond the reach of utilities and in places so thinly populated that it is possible to walk for hours without sight of another soul. Spend time in solitude here, contemplate the blue of a placid day, the sea immanent in its power but at rest, the very air benign – and feel a warming of the senses that touches the spirit; then watch as the sky comes up like gunmetal from the south-west, and the wind blows the rain in, churning up the sea so that it boils and dashes against a jagged line of slicked black rock, all the elements roused to fury and no place unexposed – and recall a time when man knelt before Nature.

To the interior lies a green, gnarled land, slashed by gorges and topped by rolling hills. Valleys are hung with a filigree of mossy bush and groves of flailing wild banana trees, but the hillsides have long since been stripped. Instead, the slopes are dotted with circular mud huts, thatched, their doors facing eastwards, with patches of maize beside. Beyond, a grave-faced child of just about school-going age, bearing a staff – and with it the responsibility of guarding his family's treasure – tends a herd of long-horned cattle. It is a scene little changed by time for, like the Wild Coast itself, the land lying between the Umtamvuna and the Kei Rivers, and extending for about fifty miles inland, is an enclave that the haste of modern life has yet to penetrate. It never quite fitted into the federation of British colonies and Boer republics that eventually made up South Africa, and is still usually known as Pondoland.

The inhabitants are descended from the Bantu migration, one of the most successful settler movements in history, which began in central Africa in the first millennium and resulted in the occupation of hospitable tracts south of the Equator within a few hundred years. However, among the numerous polygamous and patriarchal clans dwelling on the coastal escarpment of south-east Africa, the Pondo have always been a people apart, overshadowed by their more numerous and prominent kin, the Zulu to the north and the Xhosa to the south.

Elders used to talk of a time when their ancestors lived on the upper reaches of the great river called, then as now, the Umzimvubu, which rises in the snow-topped mountains to the north and courses down to the sea. No one could say for how long they were there, for time was measured not in seasons but generations, and even the precise naming of the ancestors was not always agreed upon by the old men. But the clan dated its birth to a dispute between twin brothers, Pondo and Pondomise, over who was to succeed their father Njanya. As so often in the stories of the elders, the dispute was caused by a hunt. Pondo killed a lion, and Pondomise, according to a tradition entitling the ordained heir to his choice of prize, claimed the skin. Pondo refused and, rather than submit, led his people and his herds away like a tribal Moses, beginning the descent from the headwaters of the Umzimvubu to the coastal escarpment. There they settled, in a land where the rivers were as numerous as the cattle of a great chief, and they became known as the amaPondo, the people of Pondo.* The rivers had names beginning with the warming Bantu diphthong that combines 'u' and 'm' in a sound not unlike a hum, and so, along with the Umzimvubu, there were the Umtamvuna, the Umtentu, the Umsikaba, the Umtata, and many others.

On pasturage between the rivers, Pondo's people grazed their herds. Cattle regulated almost all the clan's activity. They were more than a source of essentials, such as food and leather, or luxuries, such as milk and curds. They were more, even, than symbols of wealth and status. Cattle were the focus of the entire social order. They were a source of conflict and the means of peacemaking. They defined the institution of marriage. Although they were not quite worshipped, they did have a religious significance in their nearness to the Pondo soul.

Theirs was a magnificent and dramatic country, but it was not an easy one for a pastoral people. The steepness of the valleys and the density of the indigenous forests that clung to their contours restricted easy movement by men and herds. The quality of pasturage was variable, and that beside the sea usually poor. Some areas could not sustain full-time occupation. In short, while the numerous clans inhabiting the lush lands to the north were about to begin their rise towards the powerful centralised state that became the Zulu kingdom, and those on the equally fertile plains to the south were evolving into the confederation of chiefdoms that constituted the Xhosa, the Pondo were often engaged in a struggle for resources

* Anthropologists have offered another, more prosaic, explanation for the Pondo origin – that they were an offshoot from the Swazis and came down to the coast through the country now inhabited by the Zulus.

with neighbouring groups – the Tembu, the Bomvana, the Pondomise – and among themselves. The Xhosa regarded these smaller tribes with suspicion. They were, in a local idiom, 'poor in cattle and therefore extremely rapacious'. Prosperous families dwelt on the inland hills, the poorer ones on the coast, along with outcasts who had access to neither cattle nor crops and lived by foraging for wild fruit and molluscs.

The Pondo were also, without exception, poor in metal. Few districts along the heavily forested coastline contained deposits of the blackish gravel that Bantu smiths ground to powder and smelted in the ground. Iron was such a precious commodity in Pondoland that agricultural implements made of fire-hardened wood were still in use in the 1880s and locations of ore deposits remained a closely guarded tribal secret in the mid-twentieth century. The consequence, noted among the earliest European visitors, was that although the amaPondo were 'very civil, polite and talkative, saluting each other and asking whether they have learned any new dances or tunes', it was wise for travellers to 'go naked and without any iron or copper, for these things give inducement for the murder of those who have them.'

Pondo was succeeded by Sihula, he by Mtwa, and he by Santsabe. For twelve generations Pondo's line was unbroken; but if the paramountcy remained stable, chiefs of the kinship groups that paid allegiance to the Great House were often at odds. Disputes over cattle and land developed into clashes between warrior groups. Battles were rarely very bloody, but the frequency with which such accounts occur in the oral traditions indicates a society familiar with strife.

What gave it stability was a way of life unchanged for centuries – that, and isolation from the world beyond. As they had for as long as anyone could remember, women did the work of the fields as well as of the hearth. Girls helped their mothers, while boys tended the herds. Men, most accounts agree, did not do a great deal. Intoxicants were popular. *Cannabis sativa* has long been among the most prolific crops of Pondoland; and millet, which was the staple, being ground and baked into cakes, was also fermented in clay vessels with water to make a beer which was drunk frequently and with great relish.

Nine generations after Pondo brought his people to the coast, their isolation was interrupted.

On a day in the first weeks of 1488 – the precise date is unknown – a Portuguese named Bartholomeu Dias became the first mariner to double the southern tip of Africa, and reveal the Indian Ocean to Europe. So atrocious were conditions that Dias did not realise he had accomplished this feat until tacking north after thirteen days of constant storms and coming to an inlet now named Mossel Bay. On landing, the Portuguese were stoned by cattle-herding Khoikhoi* – until Dias took up a cross-bow and felled one of their assailants. So ended the first encounter between black and white in southern Africa.

Returning in triumph to Lisbon, Dias dubbed the gateway to the Indies *Cabo de Todos los Tormentos* – the Cape of All Storms. His successors, such as Vasco da Gama, found that name far more appropriate than *Cabo de Boa Esperanza* – or Cape of Good Hope – as it was euphemistically retitled; but within twenty years the Portuguese had established powerful trading positions at Goa and Cochin on India's Malabar coast. Although it was essential for the caravel crews to be able to obtain fresh victuals in Africa, they kept well clear of the Cape after Dom Francisco de Almeida, a viceroy returning from India, and a party of nobles were massacred by the Khoikhoi at Table Bay in 1510. Instead, the Portuguese established outposts in what are now Angola on the west coast and Mozambique on the east.

Pondo's people did not encounter mariners until 1554. A fleet of five ships was returning from Cochin with a cargo of slaves, spices and porcelain when the *São Bento* was disabled at roughly 30°E 31°S and driven on to an island near the shore. A third of her 450-strong company drowned, and when the rest reached land they found themselves in a bay with the sea roaring and dunes rising around them like battlements. They were at the mouth of the Umsikaba, a day's walk from where the *Grosvenor* grounded almost 230 years later.

An officer from the *São Bento* described the first meeting on this shore between natives and Europeans:

> There appeared upon a headland close by seven or eight men . . . but they were afraid and took to flight, so we could learn nothing but that

* Unlike the Pondo, the Khoikhoi were not a Bantu people, having been established at the Cape thousands of years earlier along with the hunter-gatherer San, or Bushmen. Both Khoikhoi and San were displaced and eventually eradicated by a combination of European and, to a lesser extent, Bantu expansion.

> they were Kaffirs, very black in colour, with woolly hair and went naked, having more the appearance of savages than rational men.

The following day the natives returned and, after examining wood from the wreck, began 'burning some pieces, in order to get out the nails'. The *São Bento*'s captain, Fernão d'Alvarez Cabral, approached them, empty-handed. '[They] became bolder on seeing us unarmed . . . and came to speak to us and Fernão d'Alvarez gave them the best welcome he could, giving them such poor provisions as we had, and caps, pieces of cloth and iron, with which they were as delighted as if they had been made lords of the earth.'

Later that day, about a hundred warriors came towards them, carrying wood-tipped spears. The Portuguese feared the worst:

> We took our arms and went to attack them, thinking such was their intention; but it proved otherwise, for on our approach they offered no violence, but showed themselves peaceful as before, and therefore . . . we began to speak to them. After spending the best part of the day, we learnt nothing from them except that from their peaceable and assured demeanour they were men who had come to see us as a novelty, showing their surprise at our colour, arms, dress and disposition. In time they rose and dispersed themselves into the wood, eating certain roots, like wild animals.

This first castaway band did not linger. Pausing only to provision themselves with food from the wreck, and as many nails as they could carry for barter, they set off northwards up the coast, a company of 100 Portuguese and 220 slaves. Just twenty Portuguese and three slaves reached sanctuary at Mozambique a year later.

They had spent only three days at the Umsikaba, but their legacy endured. Among the inhabitants a mythology was born out of tales from the fireside, establishing the pale apparitions in the collective consciousness. The oral traditions told of an object like a giant *uqwembe*, a wooden meat-tray, which came from the sea and disgorged white men. At first, they were called *izilwane* – wild beasts.

Another three generations passed. The Pondo suffered the second great schism in their history when the sons of Cabe, the twelfth king, fell out over the succession, and the eldest, Qiya, took his people south across the Umzimvubu to found a new clan, the Tshomane. Favoured by Cabe, the youngest son, Gangate, became head of the Great House. It was during the reign of Gangate that whites again came among the Pondo. This time they were to be known as *abalumbi* – the makers of wonders.

The *Nossa Senhora de Belem* was in difficulties from the time she sailed from Goa in February 1635. Her refitted masts were too heavy for the vessel and most of the crew were suffering from scurvy. In June, approaching Africa, she was assailed constantly by storms, and went aground. The place was at 29° 34´E, 31° 37´S, just north of the Umzimvubu River.

The captain, Joseph de Cabreyra, managed to bring all the 150 or so Portuguese and 100 slaves to shore. 'We embraced each other, rendering thanks to God as men newly born into this world having almost found ourselves in the next,' he wrote. The next day 'many natives came out of the woods and gradually assembled until they numbered more than three hundred. This caused us great anxiety, our number being so inferior.'

It was eighty years since the *São Bento* wreck, but Cabreyra was a tough, resourceful leader and, like his predecessor, reacted sensibly in this delicate situation:

> When the natives drew near . . . they stuck their assegais in a sandbank and then asked by signs why we had arms in our hands when theirs were laid aside. As it was a time for making friends, I resolved to go among them, giving my gun to a comrade and leaving a pistol and dagger in my belt.
>
> My first salute to them was to place my hand on their beards and smooth them well, then I sat down among them, at which they appeared well pleased, understanding that I was the captain of the company, and they showered praises upon me, calling me Umlungo, Umkulu, Manimusa, which are equivalent to great titles.

The Pondo were happy to barter millet for a brass bell, but harmony did not last. After some petty theft and harassment, Cabreyra decided on a confrontation, 'for though we might get an assegai wound, if we could kill a couple of them, they would respect us more'.

The sailors were surrounded by warriors who 'posted themselves on a bank behind us, from which they hurled down pieces of rock and clods of earth, striking many of us on the head'. Cabreyra had meanwhile posted two sharpshooters in a thicket with muskets. As the warriors closed in, one of the men 'did the first execution with a good shot, which brought down a native. Then we all fired a small volley, but it was sufficient, for every ball told. After this the natives slackened.'

Their position secured for the time being, the sailors set about salvaging rice and other food from the wreck. Facing rumblings of discontent among his crew that at times came close to mutiny, Cabreyra nevertheless persuaded them that their best hope of salvation lay in building new ships rather than making an overland march that few would have any hope of surviving. They set to work, cutting trees from the thick indigenous forest that grew down almost to the water's edge.

A clearing was made 'that there might be no cover between us in which the negroes could lie in ambush', and a storehouse built for essentials, over which a constant watch was kept – for Cabreyra was quick to see that if he was to have any purchasing power, every piece of metal 'had to be guarded as carefully as diamonds'. Within a week, the sailors had established a settlement, with straw-hut dwellings and, because there was a priest in the company, a wooden church at which the feasts of the saints were duly celebrated.

After the initial clash, dealings with the natives were marked by watchfulness, but on the Pondo side there seemed no lingering hostility, and bartering for millet resumed. For some time they were reluctant to trade cattle, and Cabreyra was on the point of launching a rustling raid when he was approached by 'a king who had brought seven very fine cows for sale'. Plied with rice in syrup, and offered a bell on a silk cord and a piece of brass, the chief agreed to the exchange. Soon others came, seeking copper objects made from the ship's cauldrons, and thereafter the seamen were never short of beef or milk. A kraal was made for their cattle and Cabreyra found that 'whereas I had given orders that we were only to kill one cow every Saturday, we were able to kill three a day'.

Cabreyra never missed an opportunity to impress the Pondo with his guns. After some weeks, the castaways were visited by 'a king who was held to be a valiant and warlike man, because these people are always at war among themselves'. This may well have been the usurper Gangate, come to investigate reports of the whites' firearms. Cabreyra laid on a demonstration, ordering a sailor to shoot down a crow in a tree:

> The Kaffirs were astonished; and if they had been plotting any treason they abandoned it. Taking up the crow they examined the wound, putting their fingers in their mouths, which is a way of exhibiting friendship, showing they would rather have us for friends than enemies.

As months went by and the fame of the settlement spread, so did Cabreyra's reputation as its chief. He was asked by one clan to act as a rainmaker, and healed a chief's skin ailment with coconut oil. Meanwhile the first ship, the *Nossa Senhora da Natividade*, was nearing completion and a second, the *Nossa Senhora da Boa Viagem*, had been begun. By now the men were varying their beef diet with hippopotamus from the Umzimvubu, and saints' feasts were celebrated with some pomp. Theatrical performances were staged and Cabreyra recorded holding a bullfight as if it were the most natural thing in the world.

In January 1636, six months after the wreck, the two vessels were launched in the river and preparations begun for departure. Barrels were made to contain water for the voyage, and beef was steeped in salt water and dried. They needed to be especially thorough as Cabreyra had decided to set his course, not for the nearest port on the east coast of Africa, but to round the Cape and proceed up the west coast to Angola.

At this point an incident occurred that spurred their departure. Whether the Pondo or the Portuguese were to blame is open to interpretation: Cabreyra claimed that he sent an armed party to reclaim items stolen by the inhabitants of a nearby kraal, but he may simply have been seeking an excuse to plunder the tribe's ripening millet crop for the coming voyage. In any event, the Portuguese found themselves surrounded: 'A sailor named Manuel d'Andrade gradually retreated with the others, and raising his gun, he shot the king, upon which his men seized their assegais and ours retreated in good order for about a league, killing several more, and among them a Negro of such high rank that they were dismayed and advanced no further.'

With the country in outcry, the Portuguese boarded their two vessels, with 135 souls on one and 137 on the other. By the end of January, they found themselves 'where none had ever thought to be, in a vessel under sail again in quest of the Cape of Good Hope'. Forty-eight days later, after further perils and hardships, Cabreyra had his reward when he guided the

Nossa Senhora da Natividade to anchor off Luanda in Angola. Having come through so much, the other half of his company had, however, finally run out of luck. The *Nossa Senhora da Boa Viagem* disappeared at sea, and was never seen again.

Back home, Cabreyra penned a lyrical if slightly embroidered account of the Pondo:

> The men are very lean and upright, tall of stature, and handsome. They can endure great labour, hunger and cold; they live two hundred [years] and even more in good health, and with all their teeth. They are so light that they can run over the mountains as fleetly as stags. They are clothed in skins which hang over their shoulders to the knees; these are cow-hides, but they have the art of dressing them till they are as soft as velvet.
>
> The kings have four, five and seven wives. The women do all the work, planting and tilling the earth with sticks to prepare it for their grain, which is millet. The women bring no dowry in marriage, on the contrary the husband pays the bride's father with cattle, and they become as slaves to their husbands.

Cabreyra had demonstrated that a man of boldness and resolve could impose his will on a desperate situation and bring those in his charge to safety. It would be 150 years before another captain came among Pondo's people to face a similar test.

8

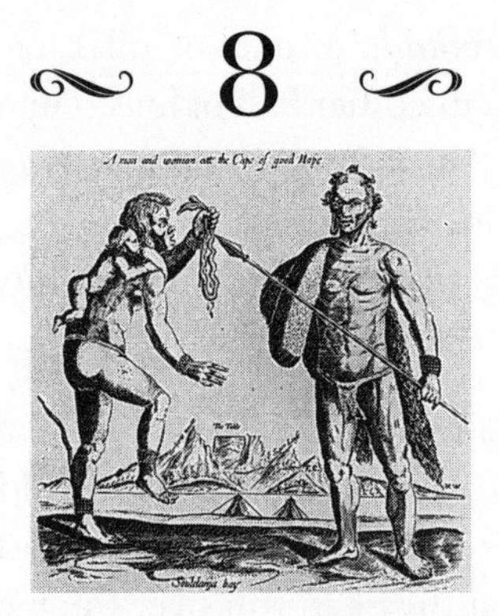

A FATAL DREAD

Lambasi, 6 August–Waterfall Bluff, 8 August

Failure to salvage powder and shot from the *Grosvenor* was to have incalculable consequences. European supremacy among indigenous peoples had always come from the barrel of a gun and when, on the evening of 5 August, William Habberley watched a Pondo warrior smash a pair of pistols on the rocks, it might have seemed an act of eloquent symbolism – the rage of a powerless people against an awesome technology. In fact, the Pondo were not interested in the pistols themselves, only the metal parts, and as Habberley noted sorrowfully: 'They were of course no utility to us.' It did not take either side long to realise that without firepower the castaways were merely mortal.

Joseph Banks had anticipated just such a predicament in 1770 when, with Cook on the *Endeavour* off north-east Australia, they came close to being wrecked. The great botanist's opinion was: 'Probably the most of us must [have been] drowned, a better fate maybe than those who should get ashore without arms to defend themselves from the Indians, the most uncivilised savages perhaps in the world.' Sir Joseph's response on hearing about the *Grosvenor* is not recorded, but his thinking is instructive.

It is easy to be overcritical of the man who had to deal with this desperately unenviable situation. John Coxon was not unusual among Indiamen skippers of the day in having a keener eye for profit than for navigation or the management of men. He was even less a soldier than he was a seaman

Africans at the Cape, a view by Sir Thomas Herbert from 1627. 'These Savages eat men alive or dead,' he wrote.

and nothing in his previous experience had equipped him to deal with such a crisis. Whatever tensions had developed in the great cabin over recent weeks – and it would have been a most unusual voyage had there been none – would now have been turned on him. He was under pressure from the overwrought passengers in his care, and understandably fearful that the sailors would simply abandon them. The fact was that while the only chance of saving everyone lay in harnessing the energies of the younger men to help the weak and injured, once they had come ashore the ninety-strong crew were no longer bound by shipboard discipline.

The captain's priorities at dawn on the second morning were twofold. First, he must act to quell the rumblings of insubordination and prevent any desertion. Second, he needed to have Logie fit and well again at his right hand. Logie knew how to handle the men. Logie was resourceful. He would see a way out.

Orders were given to muster the lascars. Addressing them, Coxon gave a warning that if they deserted, the Dutch would undoubtedly enslave them when they arrived at the Cape. If, on the other hand, they stayed with the company until they reached safety, he guaranteed to see that they were sent back to India on the first available ship. He was exaggerating both the risk to them and his own powers, but it did the trick and for the time being there was no further talk of desertion.

As for Logie, the outlook was less encouraging. The chief mate, being watched over by his wife, was unable to stand and barely conscious. Coxon, having admonished the lascars, then did nothing further to impose a sense of order and for the rest of the morning affairs were again allowed to drift. Left to their own devices, the hands wandered off to see what else they could collect from the shore.

At some point in the morning the Pondo returned, and in greater numbers than before. Having encountered no resistance, they now started to collect whatever pleased them. They also alighted upon a few pigs, which had been on the ship and had somehow been overlooked by the sailors. One man, Thomas Lewis, recalled: '[There was] particularly one boar, who thought himself the king of the place, rutting up the ground. The natives coming to catch him, he turned up his snout and grunted at them, so that they were afraid to seize him, but killed him with a lance, and the women and men cut him up.'

Encouraged to find that the sailors would not raise a hand even to protect their own food, a few Pondo now went into the camp. They gained entry to a tent and, Habberley related, 'took away some of our things'. Whether this was the women's tent, or the one being used to store provisions, the sudden appearance of the dark figures under the canvas had an all-too-predictable effect on the terrified Mary Hosea.

Coxon was again galvanised to action. He called a conference in the tent with Shaw, Beale and the other officers, and the senior passengers, Hosea, Newman, Colonel James and Captain Talbot. Lacking information on the deliberations that were to involve the senior men in the days ahead, we can only speculate on the influences each brought to bear. It would appear that Coxon, as the natural figure of authority for the sailors, was called on to assume command, although some of the others, including Talbot, may have already begun to wonder whether he was up to the task. Privately Shaw relayed to Habberley the main substance of what occurred at this meeting: a unanimous decision had been taken that in the morning Coxon would address the company and order that a start be made for the Cape.

Foraging continued for the rest of the day and a second cask of flour and a tub of pork were discovered. That night a large fire was set. While the region falls into a band of subtropical climate, August is the coolest month, with a mean temperature of 17.9°C (64°F). The seamen had little clothing and although their numerous discomforts would not include real cold, they made fires for warmth, as well as for reassurance and fellowship.

Before posting guards that night, Coxon ordered that the arrack barrels be stove in 'lest the natives, getting at it, might in a fit of intoxication, destroy [us] all'. It was a small incident but revealing perhaps of thinking in the tent. Seamen were not trusted with alcohol at times of crisis, and the captain and his passengers had begun to conflate what might be expected of sailors and natives. And although, as Dalrymple noted at the inquiry, the Pondo never offered violence at the wreck site, it seemed Coxon believed an attack was inevitable.

As the sun rose on 7 August, the third morning since the wreck, all hands were summoned. In his first speech to the whole crew, Coxon told them that his intention had been to wait until Logie recovered, but the natives' temper and shortage of food made that impossible. He had decided, therefore, that they should set out in a body, following the rising sun down the coast to the Cape of Good Hope.

He then made a bold and heartening claim: they would reach the outlying Dutch settlement in no more than seventeen days, he said, but with fortune he hoped in as few as ten. This speech concluded with a rousing call, exhorting the fit and strong to stand by their injured shipmates and emphasising the need for them all to stick together. What a cruelty it would be, Coxon said, 'for those who had escaped unhurt to leave those who were maimed to the mercy of such savages'. The captain was naturally keen to emphasise the solidarity that the officers and gentlefolk felt for the common seamen. He for one, he added, would sooner die than abandon any of them. As a company they would be better able 'to protect ourselves from the wild beasts, which we all knew this part of the globe to be infested with, and from the no less savage natives. If he might judge from their behaviour, we had no reason to expect the least mercy from them should they find us separated'. Logie, too sick to walk, would be carried on a litter.

Then the captain turned to the question of authority. As John Hynes related:

> He represented that as he had on board been their commanding officer, he hoped they would suffer him to continue his command. To this he was answered 'By all means'.

The company was immensely cheered. Familiar with the firm hand of discipline at sea, the men had been lost without a clear chain of command. Now Coxon had asserted his authority and, with his statement that they would reach sanctuary in two weeks, they could see an end to their ordeal. Few appear to have paused to reflect that the last time the captain had offered such an estimate, it was to assure them that they were 300 miles from the shore.

Once again Coxon's reckoning was fatally flawed. He appears to have thought that they had been wrecked at 29°s, when their true position was 31° 23´s. He believed that the nearest Dutch settlement was to be found as far north as 31°s, when in fact it was at 34°s. The upshot was that he calculated salvation lay within 250 miles, rather than the true distance of almost 400. To be fair, he was not alone in his ignorance about Africa's east coast. British charts were hopelessly inaccurate, and even after hearing the evidence and studying Portuguese geographical accounts, Dalrymple assessed that the *Grosvenor* had been lost in 28° 30´s. (In the process, he scorned the remarkably accurate estimate provided to him by the sailors of about 31°s.) However, the fact that these misreadings all put the Indiaman well north of her true position was a compelling reason for making for Delagoa Bay to the north rather than the Cape. If Coxon gave any consideration to the Portuguese settlement, there is no sign of it; and although he had no way of knowing what kind of country lay in either direction, he ought perhaps to have been aware that most previous castaways, faced with a similar choice, had opted for Delagoa Bay, and that a comparatively high proportion had reached it. He had been lulled into thinking that the little he had seen of the terrain – a grassy landscape of gentle contours, as it appeared from their position – was typical of what lay ahead. The choice of the Cape over Delagoa was crucial to what followed.*

As things stood, the company was just about managing. They had food for up to two weeks and unlimited fresh water. The possibilities of bartering with the Pondo had yet to be explored, and a still more bountiful source of food lay at hand. Molluscs were plentiful on the rocks – the spot is still sometimes called the Bay of Mussels. In such a place they could have established a defensive camp to be held by a majority of the 111 men, providing shelter for the injured, women and children. There was a risk of desertion, but the odds were that a core of men would respond to their officers' orders or, failing that, offers of reward for their loyalty. In the meantime, a party of the fittest men could have struck down the coast under an officer such as Shaw to raise the alarm at the Cape. A second group might have been sent north to seek help from the Portuguese.

Instead, Coxon and the senior men were goaded into hasty action, by fear partly of a Pondo attack but also of a mass desertion by the crew. The privileged inner circle of those who had dined at the captain's table were, suddenly and terribly, dependent on the sailors for their survival while at the same time having little faith that the men would stand by them. So a company that included seven women – one of whom, Lydia Logie, was in an advanced stage of pregnancy – five children, a number of grievously

* In 1552 a Portuguese galleon, the *São Joao*, went down about fifty miles further north. Of 500 or so survivors, most reached Delagoa.

injured men and a chief mate unable to stand, were set on a forced march of almost 400 miles along a tumultuous coast slashed by dozens of rivers and precipitous valleys, inhabited by wild animals and many more tribes of the supposedly savage people whom they now sought to avoid.

All was made ready for departure. The steward, Lillburne, was put in charge of distributing the food – 5lb of flour and 6lb of salt meat per head, each man to carry his own rations. It would be sufficient for eight or nine days. Coxon advised the men to throw away their heavy caps and to assemble a turban of silk or muslin against the sun. Adorned in this strange headgear, they started to gather beside the tidal pool.

One sailor, the supposedly demented Joshua Glover, had already gone off with the Pondo. A second man with misgivings now emerged. John Bryan, one of five discharged soldiers from Madras, had survived the Battle of Pollilur and could recognise a disaster in the making. He told the officers that he was unable to walk as a result of a leg injury that had left him lame. Bryan, like Glover before, appeared a doomed, pitiable figure to his comrades as they shook hands with him. Privately, he told the Irish seaman Hynes that he might as well die among the natives as starve on a march. Besides, he said, he might even prosper. He intended

> to get some pewter and lead from the wreck, of which he would make little trinkets to amuse the natives, hoping to ingratiate himself with them, and learn their language.

On Colonel James's advice the company lined up in army formation. It is surprising that, in a situation crying out for military leadership, more had not been done before to involve the former commander of the Madras Artillery, but – an opaque figure throughout – it would appear that either he had fallen out with the captain's circle or he no longer had the appetite to lead men. Shaw was in charge of the vanguard, made up of the stoutest hands. Behind them, in a group led by Beale, came the passengers and the injured, including Logie, who was to be carried in a litter. Coxon brought up the rear with the other seamen. In addition to the silk turban on his head, he brandished a curious weapon consisting of a bayonet tied to the end of a long pole, no doubt meant to impress on the Pondo that the castaways had spears of their own. To strike another military pose, they had fashioned a

Dutch standard, which was borne at the head of the column. Coxon's reasoning was that the colonists' flag would be more readily recognised than the Union Jack, and would help to create an impression of organised force.*

It was a clear morning as this caravan of all the East India Company ranks prepared to move on; nabobs formed up with soldiers, officers with tars; men in tailcoats and breeches stood beside those in shirts and linen trousers; women, in what remained of their finery were at last on terms of equality as well as intimacy with their *ayahs*. Mary Hosea and Lydia Logie had tucked away their last treasured possessions, brooches and other jewellery, in their pinned-up hair. Children, touched by the bright hope of the moment, skipped in the sun. They looked back at the wreckage of the *Grosvenor* for the last time. The ship was now 'all to pieces', Habberley recalled, with only the fo'c'sle and bow proud of the water. Then they crossed the Tezani and started for the Cape.

A beach stretched ahead; beyond it a grassy point. The sand was firm underfoot and where it ended a native path appeared. There was nothing in the slightest bit threatening in the landscape – flat, open grassland with a ridge of low green hills to the north and the sea to the south. The going was easier than any but the most optimistic could have hoped for – almost like a walk in the countryside. All they had to do was follow the coast.

Just then, the leading seamen saw the heads of Pondo warriors bobbing over the ridge to their right. While the castaways wanted to leave, the natives were determined that they should stay. The *abalumbi*, delivered to the Pondo by the sea, had been a gift – not merely the makers of wonders, but possessors of the secrets by which they were created.

There are a handful of sources for what followed. The most detailed account comes from William Habberley:

> We were surrounded by a great number of the natives who began throwing stones at us and, holding their lances in a threatening manner, seemed desirous of preventing us proceeding. Thinking them jealous of our going near their habitation, we endeavoured to

* It has been suggested that this was a disastrous miscalculation inviting attack, as a Dutch frontier war against the Xhosa had ended only a year before. However, the tribes in this region had no previous experience of the Dutch.

keep close to the sea but that was impossible . . . The natives still continuing to plunder and throw stones at us, notwithstanding we made every sign we could think of to make them sensible of our peaceable intentions.

Captain Coxon stayed behind a little, endeavouring to persuade them to desist, but they surrounded him, threw him down, and took from him a stick with a bayonet fixed to the end of it, with which they gave him some very severe blows. Our people then went and rescued him, and was [*sic*] going to revenge the usage, but the captain prevented it.

The Pondo withdrew, and the column moved on. Just over a mile after leaving Lambasi they crossed a stream, the Maviti, and suddenly progress was no longer easy. Rain had left the ground marshy underfoot and the way ahead rose steadily in a series of increasingly sharp contours. The men carrying Logie's litter had to pick their way carefully among the rocks. Within three miles they came to another river, the Mkweni, and this time there was no question of simply wading across it. For the first of many times, they were forced inland in search of a crossing.

About a mile upstream, the Pondo again advanced on them:

We were surrounded by some hundreds of the natives, all armed with lances and targets [shields]. They set up a terrible shouting and came on brandishing their lances over our heads, we expecting nothing less than to be cut all to pieces, which such numbers of them might easily have accomplished.

Instead of the massacre that threatened, however, the warriors came among them, 'stripping us of everything they fancied'. It would seem that as well as Coxon's bayonet-lance, the six cutlasses were lost in this fracas, for nothing more is heard of them.

Such feebleness is hard to reconcile with the robust tar of seafaring tradition. We are used to seeing the imperial Briton abroad as a dominant if not domineering figure in an unbroken chain of pre-eminence. The reality is far more complex. Britons abroad at this time, whether in North America or India, were invariably in a minority, often on the back foot, and strangers to neither defeat nor humiliation. And the men of the *Grosvenor*, however stout-hearted they might have been in their own element, were clearly overawed by these new surroundings. There is something simultaneously sad, comic and yet illuminating about Habberley's embarrassed attempt to explain why they had not resisted more:

> The buckles, buttons etc. we freely parted with, but when they began to destroy our provisions [they] exasperated some of us so much that we were beginning to defend ourselves, notwithstanding the captain's orders to the contrary.*

It was growing dark when the company found a point to cross the Mkweni. For a while they pressed on across increasingly rough ground until coming to a stream where they stopped, exhausted. The wood here was too green to make a fire, and they slept in the open on the side of a hill. At the end of that first disastrous day of the march, they had covered less than five miles.

The next morning, as the column wended its way with painful slowness up a steep gradient, it was approached by 'about sixty of the natives marching in regular order two deep, armed with lances and targets and headed by a chief'. The castaways recognised that these were a different people from their assailants. Taller and darker, with cheeks daubed red, they wore ostrich feathers in their hair. They were from a small clan, the Bomvana, and instead of advancing threateningly, they halted a distance off. Habberley was relieved to note: 'The chief then stepped forwards and made a short speech, they all behaving themselves very peaceable.'

Encouraged to parley with the natives for the first time, Coxon ordered the purser Hayes to go forward. Apprehensively he advanced with some gold lace, and had the happy inspiration of cutting it into pieces with which he decorated the heads of the Bomvana women. In return, they presented the castaways with sweet potatoes, maize and bread, which were divided among the passengers. The delighted Bomvana, wreathed in smiles, 'marched off in the same manner as they approached'.

* One scholar of the period might almost have had the *Grosvenor* seamen in mind when she wrote: 'By means of the sea and ships, these puny people could and did go everywhere. Ships cannot operate on dry land, however; so after landfall things for the British were always different, and usually far more difficult. This was emphatically the case as far as the East India Company was concerned.' Colley, p. 246.

No sooner had they left than another singular figure approached. Of lighter skin than the natives and with straight silky black hair, he came up clapping his hands and addressing Coxon in Dutch. On a hurried consultation it was discovered that Williams's manservant, John Sussman, had picked up some of the language in the East, and was able to interpret. Coxon, seeing that the newcomer was obviously of Asiatic origin and therefore reassuringly familiar, fell on the newcomer as a saviour.

Trout, as the castaways knew him – he would seem to have been named Traut by the Dutch – was a frontier fugitive. Little is known of his career other than that he was a Javanese slave of the Dutch who had escaped and fled up the coast beyond the colonists' reach. He had established a fiefdom among the Pondo, who valued his knowledge of the outside world. Right now, having heard about the wreck, he was on his way to the *Grosvenor*, intent on booty. His advice, given in a conclave of the senior men, was unequivocal. Told that they were shipwreck victims and intended walking to the Cape, he said that such a journey by a party including women and children was quite impossible. Habberley heard him spell out the 'unspeakable difficulties'.

> We had many nations to pass, and deserts to travel through, together with the dangers we should experience from wild beasts, and the various large rivers we had to cross.

Coxon was deaf to these warnings. He offered Trout a reward to act as their guide. Trout refused; the Dutch would kill him if he returned, he said. Coxon implored him. Among the party were men of great wealth, he said; they would pay Trout anything he asked, and sort out his difficulties with the Cape authorities. Still the Javanese declined. He gave as his reason that he had a wife and children, but it is clear that he wanted no part of a doomed enterprise.

Here, briefly, was a chance to reassess their position. The terrain ahead was already looking ominous, and Trout's description of rivers and deserts was only too plausible. At the same time, they had come among a friendly people willing to trade food. They could take stock and explore the way ahead while the sick and injured recovered; but the *Grosvenor*'s captain, increasingly aware of mutterings among the men and fearful of the break-up of his crew, was now a man incapable of reason. Coxon not only ignored Trout's 'disheartening' advice, but also, according to Habberley, 'carefully concealed it from the major part of the company.'

Trout's parting shot before he hurried north towards the wreck was that they should hold to the coast, for if they ventured inland they would encounter 'Boshemen Hottentots', San hunter-gatherers, who would undoubtedly kill them all.

If Coxon thought he could hide their rapidly deteriorating situation from the men, he was mistaken. As they resumed the climb towards the heights known today as Waterfall Bluff, the fitter seamen could not help but notice how their progress was being retarded. The pregnant Lydia Logie was having difficulty getting along, but she was not the only one. Frances Hosea, just past her second birthday, bewildered and frightened by all that had befallen them and also no doubt by the state of her strangely altered parents, was crying as she stumbled on. During the afternoon, an Italian seaman, Domenico Circanio, took the weeping child up in his arms and began to carry her.

A few men were also labouring, and before they called a halt that evening another incident occurred that prefigured events to come. A second Italian, a portly hand named Sebastiano Nardini, lay down and announced that he could go no further. A brief discussion followed about whether he too could be carried in a litter. Still trying to hold them all together, Coxon was in favour of the idea, but the sailors, already burdened with the chief mate, Logie, refused. Nardini was the first to be abandoned. The avowals of loyalty unto death with which they had set out had lasted less than two days.

9

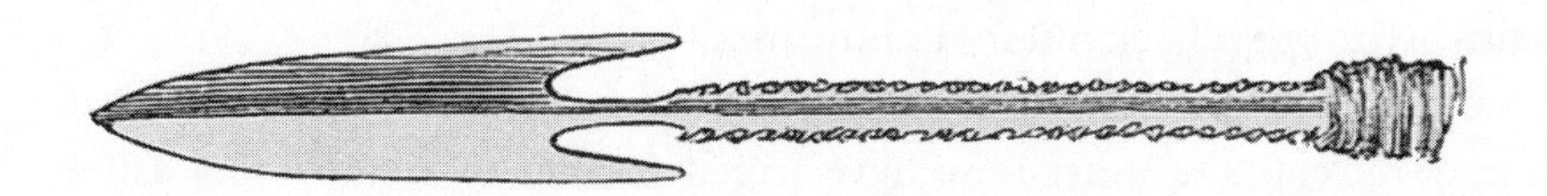

'NEVER AFTER TOGETHER AGAIN'

Waterfall Bluff, 9 August–Ntafufu River, 11 August

Dawn of 9 August came up on a scene of eerie desolation. In the early grey light, upwards of 120 figures were sprawled at the bottom of a valley like bundles on the ground, as if in the aftermath of a massacre. The previous night, the second since leaving the wreck, they had stumbled on until sunset before finding shelter in the valley and making a rudimentary camp. The passengers, shrouded in blankets, were clustered in a group. The sailors lay where they had huddled together beside the embers of their fires.

Gradually the figures came to life on the dewy ground. Fires were rekindled and flour and water baked into biscuits. Then the castaways formed up again and moved on, following a native path out of the valley. After a couple of hours of heavy slogging the straggling column reached the heights of Waterfall Bluff, a place of immense and commanding grandeur that looks out across the Indian Ocean. It was an appropriately theatrical setting for a confrontation between English seamen and African tribesmen.

The circumstances are confusing. Some men spoke of a kraal from which warriors came pouring out towards them, but Habberley stated that their assailants were men who had been shadowing them from the wreck: '[We] were marching along a path when the natives got before us and endeavoured to prevent us.' Some threw stones, others waved assegais as if to drive the castaways back like cattle.

Head of a spear, wood engraving by George Baxter, 1845

Something in Coxon finally snapped. 'One of them came up and cut the captain in the hand, which irritated him so much that he laid hold of the fellow and snatched the weapon from him,' Habberley related. Another sailor, Thomas Lewis, recalled: 'The native endeavoured by signs and entreaty to get it back but to no purpose.'

If they had not done so already, James, the Army colonel, and Talbot, the naval captain, must now have urged Coxon to action. The sailors seemed almost relieved to be at last given licence to resist. The story told by John Hynes – that they charged the Pondo, who withdrew briefly but then mustered an *impi* of 400 warriors, which fought a desperate running battle with the crew of ninety during which 'a great number were maimed on both sides' – smacks of dramatic licence. A more plausible account of events can be pieced together from the testimony by Lewis and Habberley to the inquiry. Lewis related: 'The captain put the ladies and those who were unable to do anything upon a rising ground with the baggage, and then attacked the natives.'

The Pondo retreated to a kraal. Lewis stated that the seamen pursued them among the huts and drove them away, only for them to regroup and return with shields, assegais and sticks. Habberley picked up the story:

> The [shields] being made of strong hides, about four feet long and two broad, the stones we threw had not the least effect on them, they very seldom missing us, but running off when we advanced. In retreating, one fell down and was caught and almost killed by our boatswain.

All the pent-up fury over their ill-treatment had come boiling to the surface. The bosun, Robert Rea, on-ship a strong-armed enforcer, was not used to being knocked about by anyone and was still pummelling his bloodied victim when the crew pulled him off. Coxon now went about urging that none of the natives should be killed, but a running skirmish continued for some time on the rocky hills around the kraal. Sailors were everywhere, running and cursing, as the Pondo darted away up the rocks. But these clashes were oddly bloodless. Habberley, for one, realised that the Pondo 'might easily have destroyed us all had they thrown their lances'. Although alive to the chance of plunder, the natives were not predisposed towards killing. They were also uncertain. Having been emboldened by discovering that the whites were without guns, the Pondo still appeared to be caught between a desire for their possessions and apprehension at some as-yet-unrevealed power.

The first real casualty was Charles Newman. The barrister had joined the affray and was setting about one of their tormentors when he was stabbed in the head with an assegai. The thrust was not fatal but the point entered Newman's ear and he fell insensible. As he went down, the warriors 'set up a shouting', as much perhaps in shock as triumph. Newman was carried to the high ground, where the women and children had been moved for safety. His wound was serious and he remained semi-conscious for a couple of hours. Meanwhile, the seamen, 'made a formidable charge on the natives and drove them some distance off'.

There was a stunned lull after Newman's stabbing. As if shocked by the turn of events, and the destructive impulses that had been unleashed, some of the Pondo returned to make overtures of friendship. What followed resonates with pathos and farce in equal measure. Habberley's description of it has an almost childlike quality:

> We made signs for them to leave us, first giving them the lance the captain had taken from them. They then brought the wounded man forwards and exhibited him, who certainly was badly bruised by the boatswain and others. We stayed hereabouts; the natives bringing some sweet potatoes which they exchanged for buttons, etc. They being now quite reconciled, we proceeded on.

The Pondo had demonstrated that, whatever else, they were not murderous brigands, and the sailors had belatedly fought back. But the skirmish at Waterfall Bluff came too late to have any benefit. Thereafter Coxon looked a defeated and isolated man. The sailors had lost faith in him and the spirit went out of the whole company. As Habberley put it: 'After this affray we never again opposed the natives, but let them take whatever they pleased from us.'

Newman was able to walk only with the support of a sailor on either side. At first progress continued to be slow along the cliffs, but by late afternoon they had reached lower ground and had covered about four miles when they were overtaken by Trout, returning to his village with plunder from the wreck site. This time the Javanese cut a disconcerting, even sinister, figure. He was wearing a nightgown of Coxon's that had been salvaged from the wreck, along with items of iron and copper. Trout's response to their tribulations was no less perturbing. When he heard about the skirmish, 'he laughed and cautioned us against making any resistance in future'. Forlornly, Coxon asked him in which direction the Cape lay. The same way that he was going, Trout replied, before striding off.

In the evening they came to a stream set about with bright-red blossoming trees. The water was good, and a fire was started. Looking across to where the women sat, John Hynes was moved to pity. The sources are almost silent about what had been happening to the families since the start of the march and Hynes provided little insight into their state at this point while offering a melodramatic flourish:

> What a situation this for ladies who had been delicately brought up, and lately used to all the luxuries of the East! Every susceptible heart must sympathise in their sufferings, and lament that they were out of the reach of relief.

But if there was indeed sympathy 'for the sufferings borne by delicate women of the higher ranks and the miseries of their children', as another contemporary account related, it was combined with a clear-eyed assessment of their frailties. Around the fire, the seamen had begun to talk in low tones and on one point they were agreed: although they had barely started, some of the company seemed already near the end. No one could fail to note the wild-eyed terror of Mary Hosea, the painfully laboured progress of Lydia Logie, or the effort required to carry her husband, a deadweight on the litter. At the end of their fifth full day in Africa, they were not even ten miles from where they had been wrecked. Roughly a quarter of their provisions had been consumed, yet no new source of food had been found.

One last opportunity to avert catastrophe presented itself in the morning, when they arrived at Trout's village. He lived beside the Umbotji River in a setting of sweet tranquillity. Thatch huts dotted both banks and tall grass swayed in a breeze coming off the sea. Cattle thrived on this excellent pasturage and for the first time were to be seen in numbers grazing placidly on the hillsides. As the straggling column entered the settlement, they were surrounded by a milling throng, not just of men and women, but of children who clutched for their mothers in astonishment.

Quite apart from the strangeness of these pallid figures as a whole, they were mesmerised by the sight of the seven-year-olds, Thomas Law, Robert Saunders, Tom Chambers and Mary Wilmot; and Eleanor Dennis, aged three, and Frances Hosea, two.

Trout met the castaways. He toyed with Coxon. Holding a child in his arms, he demanded a piece of salt pork for the youngster. Desperately short of food as they were, Coxon complied, then – 'pointing out the distress we were in' – asked Trout to trade one of the cows grazing nearby. That was quite impossible, the Javanese replied: he had none himself, and the Pondo would certainly not part with their animals. All pretence, all composure, were gone. Coxon pleaded with Trout one last time: guide them to safety and everything in their power to command would be his. The answer was as before. Trout would agree only to ask the Pondo to provide escorts.

Once again, the question arises why, finding themselves in a spot hospitable to habitation, the castaways did not consider staying where they were. Natives were clustering around the sailors, not with any apparent hostile intent, but rather, according to Habberley, 'desirous of holding a dialogue with us'. What might have come of this overture had it been allowed to develop is impossible to say for, Habberley went on: 'The captain would not let anybody hold conversation with them.' This episode lingered in the memory of other seamen too. Warmington and Leary told the inquiry:

> The officers and passengers would not let the seamen have any parley with the natives, thinking that they could manage better with them.

The reference to passengers suggests Hosea's influence. Signs of Coxon's desire to placate the fretful Resident flicker throughout the story of their shared ordeal; but by now they were equally fearful of the brute forces that each perceived to be at work – not only among the natives of Africa, but in the seamen of their own kind. Coxon had repeatedly squandered opportunities for treating with the Pondo and demonstrated a lack of faith in his crew. Matters were too far gone now for help to be obtained from the natives, and the seamen had been estranged. Increasingly, the men were looking to the only figure in authority who had been alert to their peril from the first, who had given warning that the ship was dangerously close to the shore: the second mate, William Shaw.

Trout returned at length with two men who, he said, would act as guides, then took his leave. He had been honest in his advice, but he had rendered neither favour nor service. Having been a slave of the Dutch, he had no reason to like Europeans, and seeing that they were bent on self-destruction, he now determined to plunder them. The seamen did not encounter him again, but afterwards he figured in the collective memory as a malign figure manipulating the events that followed. Up to now the efforts of the Pondo to get at their possessions had been blundering forays. That was about to change. As Thomas Lewis put it: 'The Malay was a rogue as he shewed the natives where [our] pockets were.'

They had scarcely left Trout's camp and crossed the Umbotji River before men, women and children came up on the rearmost, throwing stones. At first it seemed no more than petty harassment and the sailors reasoned that 'the natives would not follow far'. They carried on and around noon crossed another small river, the Umzimpunzi. By evening they had made about eight miles, comparatively good progress, and stopped when a source of fresh water was found. They were resting there when Pondo warriors appeared on the hillside above and came racing down.

Coxon ordered everyone to sit down in a gesture of passive resistance. Now the dark figures came among the company. Bags of flour were snatched and the contents scattered. Hands dived into pockets and searched greedily. The captain appeared to be paralysed. According to Lewis, the sailors urged Coxon 'to go on and not to sit still and let all their things be taken from them; but . . . he would not move, and so different people set off without him'.

Certain images were to linger in the mind: a warrior seizing Newman's watch, puzzling over the sound of ticking, then smashing it to pieces between two stones; Mary Hosea and Lydia Logie, who had concealed their jewellery in their hair and about their persons, being roughly searched before these last trinkets were discovered. Hynes related:

> What the feelings of the ladies must be on thus losing their valuable ornaments is much easier to be conceived than described. The gentlemen, as may be supposed, could not conceal their indignation at these outrages; but all they got from the plunderers in return, were blows with their lances, or with knobbed sticks.

It had happened during the wreck, and it happened again now: men were seized by an overwhelming urge to escape. In a body, the sailors burst through their persecutors and fled, 'leaving the captain, officers and ladies'. But Coxon was not far behind: 'The lascars then followed them, and immediately after the captain, officers & c.' The passengers – women, children, and the wounded Newman – were abandoned. With a candour remarkable for its dispassion, Habberley admitted:

> As everyone made the best of their way according to their strength we were soon separated; the weakest were left behind, which was of little consequence, as any resistance made against the natives would be useless. Those who got on first escaped tolerably well, but the hindermost ones were plundered of everything about them, the natives making no difference between age or sex, pillaging all and threatening to kill those who opposed them.*

Sailors made their way along the shore in groups. By evening, about two miles on, they came to another river, the Ntafufu, where a fire was started. Looking back 'they saw at a distance the ladies etc. coming over a hill'. In ones and twos the stragglers joined the seamen again. Captain Talbot came in with his servant Isaac Blair. So did Colonel James and his wife. One of the few recorded actions of the Madras Army man was some useful advice he gave to the thirsty seamen at this point: that they could obtain drinkable water by digging holes at the high-water mark beside the river.

The Hoseas had meanwhile stayed where they were, too shattered even to move. Evidently shamed by his flight, Coxon later returned to them. They must have spent an uneasy night together, though there was little left to say and one suspects that the Resident and his wife were no longer

* Accounts of such mistreatment at the hands of Africans evoked outrage when they reached England; but it is worth recalling that shipwrecked seamen could often expect no better in their native land. The Cornish coast was notorious for the activity of wreckers who looted shipping. In 1753, one witness to 'the monstrous barbarity practised by these savages', wrote: 'I have seen many a poor man, half dead, cast ashore and crawling out of the reach of the waves, fallen upon and in a manner stripp'd naked by those villains.' When the Indiaman *Halsewell* was wrecked in Dorset three years after the *Grosvenor*, a clergyman, Morgan Jones, related hearing the news at breakfast with a friend: 'The disposition of the country to plunder is well known; we therefore immediately mounted our horses, to afford what protection we could to the unfortunate.'

capable of recriminations. It was plain to both that their status had become utterly meaningless and that the man in charge of their destinies was as helpless as they. Just a week had passed since they had last sat round the captain's table in the great cabin.

Early in the morning Coxon, accompanied by the Hoseas, rejoined the rest of the company at the Ntafufu. The reunion was brief. A point had been reached where the sailors heard only the call of survival. They knew when they could do no more for shipmates on a sinking ship, and they now saw no way of helping further the weak, the sick and the young. Some must have been alienated by the captain's patent lack of trust in them. A few may even have come to feel a certain vague kinship with the natives. John Warmington, who was among those who had tried to parley with them, came after all from a Cornish family that had produced wreckers as well as seamen and might have had time to reflect that the natives were no worse than some of his own kin.

The Ntafufu was broad and deep, and they had to wait for the tide to go out before starting out. It was Warmington who recalled: 'The ladies waded over the river breast high, being supported by the sailors who carried over the children.' That was the last act of kindness rendered to the women and the young.

Hynes's version of the parting invests the moment with sentiment: 'They had shared the difficulties and distresses incident to their situation and so were familiarised to each other; to part therefore in a strange land and almost without hopes of meeting again could not be accomplished without many pangs.'

Once again, though, it is Habberley's bleak account that speaks the more convincingly. He offered no redeeming feature to the sailors' actions, stating grimly:

> Every person was desirous of making the best of their way, saying it was of little use to stay and perish with those they could not give any assistance to. By this we were completely separated, and never after together again.

Dalrymple, who was well versed in the ways of the sea, offered no criticism in his impassively worded report: 'Some of the people set out, straggling, leaving the captain and ladies behind. The captain was not sick, but out of heart when they parted.'

It would be mistaken, however, to portray the separation as a straightforward division between, on the one hand, the strong and youthful and, on the other, the weak and helpless – or, for that matter, between the privileged and the exploited. Too much had passed, on board, between the officers, and probably even among the passengers, for it to be as simple as that. The way the two groups divided was shaped by the strains that had come to the surface during the voyage.

Coxon was left behind with twenty-three of the passengers – the Hoseas, Colonel and Mrs James, Newman, Captain Adair, Captain de L'Isle, their servants and the children. Also in his group were Alexander Logie, still ailing on a litter, and his wife. So were Beale – which is not to be wondered at, given his role in the disaster – the fifth mate Harris, another member of the captain's circle, and the petty officers – who held their rank at his discretion and remained collectively loyal – Hayes the purser, Rea the bosun, Nixon the surgeon, Hunter the gunner, and Mixon the quartermaster, among others. Coxon's party numbered forty-seven in all.

Shaw led away the remainder. As the most senior able-bodied officer, he was the natural leader for the seamen to turn to; but there may well have been more to it than that. Shaw had been excluded from the captain's clique on board. Had personal antagonism persuaded the second mate to lead a breakaway from an unpopular, discredited commander? Had differences since the wreck found expression in disputes over the course of action? The break-up could not be described as mutiny, because they were no longer subject to Coxon's authority; but that is not to say it was not acrimonious.

Dalrymple never spelled out the reasons for the seamen's actions, but he had his own reasons for discretion. So did they. All bar seven of them opted to follow Shaw. Most of the lascars did as well.

More surprising was the decision of some passengers to join them. Talbot, who was senior to and more experienced than Coxon, had seen enough to convince him that the man ostensibly in command was out of his depth. He threw in his lot with the crew, although his sixty-odd years ill suited him for a forced march with younger men. So did the nabobs, Taylor and Williams, who had lost their fortunes but not their will to live, and Colonel d'Espinette. For reasons that are not known, he was leaving his compatriot, de L'Isle.

It is a further comment on Coxon's moral collapse that his own servant, Robert Price – who had recovered from his head wound sustained during the wreck – and his steward, William Couch, both chose to join Shaw. Six petty officers, including Page the carpenter and Lillburne the steward, were also to accompany the second mate. So was William Ellis, a soldier who had been servant to another in the captain's party, Colonel James. In total, Shaw's group consisted of fifty Europeans and between fifteen and twenty lascars.

As they were about to start out, it was noticed that one of the children was weeping. Thomas Law, the little Anglo-Indian boy befriended by Lillburne during the voyage and cared for by him since the wreck, was inconsolable at the prospect of being separated from the steward. The seamen went into a huddle, at which it was agreed that the boy, ever afterwards known as Master Law, should be allowed to accompany them, and that if it became necessary, they would take it in turns to carry him.

Among those left with Coxon at the Ntafufu were seven sailors. They included two Italians: Pandolpho, who had gone over the ship's side with a rope for the offer of a reward, and Circanio, who had been carrying Frances Hosea these past few days. The last had not been heard of Hosea's diamonds. Hynes related that

> induced by the great promises made them by Colonel James, Mr Hosea & c [they] were prevailed upon to stay behind with them, in order to carry what little provision was left, and the blankets with which they covered themselves at night.

At port in Madras four months earlier the crew had doffed their caps as the gentlefolk came aboard. They had watched as Coxon, in the blue and gold of an Indiaman captain, welcomed the red-jacketed Colonel James and a resplendent Newman, silver buttons gleaming on his coat, along with the bonneted girls and the wives in their best finery, shielded from the Indian sun by parasols. On the morning of 11 August, as Shaw and his party started away, they looked back for the last time and saw only a band of ragged wretches, their faces lined with despair.

10

FAULTLINES

Ntafufu River, 13 August–near the Umgazana River, 22 August

English seamen had been vaguely familiar with southern Africa since the time of Drake – as a coastal outline, turbulent, perilous, and best glimpsed on the horizon. When William Habberley and the rest of Shaw's party turned away from the passengers, they plunged into a land that no Englishman had seen before. For the *Grosvenor* castaways, the natural world of Africa might have been another planet.

As Simon Schama observes, there have always been two kinds of Arcadia: shaggy and smooth; dark and light; a place of bucolic leisure and a place of primitive panic. The two worlds may exist in close proximity. They may even be the same place, encountered at different times or seen from a new perspective. Months later the African wilderness became for some of the men, if not a place of bucolic leisure, then something close to it, a world in which they were self-sufficient, knowledgeable about the means of survival and at ease among the native inhabitants, finding a life that held its own pleasures and freedoms. At the start, however, it was primitive panic pure and simple.

From the heights of Waterfall Bluff it is still possible to discern the edge of a geological fault where 130 million years ago a tectonic shudder began to disrupt the supercontinent of Gondwanaland, separating Africa from South America, Antarctica, Australia and India. The Egosa Fault, as it is known, is one of the scars of Gondwanaland's disintegration, a great gash

Square-nosed rhinoceros, by Captain W. C. Harris, 1852

in the earth's crust running along the coast, from which emanate the series of spectacular physical features – precipitous rock faces and gorges through which rivers course down to the sea – of the Wild Coast.

Where the sandstone bluff falls away for 300 feet, the Indian Ocean holds the eye as far as it can behold. Below the surface, the fault drops deep to the seabed, producing ocean swells of such weight that it almost seems they might shift the seismic chunks of rock against which they beat. The roar can be cataclysmic. The Portuguese captain Joseph de Cabreyra, who was stranded on the coast for months, was moved to remark: 'Often it seemed to us as if there were fleets at sea battering each other with their guns, so loud was the booming of the waves.'

This elemental place held the sailors in its grip. Having expected that they would be able to press on rapidly once freed of the women and children, Shaw's men found themselves traversing with painful slowness rock formations that pressed down to the water's edge. Frequently they would cover some difficult ground only to reach a point where they were forced back by a sheer face or an incoming tide. In other places impenetrable banks of subtropical growth pressing down to the shore forced them to hold to the sea, however heavy the going. When they could forge a way inland it was to find daunting ridges and valleys where the vegetation was again impassable.

Nothing was quite as it seemed. The forests of England were places of rustic liberty, gentle oaken groves for lovers, hunters and fugitives. Here they were places of unlit menace. Soft-wooded trees grew on top of and among one another in tortuous profusion. Trunks and branches interlocked like the limbs of mangled bodies. Creepers and foliage filled the surrounding space and blotted out the sky.

Even the fruit trees were different, for although they included varieties of wild banana and fig, they bore nothing edible. Groves of *Strelitzia nicolai*, the wild banana, grew to within a few yards of the sea and in such density that they sealed the land beyond as effectively as a metal wall. Fronds of the wild date palm, *Phoenix reclinata*, whispered tantalisingly in the wind, their fruits far out of reach. Another tree, a mysterious and grotesque succulent, *Euphorbia triangularis*, clung to the edges of rivers and ocean with candelabra fingers that reached up like giant hands. A prickly shrub bore the only attainable fruit, a lurid purple berry that exuded a vile white and poisonous-looking pus when it was picked; the men were desperately hungry before discovering some weeks later that the flesh of *Carissa microcarpa*, or the *matungulu*, as it is known to the coastal tribes, was as delicious as a plum – even if it did have what Habberley called 'a purgative quality'.

The dune and coastal forest species here are so rich and diverse that they have yet to be completely catalogued. *Putterlickia verrucosa*, the warted bastard spike-thorn, is as ugly as it sounds and ubiquitous, while the Pondo coconut, *Jubaeopsis caffra*, is lovely as well as unique. River estuaries host species of mangrove, red, black and white, each with its own range of attendant wildlife hangers-on: crabs, frogs and myriad species of insect life. But it was the animal presence around them that made the deepest impression. The African wilderness produces a fantastic range of sounds at night, from the constant rhythmic chatter of cicadas to all the squeals, grunts, guffaws, cackles, bellows and roars made by the world's most extravagant collection of fauna. The tree hyrax, a small nocturnal animal, emits an uncanny shriek suggestive of dire distress. The ibis produces a bray to set nerves on edge. It is not surprising that men whose ears were attuned to the slap of the sea and the crack of canvas became fearful of beastly noises.

Seeing the animals only confirmed the men's worst expectations. They might have spotted the odd domesticated elephant in India, but that was scant preparation for *Loxodonta africana*, a behemoth that crashed through forests in herds, heedless and untouchable. Some may have heard about London's famously placid Sumatran rhinoceros, 'a very strange beast lately brought from the East Indies, daily to be seen at the Bell Savage Inn on Ludgate Hill', but none had encountered *Cerathotherium simus*, the world's largest land mammal after the elephant, an armoured colossus with a horn like a railway spike and an unnerving turn of speed. Or *Hippopotamus amphibius*, a river-dwelling monster of immense smooth grey and pink flesh that might have appeared almost avuncular but for its baleful eyes. There were deadly creatures of awful legend, prowling lions and serpents that coiled in the undergrowth or lurked among branches above; and there were others of which no one had heard – hyenas that slunk through the night like hooded assassins, or the gawkily elegant wildebeest, of which the hunter-artist William Cornwallis Harris was to write: 'A more whimsical compound than the gnoo could scarcely have been thrown together.' Tantalisingly beyond reach were a dozen species of antelope, from the eland, a creature the size of a large cow and twice as good to eat, to the tiny porcelain-like perfection of the steenbok.

Not for another fifty years, and the arrival of Harris, an Indian Army officer who observed and drew animals as assiduously as he shot them, did African wildlife gain an interpreter able to represent its majesty to an English audience. At the edge of this world of discovery, the *Grosvenor* seamen took fright. Habberley referred constantly to his 'great alarm at the dreadful noise of the beasts' at night. Fire was thought to be the only force capable of keeping these ravening monsters at bay. When an individual fell behind and was lost, his fellows had 'not a doubt that he had become a prey to the wild beasts; as not a day passed without their seeing lions, tygers or wolves'.*

The human inhabitants seemed scarcely less intimidating. Where fear of the natives echoes through the survivors' accounts, it is less because of any cruelty, real or imagined, than for a disturbing strangeness. Quite apart from their colour or appearance, they were said to be endowed with almost superhuman fleetness and strength. The sailors suspected that what one described as the 'agility which the inhabitants of Africa are well known to exhibit both in the chase and in battle' entailed some kind of necromancy: Hynes thought it came from an ointment of butter and soot; the boy Price put it down to a shoe worn on just one foot that enabled the wearer to take prodigious leaps; Lewis, too, spoke of a single shoe made of buffalo hide that gave the natives twice the speed across the ground of a white man.

In fact, the greatest peril confronting them was neither man nor beast, but nature itself. Had the *Grosvenor* been wrecked even fifty or sixty miles further south, many more of the castaways must have been preserved. As it was, the dark star that followed the Indiaman's last voyage had brought them to the most inimical stretch of the entire coast. The castaways were heading directly into an implacable place at the heart of the Egosa Fault.

* Early identification by the English of African carnivores is extremely eccentric. Usually, 'tigers' referred to leopards and 'wolves' meant hyenas; but Hynes's mention of 'twenty wolves at a time lying in the grass' would indicate the gregarious wild dog rather than the solitary hyena.

This description of one day's march came from Hynes:

> On the fourth day they came to a high mountain, the side of which was covered with wood, and they were obliged to take this route, as the rocks near the shore rendered that way impossible. In order to pass through this wood, which appeared to be of very considerable extent, they began their march before day break, and entered it just as the sun rose: And a most fatiguing day this proved. They had a new path to beat, where perhaps the human foot had never before been imprinted, and as many of the company were bare-legged, they were greatly incommoded.
>
> Uncertain which way to proceed, they were frequently obliged to climb the highest of the trees in order to explore their way; so that night approached, and they were nearly sinking under the fatigue, before they reached the summit of the hill.

Anyone venturing into this landscape today – much of it is still accessible only on foot – must marvel that they persevered as they did. On the rocky shoreline, the scarred shales tear at bare flesh while boulders the size of buses compel the walker inland – and back into the woods. Habberley's remark after scrambling through one forest, that 'it being covered so thick with underwood, we could not well penetrate it', was a spectacular understatement.

Then there were the rivers. Trout had been quite specific about the danger posed by 'various large rivers'. The high interior gives rise to eight major waterways and scores of lesser ones that they would have to cross. On 13 August they came to the first. Cresting a grassy ridge, Shaw's party was presented with a spectacular sight, a beach hundreds of feet below and stretching away for almost two miles. Beyond lay an immense brooding river, with on either side twin heights forming a vast geological gateway to the interior.

For the hiker following in the castaways' footsteps now – savouring the grandeur of sacred nature while recognising how close pleasure and fear are in our appreciation of the elemental – here is a delightful arrival, one of South Africa's most appealing spots. The little town of Port St Johns is a drowsy haven, set beside the great Umzimvubu River and beneath the majestic sandstone cliffs of Mount Thesiger and Mount Sullivan, at

1230 feet and 1040 feet. Dropouts and backpackers are drawn to its sleepy, slightly bohemian society, the miles of sandy beaches and fine surf, and the sheer beauty of its setting in the midst of wilderness. To the castaways, however, the place spelled disaster.

It is safe to say that if they had been travelling at the height of the wet season, when the rains wash down rich red topsoil and the Umzimvubu runs thick and broad as if brimming with dark honey, none of them would have escaped. At first, they turned inland in search of a crossing point; but here the forest that crowded down from the cliffs to the riverbank was so dense that after about a mile they could go no further and had to turn back. For a better overview, they climbed the cliff now known as Mount Sullivan, where they found a stream of clear water and sighted a route to bypass the thickest forest and take them upriver. Exhausted, they settled there for the night.

The next morning they followed a forested valley running parallel to the river, only to encounter another obstacle, a tributary of the Umzimvubu. It was all too much for one sailor, Thomas Wren, who lay down and said he could go no further. A dozen or so lascars, reasoning that they would do better on their own, broke away. So did two Italians – Francisco Feancon, whose pale Venetian complexion had earned him the nickname Bianco, and Sebastiano Paro – who announced that they were going to swim for it, and disappeared into the water.

By the time they crossed the tributary and regained the Umzimvubu, exhaustion had overtaken the older members of the party. Captain Talbot and Colonel d'Espinette were men of spirit but – aged about sixty and fifty-five – near the ends of their tethers. The Frenchman collapsed with fatigue. In a phrase that was to echo repeatedly through the survivors' accounts, Habberley stated: 'We therefore were under the painful necessity of leaving him behind.'

The following day, 16 August, they found a narrow point to ford the Umzimvubu. Those who were able to swam. Rafts were fashioned from branches for the others. Having taken three days to cross just one of the rivers that lay ahead, they started back towards the sea. At this stage, little Tom Law started to show signs of distress.

The plight of the child was to bring out the best in the men. Of the 'many efforts of generosity and mutual assistance' during their ordeal remarked on by Dalrymple, none was more conspicuous than the devotion to the little Anglo-Indian boy demonstrated in the weeks to come. From here on, led by the steward Henry Lillburne, who had accepted responsibility for him, the men took it in turn to carry the seven-year-old when he had not the strength, although 'in consequence being very much wearied' themselves.

It was all up with Talbot, however. The erstwhile captain of HMS *Worcester* had shot his bolt. His gold-braided blue coat was grubby and torn, his wig was gone and his breath came in short gasps as he scrabbled up another steep hillside. Grey-faced with exhaustion, he sat down suddenly and did not get up. Isaac Blair, his servant, went back and offered to stay. Blair had been with him throughout the campaign against the French, including the battles of Sadras and Providien, and his devotion was genuine. Talbot, too, rose to the occasion. Whatever the circumstances of his departure from the naval squadron, the stigma of being a dotard, it was to his enduring credit that he would not hear of such purposeless self-sacrifice and insisted that Blair go on without him.

Few others paused. A grim precedent had already been established and whatever efforts might be made to save a child, it was clear to everyone that a good many others would fall by the wayside before any of them escaped this vale of death. And so they passed by, leaving Talbot there, an elderly gentleman who had spent most of his life at sea, sitting alone on a hillside in Africa.

Disconcerted by the phlegmatic way in which the seamen had turned their backs on d'Espinette and Talbot, and having consumed the last of their own supplies, the nabobs Taylor and Williams saw now, if they had not before, that only the strongest and fittest were going to have any chance of survival. They approached Shaw and Habberley, his young but increasingly mature aide, and put themselves in their hands. Habberley never made clear the nature of this agreement, saying simply that the four of them resolved to pool their remaining flour: 'Messrs. Shaw, Taylor, Williams and self, having agreed to use ours in common, which we fortunately still retained a small quantity of, we mixed with water and made some cakes . . .'

There was almost certainly another element to the contract. From here on, Habberley was to act as guardian to the nabobs, shepherding them across obstacles and through danger, and it is probable that they had offered a substantial incentive for him to bring them home to safety.

With five of their number lost and the lascars gone, Shaw's party was down to forty-five. Perhaps this made them appear a less formidable body, for two days later they had their first stroke of fortune. Soon after regaining the sea, they encountered a group of men, perhaps Tembu, who, Habberley said, 'behaved very peaceable'.

> They drove a fine young bullock to us, for which we gave a gold watch-chain. The natives condescended to kill it. Afterwards they lent us a lance to cut it up with, and in the meantime fetched some milk, which was cheerfully exchanged for buttons. We now readily set to making fires for the purposes of broiling a part, which we ravenously devoured.

The Tembu were not only peaceful but sociable, and the two groups shared the meal in a feast of goodwill. Optimism swept through the seamen. With their stomachs full, and reasoning that they had 'reached a more hospitable part of the country, where we should be able to procure provisions', as Habberley put it, they could lie back on the grass, a contented company, to appreciate for the first time the sun on a lush landscape, and enjoy a soft breeze coming off the sea on a golden afternoon. The bullock served another purpose too. Some of the men had been without shoes since the wreck, and had suffered agony traversing sharp rocks. They were now shod with wrap-around sandals made from hide and when they stepped forth again it was as men rejuvenated. At the next river they came to, the Umgazana, they stripped off their clothes and bounded across joyfully like naked schoolboys.

That was on 19 August. No sooner were they on the other side than they ran into country as difficult as the area around the Umzimvubu. Once again doubts began to play on the men's minds. No more of the friendly Tembu were seen and optimism that they would soon be able to barter more food evaporated. They had, in fact, been wrecked not only along the most inhospitable stretch of the coast, but also at the leanest season of the year. While the rains had just begun and would increase in frequency over the coming weeks, resources among all the coastal people were stretched in a way that made them naturally reluctant to succour refugees.

On 22 August the men ate the last of the beef. This act – the exhaustion of their food – precipitated a new crisis.

The survivors' accounts offer little insight into individual characters. The word that recurs most commonly is a general 'we' and there is a tendency to see the band of sailors as a homogeneous entity when, like any ship's company, they included hard men and sages, jokers and pessimists. Fundamentally, however, the qualities that mattered now were youth, strength and the indefinable capacity to endure, and the fact that they shared a terrible plight was not sufficient to bind them as one.

Shaw was convinced that their best prospects of survival lay in finding native kraals, and that to do so they ought to strike inland towards the higher grassland where pastoralists were likely to live in numbers. He probably argued as well that they would make faster progress in open country among the hills. It was time to take a chance and leave the coast.

Not everyone agreed. As seamen, their instinct and inclination were to stay close to their old habitat. Shaw might argue that, navigating by the stars, they need never lose touch with the sea; but there remained something that drew the men to the constant, reassuring crump and hiss at the edge of Africa. There was another, more practical, reason to stay at the coast. Its most persuasive advocate was Thomas Page, the ship's carpenter, who pointed out that beside the sea they were at least able to collect molluscs. Although little use had so far been made of this food source, there could no longer be a question of ignoring it.

'After many arguments', a third division took place, eighteen days after the wreck and still less than fifty miles from where it had occurred, probably between the Umgazana and Umpande Rivers. The group heading inland under Shaw numbered twenty-one and included the trusty Habberley, along with Taylor and Williams, and the latter's servant John Sussman. They were joined by the fourth mate, an anonymous figure named Trotter, three soldiers including William Ellis, who had started the voyage as Colonel James's servant, and ten sailors, among them Hynes, Warmington and Lewis. Shaw kept the last valuable utensil that they had between them: a gun flint to start fires.

As Shaw's group started towards the green mossy hills of the interior, Page led off with his party of twenty-four. As well as Tom Law and his protector Lillburne, it included the injured teenager, Robert Price, and Francisco di Lasso, who had taken him under his wing since saving him at the wreck. Each member of Page's party left carrying a firebrand that he would have to hold aloft through rivers and protect in high winds, to keep a flame alive.

11

HABBERLEY'S MISSION

The second mate's party: 22 August–2 November

For all its human elements, much of the *Grosvenor* story is signally deficient in heroes. Were it not for the consequences, the succession of blunders by Coxon and his circle before and after the wreck has the makings of an especially black farce. Once the seamen broke away and began their march down the coast, however, figures of more substance emerged. Most conspicuous of these was William Habberley.

William grew up in Finsbury, a part of London's City just far enough west of Shoreditch for respectability but still a comedown for the once-prosperous Habberley family, who appear to have been descended from merchants and civic dignitaries in Portsmouth. His parents had nevertheless managed to provide William with a good education, and he never lacked confidence. Although still only rated able, he was no ordinary seaman, for his apprenticeship to Shaw had been a path to shipboard rank and perhaps, in due course, a command of his own. There is no record of his appearance but his physical prowess is not in doubt and we may imagine him as a lithe and strong fellow, just turned twenty-two. He was also enthusiastic and dutiful, and probably a little condescending in his dealings with the other hands, demonstrating disapproval of indolence or anything that smacked of ill-discipline. Yet he was by no means without human warmth and, to judge from his later life, had an earthy, gregarious side to his nature. Two other characteristics stand out: a phenomenal

The Keiskamma river with Amatola mountains in distance, lithograph from sketch by Thomas Bowler, 1864 memory and a steely will. Both were apparent in the trials that befell the second mate's party.

Shaw's gamble to go in search of another friendly tribe was soon seen as a mistake. On 22 August his twenty-one-strong group separated from the carpenter's party and marched inland, where they found tribal kraals. All were deserted. That afternoon, they ate their bullock-hide shoes. 'Our hunger compelled us to devour them,' Habberley recalled sorrowfully. By nightfall they were ravenous and, on coming to another abandoned kraal with what looked like the remains of a cabbage patch, they set the stalks boiling in a discarded earthen pot. These tasted even worse than the shoes and most of the men were violently sick. Their misery was compounded by 'the beasts howling dreadfully' as they sheltered in the huts that night. When the long grass was set ablaze it revealed glittering eyes and spectral shapes.

Seafarers were familiar enough with famine at sea; towards the end of a voyage the salt meat had become rank and the flour run short. Rations on land were another matter, especially in tropical climes, where men ate better than they did at home. Shaw and Habberley had sailed to the Caribbean; others had touched at the East Indies.* Now they found themselves in a land seemingly fecund, yet somehow barren. When, the next day, they again encountered only a series of deserted kraals, Shaw recognised his mistake and they started back for the coast. After a day without anything to eat at all they got back to the sea on the evening of 24 August and gorged themselves on raw periwinkles. At dawn they started again to grapple their way down the coast.

Early on a routine was established that became a pattern for all the marchers. They would rise at first light and get on as best they could until a halt, dictated by the tide, for collecting mussels and other shellfish exposed on the rocks. As freshwater springs were common on this part of the coast, thirst was not yet a problem. Towards evening they would start looking out for firewood and a spot to rest. Wherever possible they slept on the beach, for the comfort of warm sand and to keep a distance from wild animals. A large fire was always banked up before they settled for the night.

* A sailor of the time described the fare in Timor: 'Buffalo, sheep, hogs, fowls, maize, rice, limes, oranges, mangoes, plantains, watermelons, tobacco . . . the natives showed us the greatest possible inclination to supply us with whatever they had.'

With not so much as a knife between them, they were ill equipped to deal with the windfall of a dead whale that was found on the beach a few days later. Slabs of the putrefying flesh could only be hacked away with oyster shells. Matters improved after they came upon a wooden spar from which long nails protruded; the discovery gave them new insight into the lives of the natives whose desperate need for iron they now shared:

> Elated with having obtained what was now esteemed as valuable by them as by the Caffrees, they set fire to the planks, and having taken out the nails, flattened them between stones and shaped them into something like knives. This was a most valuable acquisition.

They were at last just starting to find the terrain becoming easier when, on 27 August, they came to another large river. The Umtata was not quite as formidable as the Umzimvubu but it was bad enough and, as so often when the men encountered a serious obstacle, it caused a new division. On this occasion the breakaway was by a group able to swim. First, six men, including the Irishman John Hynes and John Warmington, set off into the water with their clothes on their heads. 'But being greatly deceived in their strength, they were nearly drowned and lost most of their clothes,' Habberley wrote. The next day, another four men including Thomas Lewis, managed to cross at low tide. They had given no hint of their intentions, for when the others returned from collecting mussels to find them gone and spotted clothes floating on the river, it was concluded that they had drowned.

This pattern, of men breaking away from their fellows at moments of crisis, often to form up again later with others further down the coast, was to be repeated constantly; but if Habberley's loyalty was tested, he never showed it, even though as the youngest and fittest of those left with Shaw, a strong swimmer who had got the measure of the terrain, he must by now have been confident of winning through on his own. From the slow rate of progress by a party now reduced to eleven, it is clear that the older men were holding him back.

For two days they clambered along the banks of the Umtata, heavily forested and spiked with mangroves. They killed a fine fat snake and ate it, and were terrified when they spotted grazing hippopotamuses in daylight for the first time – 'monsters', Habberley thought. At last, on 30 August, they found a fordable part of the river and reached the coast again at sunset the next day; but one of the party did not get across. 'We had the painful task of leaving Jacob Angel, who was unable to proceed,' he wrote.

In ten days since splitting from the carpenter, Shaw's party had been halved and had advanced in real terms by no more than thirty miles. Much of their energy had been dissipated on inland detours and many more rivers lay ahead. It is just as well they were unaware that the nearest Dutch farm was still 300 miles away.

But the going was now definitely becoming easier. Tracts of firm sand broke up the rocky coastline and where the men were driven inland it was on to grassy hills. Forests were scattered and avoidable. The remaining men had covered about twenty miles in two days and were daring to hope that they might have put the worst behind them when, on 3 September, they came to yet another daunting river. The mouth of the Bashee was surrounded on either side by forested heights. No one could bear the thought of another inland detour and they set to making a raft from driftwood, bound together with their ragged clothing and creepers. It was a month since the wreck when Habberley, the last swimmer in the party, started to ferry his companions across, one by one. They had just been caught up by a lascar and were again eleven in number:

> I swam them over one at a time, each having a person on it, none of the party being able to swim but Mr Williams and myself, and unfortunately he was extremely ill, which prevented him lending any assistance. However, we all got safe over, and proceeded.

For a few days they again made reasonable progress, before being faced with a new crisis. Williams had recovered, but now Shaw was ill. The second mate had never been a robust figure and, although still only in his early thirties, was worn down by strain and malnutrition. By 11 September he was holding back the rest of the party. The following day his condition had deteriorated and they called an early halt. All that night it poured with rain. Habberley feared the worst:

> Friday, 13 September: In the morning we persevered along the beach but very slowly, Mr Shaw being no better. We at length came to a small river which we crossed, and on account of our invalid we retired early in a thicket.

Even as Habberley watched his friend and mentor sinking, the leadership of their party was passing to him. Though the fourth mate, Trotter, was nominally the senior man after Shaw, it was to the former apprentice boy that the others now turned. On 15 September, seeing that Shaw could go no further, being 'worn down to a mere skeleton and his strength quite exhausted', Habberley called a halt.

The next day Shaw could no longer stand. Still Habberley would not leave him. Molluscs and water were at hand, and it was agreed that they could wait for up to three days. If at the end of that time Shaw was still unable to walk, they would abandon him. For another day he lay on his back in the sand, a pitiful, half-naked scarecrow.

On 18 September Habberley recalled:

> Mr Shaw, second officer of the *Grosvenor*, died, greatly lamented by the whole party, but more particularly by myself, who had been bound apprentice to him in the year 1778 and sailed with him to the West Indies, and had constantly attended him on his travels. I therefore respected him as a father and a friend. Mr Shaw was a gentleman . . . possessed of great amiableness, and bore his misfortunes with uncommon fortitude.

They buried Shaw in the dunes. The next day another body followed him into a sandy grave. William Ellis, the former soldier-servant to Colonel James, had survived the Mysore wars, only to leave his bones in Africa. A band of twenty-one when they had parted from Page was reduced to nine: Habberley, Williams and Taylor, the latter's servant John Sussman, the fourth mate Trotter, Jonas who had been Beale's servant, James Stockdale a soldier, John Howes a seaman, and the lascar.

Habberley referred to the region between the Umtata and Bashee Rivers as 'the uninhabited country'. In three weeks the castaways had not seen a single native. They had long since passed out of Pondo country, crossed the territory of the Bomvana and Tembu, and were approaching the land of the cattle-rich Xhosa. Once again, however, the Africans' responses to them were to be unnervingly unpredictable.

On 20 September they spotted a kraal on the far side of a large river – the Qora – and set off towards it. As always when crossing a river, they stripped naked and carried their clothes on their heads, and were approaching the far bank when they saw that the villagers had gathered to await them.

> About twenty of them surrounded us before we could get on our clothes. They then rifled them of whatever they pleased, and afterwards drove us away by throwing stones. Seeing cattle grazing we made motions for something to eat, as a remuneration for what they had taken from us, but they threatened to throw their lances in case we did not depart.

For the next week they encountered neither rivers nor natives. Men previously used to handing themselves up ratlines now spent their days simply putting one foot in front of the other with the constant hiss of the surf away to the left and grassy ridges lying to the interior. The days blended into one another, but the men must have noted the rising temperature of the African spring under an opal sky, even if they were regularly drenched by thunderstorms. Coxon had estimated that they would reach sanctuary within three weeks and faulty though his judgment was seen to have been, they were nevertheless hopeful, Habberley recalled, that almost two months after the wreck, 'we must be near the Dutch settlements'.

In fact, they had just entered the most densely populated of the tribal territories. On 2 October, at the Kei River, they came to a large kraal whose inhabitants at first seemed friendly. They 'brought out some milk, offering it to us for such copper trinkets as they wore, and, as we had not any to give them, they put it down to their dogs, at the same time pointing to us to be gone'. At the next kraal, Williams offered buttons for milk, but the trade was declined, 'and when we retired, they followed throwing stones at us'.

The castaways were thrown into wretched gloom, 'so much that we were now careless whether we proceeded on or not, or even of endeavouring to support life'. Some had indeed lost the will to go on. The lascar, whose name was never recorded, fell and was left. Before they crossed the Kei, John Howes, able seaman, died 'through great weariness'.

Bearded and tattered, with matted hair and smelling of wood fires, salt and sweat, they were distinguishable now only by the colour of their skins from the poorest of the tribal poor, the wretched and despised coastal scavengers who, cast out for whatever reason from the mainstream of clan life and denied access to cattle or crops, also survived by gathering shellfish along the shore. Even the once-proud nabobs were without shoes or stockings. Their breeches were tattered and George Taylor's shirt had been lost; his torso was covered by a woman's shawl. What rags they had were used to clothe their feet, to avoid being flayed when crossing rough ground.

They were always hungry. Habberley recollected daily foraging for food, water and firewood, and details of a diet in which the salt meat of shipboard life had been replaced by the equally monotonous fare of salty molluscs: 'Sept 28: mussels; Sept 29: a little wild celery and sorrel; Sept 30: shellfish; Oct 2: a few bramble berries; Oct 3: black berries, shellfish.'

The shellfish were small crabs, periwinkles and limpets, occasionally conch. Every now and then there was a windfall: 'Oct 5: plenty of the largest mussels that we had yet seen, and likewise some fine oysters which we laid on the fire until they opened.'

Often, though, there was discomfort and sickness: 'Oct 14: we found a vine bearing a long pod of which we ventured to eat, but was so extremely ill that we thought we should have died, they making us reach [*sic*] violently.'

In privation, social distinction was lost and a fellowship born. When the discharged soldier Stockdale fell ill, on 5 October, Taylor and Williams were agreed that he could not simply be left. Over the next few days, the six relatively able-bodied men would go forward just far enough to locate a source of fresh water or food – a stream or a tidal pool containing shellfish – before starting a fire, to await Stockdale, following with painful slowness. On the third day the soldier came up 'just as we had done gathering our shellfish, but in so weak a state that he was almost dead'. The following day Habberley recalled:

> Wednesday, 9 October. This morning Stockdale was no better but said he would endeavour to follow us if we would halt for him at the ebbing of the tide, which we readily consented to . . . Under these ideas we continued on, and never saw nor heard of him more.

Yet the worse their situation became, the more it seemed to bring out qualities of determination and endurance in the nabobs. While others were nearing the ends of their tethers, George Taylor and John Williams, both aged around forty, had found new resources within themselves. Taylor had once been the junior partner. Now he emerged as the stronger, able not only to support his brother-in-law but to rally morale, so that when Habberley became despondent, the trader took over – urging the others on with assurances that they just needed to keep going, and that now, surely, they were nearing sanctuary. The same spirit that had inspired the nabobs to adventure in the Orient was keeping them alive. Five great rivers had been crossed – the Umzimvubu, the Umtata, the Bashee, the Qora and the Kei – when they reached a sixth, the Buffalo, just to the east of where the modern city of East London stands. After making a detour upriver, Habberley recalled:

> Saturday, 12 October. We at daylight crossed the river and travelled towards the sea. Not being able to reach it before dark, we halted in a thicket about three miles from it, and there found some well-tasted plums. We met with some wild beasts in the day, who seemed as willing to avoid us as we were them, owing as we supposed to the firebrands we carried.

While they circled river mouths to avoid herds of elephant that were becoming increasingly common, no action was taken to evade the natives. Despite their difficulties, the men remained hopeful of finding a friendly tribe. What they did not know was that they had crossed into the land of the Rarabe Xhosa, the easternmost of the Nguni tribes, who had recently been raided by Cape settlers in the First Frontier War. For the first time, the castaways were in real peril from hostile people.

On a sunny day in mid-October, the six men were tramping down the beach when a band of about twenty Xhosa, including women and children surrounded and beat them with sticks. Neither on this occasion, nor the next day when they were again attacked, did these assailants show any interest in their possessions, though by now they had nothing left worth the trouble of taking. Instead, the castaways were left 'hardly able to move with the cuts and bruises they inflicted on us'.

Their injuries, on top of their abject physical state, made walking difficult; but Habberley had seen enough to know that they needed 'to get out of the reach of these savages'. Once again a river lay in their path. On 18 October they came to the Keiskamma, a rain-swollen cauldron that they would have to cross by raft. Elephants crashed about on the banks. Here they enjoyed a rare treat when they spotted a scrawny native dog. 'This dog we were rejoiced in meeting with . . . When it was dark we took the opportunity of hanging him with a piece of handkerchief, afterwards cut him open with mussel shells, then broiled and eat part of him.'

The feast came too late for Williams's servant, John Sussman. A Londoner who had been with the merchants throughout their adventures in Canton and Calcutta, Sussman had for some time been too sick to help with daily tasks. On 20 October, their eightieth night in the open since the wreck, Sussman 'died without a groan'. Fresh water had meanwhile become another concern, and the following day Jonas was so thirsty when they came to a brackish pool that he could not control himself. He was found 'speechless, having drunk to such an excess that his belly was almost bursting, in consequence of which he died'.

That night the fourth mate, Trotter, drank from the same pool and became delirious. In the morning he was unable to move and pleaded with them not to abandon him. A raft was fashioned, but at first Trotter could not be persuaded to risk the crossing; Habberley pushed the raft with Taylor and Williams out into the Keiskamma, swimming with it as the tide flowed in and carried them upriver. As they walked back towards the mouth, Trotter cried out for Habberley to return, but the raft had been swept away. The last of the *Grosvenor*'s officers was lost, and they were just three.

Although Habberley was still holding up, Taylor and Williams had exhausted their last reserves. It took the trio almost a week to cover about thirty-five miles between the Keiskamma and Great Fish Rivers as first Taylor and then Williams became increasingly feeble and the task of finding shellfish and firewood fell wholly on Habberley. On 29 October the two merchants were feeling a little stronger and they made some progress, coming to a spot where a few Xhosa women had found a dead seabird 'which they kindly gave us'.

Two days later they were overtaken by more Xhosa at the Great Fish River. This time they were warriors, with assegais and shields, and their antagonism was clear:

> Some of them made motions and talked much, which we could not possibly understand. They then began throwing stones at us, at which we implored their mercy . . . They then took hold of Mr Williams and dragged him down to the river and there threw him in. When he rose again and endeavoured to reach the opposite shore by

> swimming, they again threw stones at him, and before he was half-way over, some of the stones striking him on the head, he instantly sunk, when the savages perceiving it they all shouted.

John Williams was dead, his body carried away on the tide into the ocean where he had ventured and lost. Appalled and terrified, Taylor and Habberley fled to hide in the undergrowth, but the older man was chased to ground with dogs. From his hide in a bush, Habberley could hear the merchant pleading as he was beaten, and when his cries faded concluded that he was dead. For the rest of the day Habberley stayed in hiding, emerging at sunset to find Taylor cut and bleeding but still, astonishingly, alive: 'I bound up his wounds with pieces of our clothes, which he was grateful for, and seemed much rejoiced at my appearing, for he conceived that I had been murdered.'

In the morning Habberley got his companion on to a raft, and across the river. Taylor could manage to hobble only a short distance down the beach. The next day he was unable to move. Habberley set off and returned with water in a shell. This revived his companion a little and again Habberley went foraging. Great was his joy when he found a dead turtle. Cutting away at the underbelly with a shell, he extracted eggs and organs which, after dragging the creature above the high-water mark to await his return, he bore back in triumph.

Taylor was alive when he got back, but only just. He could not speak and was unable to swallow even the soft turtle eggs. During the night, the nabob of Walthamstow died quietly. Habberley was even more deeply affected than he had been by the death of Shaw:

> Not a night since the ship was lost could equal this. I had hitherto by Mr Taylor and my conversation been encouraged on with the hopes of seeing Dutch settlements, and that there would be an end to our sufferings. Grief overpowering me, I laid myself down.

Three months almost to the day since the *Grosvenor* went aground, William Habberley was utterly alone.

1 *Wreck of the Grosvenor, East Indiaman.* The artist, Robert Smirke, drawing on first-hand accounts received in London in 1783, portrayed the miraculous salvation of the passengers after the ship broke up and moments before the stern section was swept in to the shallows at Lambasi.

2 Thomas Chambers, painted by John Hone, just before his departure aged seven on the *Grosvenor* for schooling in England.
3 Sir Robert Chambers, Calcutta Supreme Court judge and father of the castaway child, from a portrait by Sir Joshua Reynolds.
4 Warren Hastings, the Company's first Governor-General, from a portrait by Reynolds.
5 Richard Blechynden, Calcutta diarist and brother of Lydia Logie, by an unknown artist.

6 *Calcutta from Garden Reach with shipping in the Houghly*, by Thomas Daniell, 1797. Company gentry, borne on palanquins, lived in mansions set back from the river. Larger Indiamen like the *Grosvenor* were unable to safely navigate so far up the Houghly and anchored downriver at Kedgeree Roads.
7 *Indiaman in a Breeze* by Charles Brooking, c. 1750. Indiamen at this time tended to be smaller than those of the *Grosvenor* era.

8 John Coxon – a captain with a shrewder eye for commercial opportunity than for the elements of seamanship.
9 Lydia Logie – wife of the *Grosvenor*'s first mate and 'the finest lady' according to a fellow passenger.

10 *African Hospitality*, mezzotint by J. R. Smith from the painting by George Morland, London, 1790. The artist's vision of the immediate aftermath of the *Grosvenor* wreck was coloured more by the emergent anti-slavery campaign than survivors' accounts.

11 *All Among the Hottentots*, by George Cruikshank. Almost forty years after the *Grosvenor*, British migrants were being sought for the Cape Colony but public opinion was hostile. This cartoon, from 1819, is captioned: 'To be half roasted by the sun and Devoured by the Natives!! Recommended to the Serious consideration of all those who are about to emigrate.'
12 *The Hippotame*, an English engraving of 1798. Fanciful images of the 'wild beasts' encountered by the castaways remained the norm until the mid-19th century.

13 *Kaffers on a March*, engraving by Samuel Daniell, 1804. The ostrich-feather head-dress is typical of the Bomvana, a small tribe who gave the castaways hospitality within days of the wreck.
14 *Scene in Sitsikamma*, aquatint by Samuel Daniell, 1805. The primordial nature of much of the Cape coastline is well captured by the only one of the three Daniells to travel in South Africa.

15 *Swellendam*, the outlying Dutch settlement where the survivors recuperated after their rescue, by William Dickes, c. 1850.

16 Objects salvaged from the wreck site, including a brass protractor by the London instrument maker, J. Bennet, the gold case of a fobwatch by Jules Le Roy of Paris, gold star pagodas and silver rupees.

12

'A SACRED CHARGE'

The carpenter's party: 22 August–29 November

Habberley had been unusual in allowing his pace to be dictated by his charges, but a still more noble exception to the instinct for self-preservation was to be found in the party led by Thomas Page, the carpenter. While Habberley had been shepherding Taylor and Williams, an epic of self-sacrifice was being enacted three or four days' march ahead.

Charles Dickens thought the story of Thomas Law 'the most beautiful and affecting I know associated with a shipwreck'. Alexander Dalrymple obviously had it in mind when he expressed satisfaction at finding 'so many efforts of generosity and mutual assistance' among the castaways. He heard about it from the survivors and his report gives an account of the little Anglo-Indian boy. However, the principal version of the story, and the one that made such an impression on Dickens, is contained in George Carter's *Narrative of the Loss of the Grosvenor*.

Carter was a hack artist who, in 1785, took passage to try his hand in Bengal. The *Grosvenor* wreck remained fresh in the public mind and with information that he had gleaned on the voyage out, Carter painted at least two scenes from the drama. To judge from the only one that survives, *The Shipwreck of the Grosvenor*, a gouache in the vaults of the National Maritime Museum in Greenwich, it is no surprise that he is entirely forgotten as an artist. Competition was especially keen in Bengal, where the rewards for the successful in any field were spectacular; Zoffany, the society portraitist, and

The Death of Master Law, copperplate by George Carter, 1791

the uncle-and-nephew team of William and Thomas Daniell, in the field of topography, made fortunes as well as names for themselves. Carter meanwhile gave up after a few years and sailed back to London.

But Britain's awakening curiosity in far-off lands, and the interest in seafaring dramas, shipwrecks and castaways – an appetite fed by the phenomenal and enduring success of Defoe's *Robinson Crusoe*, published sixty-five years earlier – had given Carter an idea. In 1791 the firm of John Murray published his account of the *Grosvenor*. Readers were promised . . .

A Variety of Matters respecting the Sufferers,
Never before made Public:
With Copper Plates descriptive of the Catastrophe
ENGRAVED FROM MR CARTER'S DESIGNS

The *Narrative* was a huge success. From the time that news of the wreck reached England, public fascination with the *Grosvenor* had been matched only by the paucity of information about the subject. Dalrymple's inquiry produced a taut document, sparing in detail and limited in circulation. Now here, after a silence of eight years, was the first widely available account of the disaster. Moreover, it turned out that Carter was a very much better story-teller than he was artist. He allowed his imagination to run free and he seized on the big moments. Biggest by far was the story of Tom Law.

The sailors could have had no illusions about what was involved when they decided to take a seven-year-old boy with them. As Habberley noted, Tom had required help from the outset, 'being carried by the party and they in consequence being very much wearied'. When he was able to make his own way, the others had to slow their pace to his. At no stage is there mention of any objections to this, and while the steward Lillburne was Tom's principal protector, others sacrificed themselves for the lad too. Thomas Lewis told the inquiry:

> Master Law was first carried by William Thomson, midshipman, and then by each of the party by turns; and when they were knocked up, Mr Lillburne said he would save the boy's life or lose his own.

The carpenter's decision to stay by the sea was soon vindicated. While Shaw's group were stumbling inland, the twenty-four men led by

Page made comparatively good headway, although the strain of carrying the child was too much for Midshipman Thomson, who died early on. Two days after parting from the second mate they reached the mighty Umtata.* Carter's narrative is short on details of how such obstacles were overcome, but Page's party seem to have made better use of rafts than the others. After that the worst of the broken country was behind them and hopes rose. With the sand firm beneath their feet and the sun on their backs, they could cover up to fifteen miles in a day. They discovered simple new pleasures – bathing naked in a river, a bed in the warm, soft beach sand at the end of a day – along with exultation in the odd unexpected find, such as berries ripening in the sun. In the evening there was time for reminiscences of life before the wreck, for anticipation of debauches to come at some Thames inn – Lord, how fine a tankard of ale would taste! – and, perhaps sometimes, enough spirit left in the sailors for one of their songs.

Henry Lillburne's background and age are not known. As steward, he had been in charge of the *Grosvenor*'s provisions and, endowed as he was with authority, the men looked to him for orders even though the carpenter was acknowledged as leader. Lillburne was a literate man, able to sign his name in the ship's impress book, but not necessarily an educated one. He was strong enough to carry a child on his back across heavy ground, and we can imagine him as burly as well as gentle, epitomising the fondness found among some elder crewmen for youngsters. Ships' boys were intrinsic to British seafaring and in our cynical age it is easy to see something unwholesome in this tradition. In a more innocent time, the old salt was almost synonymous with indulgence towards youth. For many men, such ties were the closest they would come to the father–son relationship of home life. In the case of Lillburne and Tom Law, the evidence points to an act of simple devotion, and the natural response of a child in a crisis to a strong, paternal figure.

A handful of other individuals also attract our attention. Francisco di Lasso, a native of Genoa, was another father-like figure. He had saved Robert Price, servant to Captain Coxon, when he was dashed on the rocks, pulling him from the sea by his hair, nursing the lad as he lay

* This was on 24 August. Shaw's party reached it three days later, after returning from their inland detour.

unconscious for almost two days, and keeping an eye on him when the march began. Price, now aged about fourteen, had opted at the parting to follow his guardian rather than his master and, having recovered fully, was repaying Di Lasso and his shipmates with his abilities as a forager and diviner of drinking water. Price's closest friend was another youngster who had been in Coxon's entourage: his steward William Couch.

Jeremiah Evans, born amid the lanes of Wapping, was aged eighteen, a wiry hand whose experience clambering up rigging had served him well in tackling the sandstone heights and forests on those desperate days early in the march. Barney Leary was a bullock of a youth, with 'a very robust habit of body'. He had started the voyage as the only sailor with the novice rating of landsman, indicating that he too was still in his teens. Even so, these young men regulated their pace to the child – and were duly caught up by some of the sailors from whom they had separated about a week earlier.

It may be recalled that Shaw's company had been left at the Umtata by two groups of men able to swim. The first included Hynes and Warmington, the second Lewis. These men, ten in all, were soon reunited and caught up with Page towards the end of August. For a couple of days the party was increased to thirty-four, before the pattern of disintegration resumed. Carter, trying to make sense of the random break-ups, interjected exasperatedly into his narrative: 'I cannot help lamenting that persons in so perilous a situation as these poor shipwrecked wanderers, should be wanting in that unanimity which alone would ensure their preservation.'

In the 140 miles or so that lay between the Bashee and Great Fish Rivers, bands of men appear to have been breaking up and reforming almost daily. By the beginning of September, Page's party had splintered into at least half a dozen bands. What acts of heroism and betrayal went unrecorded will never be known. We are left with a pattern of human behaviour in crisis. A group would fragment as a few sailors, almost invariably the younger, found that they had to moderate their pace to allow the others to keep up, and gradually would forge ahead. This winnowing of the weaker men was so undramatic, a slow widening of space between two groups, that it might not have occurred to anyone that they had actually been abandoned until their fellows were, quite suddenly, out of sight.

To follow each group is not possible, and on the basis of the limited evidence available would not add to the overall picture. Percival Kirby, who studied the *Grosvenor* sources minutely, commented wryly: 'The evidence of the survivors at this stage of the journey is so conflicting that one can hardly say more than that the whole of the coastline from the Bashee southwards must have been dotted with small parties of men, separated from each other by several miles, and making their way slowly in the direction of Algoa Bay while struggling desperately to find sufficient food to keep body and soul together.'

We are on safer ground in following what became of a core group that stayed with the carpenter. Within a few days of crossing the Bashee they had been reduced from thirty-four to twenty, including Page himself, Lillburne, Di Lasso, Price, Couch, Evans, Leary and Tom Law out of the party that had separated from Shaw in the first instance, and Hynes and Warmington from those who had left the second mate's company at the Umtata.

A month after the wreck, they had entered the Xhosa country and were 'passing many villages without being molested' while still finding little willingness among the inhabitants to part with food unless it was for barter. Jealous of their livestock, the tribesmen were also in no position to make free with the remains of the previous harvest when it would be at least another two months before new crops were available. Dalrymple, with the benefit of both hindsight and objectivity, went some of the way to understanding their wariness. The natives, he wrote,

> treated the individuals that fell singly among them rather with kindness than brutality, although it was natural to expect that so large a body of Europeans would raise apprehensions; and fear always produces hostility.

By now it seems that the seamen were themselves so suspicious that they did not always respond even when friendship was offered. They were among the Gcaleka Xhosa, a people who – unlike the Rarabe Xhosa, who had killed Taylor and Williams – had no record of conflict with whites. A band of young men approached Price with his friend William Couch on the beach one day, and offered him a spear. As Price himself recognised, this gesture was 'by way of making friends'; they took him by the arm, indicating that they wished him to accompany them. Price, however, was so traumatised that he began to weep. Couch and the others started crying too, whereupon the unnerved Xhosa retreated.

The Irishman Hynes was more perceptive than most in realising that behind what seemed to be the natives' indifference to the castaways' plight lay a real fear for their most treasured possession, their livestock. Noting how even in this fine cattle country, the Gcaleka 'would neither bestow any, nor suffer [us] to purchase any by way of barter', he related: 'So apprehensive were the natives of the strangers stealing their livestock, that they constantly drove them away as they approached the Kraals.'* But although the Xhosa refused to feed so large a party, Hynes also noticed how Tom Law would be singled out by women when they came to a village and given milk 'contained in a small basket, curiously formed of rushes, and so compact as to hold any liquid'.

The discovery of a dead whale provided another occasion on which the Xhosa demonstrated goodwill. The castaways' joy at the find turned to apprehension as they saw a large party of men approaching with assegais. 'The natives, however, no sooner saw in what a deplorable situation they were, and how unable to make any opposition, than they conducted themselves in so pacific a manner as to dispel their fears. One of them even lent those who were employed on the whale his lance to cut it.'

After almost two months on a diet of molluscs and water, their greatest enemy had become malnutrition. At just what point it did for Page is not known, for Hynes became detached from his party, and when he rejoined them some days later it was to find that the carpenter was dead. He had been buried in the sand near the Keiskamma River towards the end of October. At this point his group had covered almost 250 miles, were within half that distance of refuge and were on the easiest terrain they had yet found. Now under the leadership of Lillburne, they stepped forth each day on clear sand that curved away into the distance. Yet two daunting obstacles still lay in their way: a river and a desert.

* Such symptoms reflect the tensions over cattle raiding – by both settlers and Xhosa – which, more than land hunger or any other factor, had triggered the start of the Cape frontier conflicts.

The Great Fish River was reached within a few days of Page's death. Yet again in the face of crisis the men fell out, or in any event fell apart. The nineteen-strong company split into three. Five men stayed behind to die, including Isaac Blair, the servant whom Captain Talbot had urged to carry on. Two groups of seven crossed separately on rafts. The first included Di Lasso, Price, Couch and Leary. Among the second were Lillburne, Evans, Warmington, Hynes and Tom Law.

Tom, according to Hynes, had 'borne the inconveniences of so long a journey in a most miraculous manner'. For weeks he had pattered along beside the men, although there were still places where he had to be helped: 'When they came to deep sands, or passed through high grass, which was often the case, the people carried him by turns.'

Lillburne it was who 'chiefly endeavoured to alleviate that fatigue which his infant limbs were unable to bear, who heard with pity his unavoidable complainings; who fed him when he had wherewithal to do it; and who lulled his weary soul to rest.' For his part, Tom had taken on a measure of responsibility, and towards the end of each day, when the men went off to collect molluscs, he was left to keep the fires alight.

All through October their little band trudged on across open country. This stretch of coast has since become a favourite of holidaymakers, with the retreats of Port Alfred and Kenton on Sea set amid more than fifty miles of perfect beaches fringed by dune shrubs. The sailors crossed the Bushman's River, and met Thomas Lewis, a seaman who had been with another party, only to be left when he fell sick. Although urged by Lillburne to join them, Lewis said he could bear no further hardship or fatigue and had decided to head inland to the nearest kraal and throw himself on the mercy of the Xhosa. Sure that he was doomed, they carried on and soon passed – oblivious though they were to it – the spot where, in 1488, Bartholomeu Dias had landed as the first mariner to double the Cape. A few days later, and again unknowingly, they entered the most treacherous part of their trek.

What the sailors called 'the sandy desart', begins a few miles east of Cape Padrone and runs towards Algoa Bay as far as the Sundays River. It is not very considerable as deserts go, about forty miles of coastline in length, extending inland between one and four miles, and is now known by the benignly bucolic name of Woody Cape Nature Reserve. It is nevertheless a true desert, barren of water, with heavy, energy-sapping dunes 100 feet high. Had Lillburne followed Lewis's example and struck inland at this point, they too would have come upon friendly Xhosa and their story would have had a different end. As it was, they could no longer bear to turn their backs on the sea that had fed them. Tramping along the beach, they may not even have noticed how the shrubs on the dunes thinned out and disappeared. By then they were in the desert, stumbling along in sand that sucked at their feet and made each step a labour. After a while they abandoned the effort; henceforth they would walk only when the tide was out and the sand was firm under foot.

On 2 November, after a night near Cape Padrone, both Lillburne and the lad were unable to get up, having eaten what seems to have been some rank whale meat. Lillburne asked his shipmates to stay with them for a day, just long enough for him and the boy to get over the worst. The others agreed. After another night Lillburne was better, but Tom was not. Once again, the steward prevailed upon the others to wait. They must have known that there was no hope, but all agreed. During the day Lillburne scanned Tom's face for signs of improvement. He had made clear that he would not leave without the boy, but his vigil would be a solitary one, for the men had said that if Tom were no better in the morning, 'they would be under the disagreeable necessity of leaving them'.

Carter painted the scene around the fire that night, as it was described to him: two ragged sailors attend in attitudes of prayer; a third proffers morsels of food; the faithful Lillburne comforts the unconscious child. Carter said that he did his best to portray his subject 'in as just and striking a manner as my abilities would enable me', but in his hands the child became an incongruous as well as unconvincing figure, a rigidly reclining 'Blue Boy' in satin suit and ringlets. Carter had overlooked the fact that Tom was Anglo-Indian.*

* There is a slight but distinct possibility that the painting was commissioned by the child's father, Thomas Law, who was still living in Bengal after Carter's arrival. It was in any event sold in Calcutta, although its present whereabouts are unknown. Thomas Law left India and in 1793 went to the United States and married George Washington's granddaughter, Betsey Custis. He made it known that he had had three sons by a previous marriage, but that all had died.

When they awoke in the morning, Lillburne left the child to sleep a little longer while they rekindled the fires and mustered a rudimentary breakfast. On going to wake him, the steward found that the curled up body of Tom Law was cold.

The mission of saving the boy had been the only thing keeping Lillburne going. All the men were profoundly depressed, but he simply gave up. Far from being a burden, the lad had become his purpose. According to Hynes, 'it was only with the utmost difficulty that his companions got him along' at all.

That day Robert Fitzgerald drank two shells of water, then 'laid himself down and instantly expired'. In the afternoon, William Fruel said he could not go on and was left.

The next day was 6 November. It was exactly three months since the wreck. They had eaten and drunk nothing for two days. Henry Lillburne stopped abruptly amid the dunes. For a moment he stood motionless, then fell. He never rose again.

Carter's verdict on the steward was that conduct 'so humane and generous will most assuredly atone for many a misspent hour'. Reading his account, Dickens was struck how the child had been 'sublimely made a sacred charge'. His own version of the story, in an essay from 1853, 'The Long Voyage', provided a liberal and characteristically sentimental improvisation of the facts. Describing how Lillburne had accepted guardianship of the child, Dickens wrote:

> God knows all he does for the poor baby; how he cheerfully carries him in his arms when he himself is weak and ill; how he feeds him when he himself is gripped with want; how he folds his jacket round him, lays his little worn face with a woman's tenderness upon his sunburnt breast, soothes him in his sufferings, sings to him as he limps along, unmindful of his own parched and bleeding feet.

But if the author was betrayed by his tendency towards mawkishness, his judgment on Lillburne was none the less apt. The steward, wrote Dickens, 'shall be re-united in his immortal spirit – who can doubt it! – with the child, where he and the poor carpenter shall be raised up with the words, "inasmuch as ye have done it unto the least of these, ye have done it unto Me."'

Of Tom's companions only Hynes, Warmington and Evans remained and all were nearing the end. After a third day without water, they began to drink their own urine, and 'when any could not furnish himself with a draught of urine, he would borrow a shell full of his companion who was more fortunate, till it was in his power to repay it'.

Their state may have left them susceptible to hallucination, for there is a surreal quality to an incident related to Carter by one of the survivors. On the beach, he wrote, they found one of their former shipmates dead, face down in the sand with his right hand cut off at the wrist. This man had supposedly been given to exclaim: 'May the Devil cut my right hand off if it be not true.' No further explanation was offered for an episode that had, perhaps, a touch of the seaman's love of allegorical yarns about it.

The following day even their urine was exhausted, and they started to think the unthinkable. For the first and, so far as is known, only time, the custom of the sea was raised. Warmington said they had no chance together. Only by casting lots to determine who should be sacrificed might the other two survive by drinking the loser's blood and eating his flesh. Hynes, grown by his own admission 'so weak that he was almost childish', burst into tears. If he should die, he said, his companions might dispose of him as they saw fit, but while he could stand he would never submit to the drawing of lots.

The practice had long been an unspoken code among seamen. As recently as 1765, the starving crew of a cargo vessel, the *Peggy*, disabled and drifting in the Atlantic, had first butchered and eaten an African slave, then agreed to draw lots to decide who would be next. It fell to a foremastman named David Fell, who asked for a day to prepare himself for death; although his mates agreed, the strain of the impending sentence overwhelmed him. The next day the *Peggy* was sighted by a rescue vessel; Fell, however, had gone insane.

Nothing other than rescue would have saved the *Grosvenor* trio either. Warmington said that if they would not draw lots, he could go no further. Hynes and Evans shook him by the hand, and left him. They had not gone far before spotting something that, in the haze that now blurred their vision, they took for large birds but turned out to be four men, remnants of the other band from whom they had become separated at the Great Fish River.

They too had remained loyal to one another. The boy Price had repaid Di Lasso many times for saving him at the wreck, having become an able scavenger and scout. Leary and a man named Reed, the armourer, were also alive, but Price's great friend William Couch had died a few days earlier. At that point, Price told the inquiry, 'they buried him and said prayers over him; and shook hands, and swore they would never separate again until they got into a Christian country'.

Price had a gift for finding water and had just located a fresh spring. The desperate Hynes and Evans were guided to it, while two men went back to collect Warmington. For the time being they were a party of seven, but before proceeding, a decision was taken to go back to Lillburne's body. There was to be some suggestion that they intended to cannibalise the steward, although Hynes stoutly maintained they only wished to take his clothes. The result, however, was the loss of another member of the party: Evans and Reed set out but only Evans returned.

The remaining six went on. Now, on long stretches of beach, no mussels were to be found, but by watching how seabirds pecked at the sand, they found a variety of cockle. These creatures burrowed almost as rapidly as the men could dig for them, but they were reasonably plentiful.

In about a week, the men were rewarded with a sight of distant green hills: they had reached the end of the desert. Ahead, Algoa Bay opened out to the far hazy point of Cape Recife. A couple of days later, their mood brightened further when they came upon a whale carcass. Intending to exploit this resource to the full, they established a camp in a nearby thicket that provided shelter and water.

In the morning Di Lasso was sleeping under a bush and Price was on a hill looking for fruit, when he spotted a man whom, as he later related, 'he first took for one of his companions'. Then he saw the gun on the man's shoulder. 'Immediately he ran to him as fast as he could, which was not fast, his legs being swelled, and fell down at his feet for joy, and then called to De Larso.'

Price could make no sense of what the fellow said, but Di Lasso established that he worked on a Dutch farm. The newcomer, who turned out to be a Portuguese named Battores, cast a horrified glance at the chunks of foul-smelling whale flesh that these apparitions had harvested so avidly, and then told them of the comforts that awaited them at the nearby homestead of Mynheer Christian Ferreira, whereupon

> the joy that instantly beamed forth in every breast [was] scarcely to be conceived. And the effects it produced were as various as extraordinary. Every faculty seemed to be in a state of violent agitation: one man laughed; another cried; and another danced.

The date was 29 November 1782. One hundred and eighteen days after being wrecked, and having walked a little less than 400 miles, the first six *Grosvenor* survivors had reached safety.

13

CALIBAN TRANSFORMED

Caffraria, 3 November 1782–the Cape 30 May 1783

Forty miles up the coast from where Lillburne was watching over the dying child on 3 November, William Habberley sprawled among the dunes beside the Great Fish River. A few feet away, the body of George Taylor was spread out in the shade of a thicket, where it had lain since the previous evening.

When he felt strong enough, Habberley stripped Taylor's body of its clothing. The breeches that had once proclaimed the status of a gentleman were as tattered as his own seaman's trousers, but would still serve to protect his head from the sun. He also took the shawl that Taylor had used to cover his torso. Then he bore the body down to the river and set it out on the tide, to be carried off with his brother-in-law Williams into the Indian Ocean. It was an apt ritual – perhaps a tribute to their shared adventure. Though the nabobs would never flaunt their triumph in ostentatious splendour among those who had stayed at home, they were among that breed of men who had dared – in Jan Morris's words – to break out of prosaic realities and live more brilliant, dangerous lives in Xanadu.

As it grew dark, Habberley was assailed by visions. Even a hearty blaze failed to dispel the ghastly thoughts that crowded his mind, a waking nightmare in which he relived the deaths of his companions and foresaw what now seemed his own inevitable fate. Habberley was suffering from a terrible sense of solitude. Whatever the hardships and dreads over the three months since

Caffres, engraving by Jules Ferarrio, 1832

the wreck, they had been faced in company with others. Now, as he crouched near the fire, he was overwhelmed by the fear of being alone, and the familiar sounds of night in the wilderness acquired a new menace. He had come to a point of solitude and isolation that mirrored almost exactly the circumstances described by Defoe in the journal of his fictional hero, Robinson Crusoe:

> In despair of any relief, I saw nothing but death before me, either that I should be devoured by wild beasts, murdered by savages, or starved to death for want of food.

The following day, 4 November, Habberley resumed his march down the beach. He had so far covered about 270 miles – including inland detours that accounted for thirty miles or so – in ninety days, an average of just three miles a day; so for every day that their party had got along well and walked ten miles, there were many others when they had made little or no progress at all. Caring for Taylor and Williams had, in fact, drained Habberley's last reserves. For the next eight days he stumbled on, managing little more than three miles a day even though the conditions were perfect on the firm beach east of the dune desert. His legs were swollen and his skin blackened, a sure sign of scurvy. He had lost all sense of taste and smell, and his sight was blurred by the glare of sun on sand. For the first few nights on his own he was unable to sleep, and only dozed off when the first rays of sunlight streaked across the sea.

By 9 November he was forced to recognise that he was near the end. Collecting wood left him exhausted, and it took almost the entire next day to gather fruit and mussels before getting on for a couple of miles. Scurvy so afflicted him that his bloated black skin looked ready to burst. All hope and fortitude gone, 'I gave myself up to grief, unheard and unpitied by any but the Living God of all Nature, who closed my eyes for the night.' This final failure of resistance saved him.

There had been no sign of the Xhosa since the attack at the Great Fish. When, on 10 November, Habberley saw a kraal, it did not excite dread, rather a willingness to embrace fate. 'I was determined to find the inhabitants, being easy as to what reception I might meet with, for if they should kill me, then my sufferings would be over.'

At first, though, the Xhosa were more fearful of him than he was of them. At his approach, herdboys fled and, as he entered the kraal, 'the women and children left the huts, all making a great noise and running off'. There remained only an elderly couple, whom Habberley tried to reassure by sitting down, gesturing that he was desperate for food. In a while the old man brought him milk.

His passivity encouraged the women to return and he found himself surrounded by curious faces, gazing 'with as much fear as if I was some dangerous monster'. He had to admit to himself that his wild appearance and strange garb – trousers torn off at the thighs, Taylor's shawl worn under his waistcoat – were enough to startle anyone, and when he made to rise they fled again. In the process, one woman dropped her child and was too terrified to return for it. Habberley's narrative of what followed is curiously affecting.

> So I went and, carefully picking it up, brought it to the old people. The mother came back but not near enough to receive it; so I got up and walked away, and made motions for her to take it which she did. The old woman gave me a small earthen pot full of boiled meat, and some of the women produced pieces of meat, which they laid down for me not daring to give it me themselves. The woman whose child I had picked up fetched some milk, and was bold enough to give it me herself. After this they came and sat down by me.

Towards sunset a great hue and cry went up and Habberley was at first mortified to see twenty warriors with shields and assegais enter the compound with baying dogs, greeted by ululating women; but the hunting party, returning with carcasses of antelope and baboon, were unsurprised to see the tremulous sailor and it even seemed, as the old couple explained his presence, that the warriors 'noticed me with some pity, which was contrary to what I expected'. At length, the chief summoned him to the cattle enclosure. 'He sat down, and made motions for me to do the same, and talked a good deal but of which I could not comprehend. When they milked the cows he gave me some of the new milk.'

After another feast of boiled meat, Habberley made himself comfortable beside a fire while his hosts retired. Replete and rested, but still not able to take it all in, he could not sleep and spent the night looking at the stars in a delicious daze. 'My situation was so different to what it was the night before that I often fancied myself in a dream.'

This sudden hospitality was all the more remarkable, given the region's turbulent recent history. Habberley's hosts were an outlying Xhosa clan dwelling to the east of the Bushman's River, an area which had been at the heart of a growing storm over the previous decade, and the inhabitants had no reason to offer kindness to a solitary white man.

The first century of Dutch settlement at the Cape had given no indication of expansionist intent. A surgeon named Jan van Riebeeck had landed in Table Bay in 1652 with ninety men and orders to build a fort and cultivate the soil to supply Dutch shipping. Beyond bartering cattle he was forbidden to have contact with the natives and for the first forty years of its existence Cape Town was no more than a fortified camp. As well as cultivators and officials, however, the little colony bred a tough band of frontiersmen who ventured eastward beyond the Langeberg and Zwartberg mountains, as hunters and – like the tribal people they came increasingly to resemble – nomadic pastoralists, known as trekboers. The trekboer vanguard encountered the outlying Xhosa, who were moving westward, in about 1770. This eastern frontier, between the Kei and Sundays Rivers, was to be the crucible in which modern South Africa was cast, the collision point between black and white. Between 1779 and 1878, nine conflicts flared up in what one historian has called the country's Hundred Years' War. Echoes from what amounted to the opening volleys had just died away when Habberley came on the scene. Rustling on either side of the frontier by clans of Xhosa and trekboers brought organised incursions by Cape militia in 1780 and 1781 that were supposedly to subdue the Xhosa, but in reality became little more than glorified cattle raids.

Habberley's hosts evidently did not know quite what to make of the solitary, tattered white man, who had neither gun nor mount, nor even shoes. The next day he was again plied with meat, milk and curds while the old chief, who was extremely attentive, questioned him closely – to no effect for, as Habberly noted sadly, 'neither of us could understand [the] other'. At the same time, men from neighbouring kraals came to inspect the curiosity, and went away equally baffled.

The effect of all this good living had an unfortunate outcome. Habberley found himself 'much troubled in my bowels'. He went to the cattle enclosure and 'eased myself among the cows who were very tame'. On finding his excrement, the Xhosa 'pointed out to me my indecency, at which they were highly offended. They instantly turned the cattle out, and refused giving me any milk.' In defiling the cattle kraal, he had committed a grievous breach of etiquette, and despite appealing to the old man, Habberley could obtain no more milk. Sadly he went on his way.

His discomfort was short-lived. That same day he came to another village, and once again was taken in, fed and subjected to a lengthy but one-sided interrogation by the chief. In two days the swelling of Habberley's legs eased and he slept the sleep of the righteous. With his strength returning, and sure by now that the natives' familiarity meant he was nearing Dutch farms, he thanked the chief and started again west across fine open country.

Increasingly now his problem became an excess of hospitality. When, at the next kraal, he offered his ragged shawl to the chief's wife, she was so overwhelmed that he found it almost impossible to get away. He was given his own hut and fed, while the chief gestured that he ought to stay, as the way ahead was difficult and 'the distance was great to people of my colour'. He left anyway, only to find himself caught up in festivities at a nearby kraal. A bullock had been slaughtered and all the inhabitants of the vicinity invited to the feast, and nothing would do but that the itinerant white man should join in. Habberley ate his fill before stealing away again later that night from his hosts.

On 20 November he entered another kraal, and came face to face with another gaunt, bearded white man in rags. It was the seaman Thomas Lewis.

Lewis, it may be recalled, had become separated from Habberley's party and had last been seen at the end of October when he had declined to join Lillburne and instead thrown himself on the mercy of the Xhosa. As he and Habberley rejoiced at meeting and exchanged their stories, they realised that each had found salvation in the same way. Lewis related that 'the natives had always behaved extremely well to him, that they gave him plenty of milk, and that his employment was to bring home wood for them, and attend the calves'.

Lewis was able to fill in some of the gaps in Habberley's knowledge about their shipmates. The carpenter Page was dead, of course, and many more; but miraculously the two Italians, Francisco Feancon (known as

Bianco) and Sebastiano Paro, who had gone their own way months ago at the Umzimvubu, had won through and were living at a nearby kraal.

From the Italians Habberley was astonished to hear about a journey that was the antithesis of his own sufferings. Early on Bianco and Paro had met a chief with a leg ulcer, for which they prescribed an Italian peasant remedy – a poultice of the contents of a bullock's stomach. On being cured, the chief's delight with these alien medicine men was great, and as they went on their reputation preceded them, so that their trek became more a triumphal procession with a warm reception awaiting them at each village along the way.

All these men had cause to reflect on the grim misapprehension in the initial diagnosis of their position expressed by Coxon at the wreck site: that they had to stay together for 'we had no reason to expect the least mercy should the savages find us separated'. As Dalrymple rightly perceived, it was only once the whites were no longer seen as a threat that the Africans felt safe in extending the generosity for which they were known among other early visitors, such as the Frenchman François Le Vaillant.

Habberley carried out work allocated to him at the kraal that had taken him in. Males in tribal society were organised into age groups for labour and military purposes and he joined other young men in milking and collecting wood, and afterwards for meals and recreation. He picked up some of the Xhosa tongue, with its awkward fricative clicks. When visitors arrived and feasts were called in their honour, Habberley joined in slaughtering a bullock, and participated afterwards in dancing at the fireside and tests of strength. Later he would recall how he once engaged in a rough bout with 'cudgels' (knobkerries) with a visiting youth, and took some rough blows:

> Some of my friends hinted to my adversary not to strike so hard, but that had no effect, for he shortly after gave me a severe blow which cut my head, and as soon as I felt the blood run down my neck I forgot my dependent situation and threw away the stick, closed in and fisted him. He not being acquainted with that kind of sport, I gave it him pretty handsomely.
>
> The spectators now shouted more than ever, which put my opponent in such a rage that he would inevitably have killed me, if it had not been prevented by the people of our village.

If Habberley was content enough for the moment, his thoughts nevertheless turned to how he might resume his journey to the Cape. Not so Lewis. The Irishman, a native of Belfast, saw no reason to abandon his newfound life of ease. Aged about thirty, he had spent long enough at sea and seen sufficient of the world to recognise a comfortable berth. It was not just that the land was green, plentiful and blessed by the sun. A more powerful notion had struck some of the seamen: as Joseph Banks had noted during Cook's voyage to Polynesia, the natives did not have to work to live – at least, not as Europeans knew it, and certainly not in the harsh and hazardous ways of the sea.

Another factor came into consideration. Sex is unmentioned in any of the sailors' accounts, but it could not escape their attention that the young women with whom they came into daily contact were almost nude. Carter hinted at alluring displays of female sexuality: 'The women, who are likewise well proportioned, and their countenances not unpleasing, go nearly naked. They wear no manner of cloathing, except a kind of net around the middle, which reaches halfway down their thighs; but the meshes of these nets are so wide, that it can scarcely be called a covering.'

While a high price was placed on virginity, young people were allowed to enjoy sexual play from adolescence onwards. Among the tribes of south-east Africa, mutual stimulation and a form of external intercourse, known as *ukumetsha* among the Pondo and *hlobonga* to the Zulu, were widely practised in an unselfconscious acceptance of sensual pleasure and freedom.

Whatever temptations there may have been, Bianco and Paro announced in mid-December that they were going to resume the march. Habberley was tempted to join them, but Lewis stated flatly 'that he would sooner live and die where he was than chance travelling the beach again'. The Italians set off together. Three weeks later Bianco returned, alone and nearly dead. He and Paro had soon become bogged down in the dune desert that had accounted for Lillburne and Tom Law. They had turned back when their water ran low. Paro had died nine days earlier, and Bianco was alive only because of his strength.

That might have been the last escape attempt. Habberley and Lewis often went down to the beach, more in the hope of intercepting stray castaways than anything else, but there was no more talk of venturing into the dune desert. Then, on 11 January, two months into his residence among these friendly folk, Habberley was in his hut when he was summoned. Three strangers had arrived.

He hastened to Lewis's kraal, expecting to find more castaways, and was taken aback to see three black men. But something set them apart from the Xhosa: Habberley noted that they were fully clothed in sheepskins, and their leader smoked a Dutch pipe which he lit with a brass tinderbox. He gestured down the coast towards the Cape and indicated that the seamen should accompany them. In some inexplicable way, the strangers clearly knew about their plight and wished to be agents of their delivery.

While Habberley and Bianco did not hesitate, Lewis was loth to quit his idyll and had to be won over. In the end, the tug of his shipmates and the prospect of a return home were the stronger. The Xhosa did not want them to go either, and 'were continually endeavouring to persuade us from leaving them. The chief in particular took uncommon pains to induce me to stay.' It is tempting to interpret this as simple friendship; it is equally feasible, however, that the kraal welcomed white inhabitants as having a talismanic effect against Dutch raiders. Yet a human bond had been established. In an unusual departure from his phlegmatic nature, Habberley recalled: 'I could not help from shedding a tear at parting from those people who had behaved with such kindness to me.'

The guides, Khoikhoi from the western Cape, escorted the castaways inland, crossing rivers and mountains and bypassing the desert that had swallowed up their shipmates. The Khoikhoi were silent men and, their baggage loaded on three bullocks, swung along at such a pace that the seaman were left gasping in their wake. At first Lewis objected that they had no provisions; that night one of the men went out and came back with honeycomb. Then they slaughtered a bullock, broiled steaks over a fire and cut the remainder of the meat into thin strips, which were spread on bushes to dry. When they spotted a lion at a distance of no more than forty paces, which set up a furious roaring, the seamen were poised to flee when the Khoikhoi gestured for them to hold their ground and responded with a barrage of halloos from cupped hands – at which the lion slunk away. Thereafter the sailors submitted to their guides without question.

Just two days after leaving the Xhosa, on 14 January, Habberley was walking ahead when he saw what could almost have been an advancing army – a vast caravan of wagons, cattle and 'a body of men on horseback with firearms on their shoulders'. Torn between hope and fear, he felt so weak that he thought he might faint, until he saw in the midst of this rough band his shipmates Evans and Di Lasso, and realised that he had been saved.

Dazed, Habberley and Lewis were guided to a wagon and, fortified by biscuit and wine, given an explanation. Di Lasso and Evans related how their six-strong group had reached the Dutch farms on 29 November. While Price, suffering from scurvy, was left to recuperate, the others had been taken by wagon to Swellendam, a tiny outlying town about 150 miles from the Cape, where they startled the burghers out of their sleepy reverie.

The Dutch response to news of the shipwreck had been as noble-spirited as it was prompt. Although his country was at war with England, and the sailors were, in principle, prisoners, the local magistrate was so affected by their pitiful state and accounts of the women and children left behind that he had despatched an orderly to ride to the Cape with a plea for permission to send out 'a strong commando to save those unfortunate people from their wretched plight'. The Governor, Joachim van Plettenberg, had not only given immediate assent but had offered a reward for every survivor found, ensuring enthusiastic enlistment. By 20 December a large mounted expedition under the command of Heligert Muller, the Captain of Horse in Swellendam, had mustered, consisting of about a hundred Dutch, mainly farmers, and 170 Khoikhoi. Supplies were contained in forty-seven wagons.

At this point Di Lasso and Evans revealed themselves as true heroes. Di Lasso had already given selflessly of himself to save the boy Price, but did not stint when Muller said he would need guides. While four sailors went on to the Cape, Di Lasso and Evans agreed to retrace their steps on that hellish march. Muller sent messengers ahead to advise Xhosa chiefs that the whites were coming, 'but we would treat them with the greatest friendliness, as our purpose was only to go and see the wreck of the English ship and take away the survivors'. It was three of these messengers who had found Habberley and his companions.

Once they had been fed and given new clothes, Muller asked Habberley and Lewis to join the rescue effort. Both refused. Habberley pointed out that the expedition already had two sailors as guides, while the Irishman stated flatly that 'he had suffered enough'. Habberley did, however, warn Muller of the difficulties ahead, and that 'he could not pass the rivers I had crossed with his wagons, nor ever reach the wreck, the distance being so great'.

Muller, he related, simply laughed. Whether or not this was bravado, it boded ill for the mission. Although a few hardy Dutch hunters had ventured beyond the Kei River, the colonists were entirely ignorant of the distant Pondo territory. Muller's party was breaking new ground. Whether Habberley might have made any difference to the outcome had he gone along is impossible to say, but in Evans and Di Lasso the commando did have two guides who were genuinely dedicated to finding their shipmates.

Meanwhile the others surrendered to comforts so long absent from their lives. In the farming district, they were taken in by Karl Scheepers, a bearded patriarch with seven children, including two teenage daughters. The farm was set amid the bonny pastures of the Zuurveld and once again it seemed that they had found an Elysium:

> The weather was fine, the house being on the side of a hill, a fine river running in the valley below, the gardens watered by a small stream which turned a little flour mill. In the garden were plenty of grapes, figs, peaches, melons, which all being ripe we had an abundance of.

Lewis revelled in this tranquil land of plenty. Habberley noted that his companion showed not the slightest interest in leaving and put this down somewhat priggishly to Lewis's 'indolent disposition'. Once again it was only with the greatest difficulty that he could drag the Irishman away when a wagon came for them. All along the way they encountered 'the greatest humanity from the farmers' and were welcomed to the lovely little town of Swellendam by the kindly magistrate who had raised the commando and who arranged their accommodation among the little whitewashed cottages in the lee of the Langeberg mountains. Here Habberley was reunited with Hynes, whom he had last seen at the Umtata River at the end of August and who related what he knew of the other survivors: Warmington and Leary were at the Cape; young Price had recovered from scurvy; Evans and Di Lasso had, of course, gone in search of other survivors. But they must have had a good idea by now that they were pitifully few in number.

They were still at Swellendam when Muller returned at the end of March.

However well-intentioned, the mission had been ill-conceived and feebly executed. Habberley's warnings, so blithely dismissed, soon came back to rebuke Muller. While there was no danger that such a large body of men would come under attack, or that, supplied by almost fifty wagons, they would go short of anything, the commando was like a lumbering beast, too cumbersome to approach coastal areas where survivors were most likely to be found. Riders made only intermittent forays to the sea. Worst of all, just when Muller reached a point where the wreck site was within striking distance, he turned back.

Early on, riders brought in the only other castaways to be rescued: eight lascars and the two Indian women, Hoakim and Betty, the maids of Mary Hosea and Lydia Logie. Muller seems not to have questioned them. Although it was five months since the *ayahs* had left their mistresses, this was a critical oversight. Only Habberley, who met them in Swellendam, took any interest in the light they could cast on the fate of the other passengers. What he heard about Captain Coxon's party exposed the extent of Muller's negligence.

Progress was meanwhile becoming increasingly difficult. At the Kei, the wagons had to be left behind. Word had spread among the Xhosa that the whites were offering copper, iron and tobacco for information about castaways. Chiefs duly obliged with any amount of vague data, and went away happily with their payment, leaving Muller to curse them and his own gullibility. Although he rode on into February, the commando had nothing further to show for its efforts but two sets of grisly remains: five skeletons north of the Kei, and, just beyond the Qora, three more skeletons, including one in woman's clothing, probably the remains of Sophia James's maid Sally.

With his difficulties mounting, Muller first became dispirited, then persuaded himself that there was no one left to rescue. When, on 5 February, a chief presented him with a number of cattle, he decided that it was 'payment for the wrong the Caffers had done to the Englishmen'. Perhaps so. Less sustainable was his conclusion that it was 'proof that they were guilty of murdering the English'. It all ended at the Umtakatyi River, where a Tembu chief told him that the *Grosvenor* had been wrecked five days' journey to the north: 'All the people from the ship had passed along the beach in groups, and some of them had been to his kraal, and he had given them food: and finally there were no shipwrecked people in his country, but that they had all passed on.'

Muller crossed the river, but found the country – 'overgrown with unusually high thickets, great bushes and thorn trees' – too difficult even for horses. Here, on 18 February, he turned back. They had not got as far as the Umzimvubu, and were still fifty miles from the site of the wreck. The decision to withdraw was not unanimous. Evans objected vociferously, as did another rescuer, Louis Pisani, an Italian employee of the Dutch East India Company. Both said there was a chance that survivors were still holding on near the wreck. Pisani, a turbulent, contrary Venetian – twelve years later he led a rebellion against the Cape authorities – made a tremendous fuss when they returned to the Cape. He was to lobby for a further rescue effort, insisting that Muller's decision was a mistake,

> . . . as they had not waited to learn whether any of the shipwrecked people were still there; the commando turned back because of the reluctance of some persons to ride further, and reported that none of the people could be found; but the commando turned back when they were still three days' journey from the wreck; the Englishman who accompanied them [Evans] was very much dissatisfied, and wished them to go further, but they would not.

Nobody took much notice of Pisani's outburst, although the shortcomings of Muller's efforts were not long in being recognised. For now, the Cape authorities had enough information to send to England that made clear the extent of the disaster.

It had become clear early on that only the youngest and fittest would survive and now that they had reached sanctuary the pitilessness of that march was as evident from their ages as it was visible in their gaunt faces and spare frames. Not one of them was yet thirty. John Warmington, aged twenty-nine, was the oldest. Thomas Lewis was also in his twenties. William Habberley was twenty-one, John Hynes roughly the same. Jeremiah Evans was eighteen. Barney Leary was not yet out of his teens either. The youngest, Robert Price, was about fourteen.

They were homeward bound in various groups. Warmington and Leary sailed from the Cape on 14 March in a Danish vessel. Habberley, Hynes, Di Lasso, Feancon and Price went in another Danish ship a month later, as did Lewis, who decided in the end to return to what he knew, and lost for ever his African idyll. Not so Evans. The young hand from London's squalid Wapping docklands had been stirred by the majesty of the country while journeying with Muller's party and, confiding to Price that he feared being pressed into the Navy on returning home, had resolved to settle as a Cape farmer.

Out of the twenty-five lascars on the *Grosvenor*'s last voyage, eight had survived. All that was ever known about them was their names, recorded at the Cape as 'Allex, Foikan, Roman, Ramat, Imat, Mamaretta, Matthys and Matteroe'. It would be gratifying to record that they returned safely to their homes; but of all the catalogue of misfortunes that had befallen various individuals on the Indiaman, they were to suffer the blackest twist. On 10 July they embarked at the Cape with the maids Hoakim and Betty on the *Nicobar*, bound for Bengal. The very next day the *Nicobar* was wrecked east of Cape Agulhas. Five lascars and one of the maids were drowned. Remarkably, the surviving maid and lascars did not vow then and there never to step aboard another ship. They were to sail again later in the year, although which of the women, Betty or Hoakim, got back to relate her tale in Calcutta, was not recorded.

When the final count came to be made, of the 140 men, women and children who had sailed from Trincomalee in the *Grosvenor* on 13 June 1782, only these nine European sailors, three lascars and one maid ever reached home.

Although they had been the last to see their mistresses, no one had shown much interest in what the *ayahs* had to say. Fortunately, William Habberley had questioned them, and discovered what had become of the captain's party.

14

THE FATE OF WILLIAM HOSEA

Ntafufu River, 11–12 August 1782

Coxon's party had been abandoned on a grassy knoll south of the Ntafufu River exactly a week after the wreck. The women and children had just been carried across at low tide when, on the morning of 11 August, they watched most of the crew disappear over the next ridge. They were left with a discredited captain, a dying chief mate, and supplies of food sufficient to last only a few days. But the worst was still to come.

Coxon was said to have been 'out of heart' at the time of the breakaway. At some point in the morning, however, his spirits revived – or at least his will to live. Within a few hours, the captain led away the remaining crew. He abandoned his passengers William and Mary Hosea and their baby Frances, Colonel and Sophia James, the heavily pregnant Lydia Logie, the other three children and the four maids. Colonel James managed, by pleading and the offer of rewards, to prevail on just four men to stay with them.

This final act of betrayal remained hidden for some years. None of Coxon's party ever emerged from the wilderness, and only two of those he abandoned lived to tell of it. The passengers' fate remained a mystery that bred speculation and rumour, and inflamed a lurid prose style in the press and popular publications of the day. Narratives dwelt on the fate of the gentlemen, 'lately blessed with ease and affluence, becoming a prey to hunger, nakedness and slavery', and 'beautiful and delicate women, wandering through unfrequented wilds, subjected to the rapine and

Caffres, engraving by an unknown artist

licentiousness of unfeeling savages'. As for their families: 'What pangs must the friends and relations of the unhappy wanderers hourly experience!'

Empurpled narrative was one thing; facts were another. The inquiry report, published a year later, could cast no light on the fate of Coxon and his passengers. Having examined four of the surviving seamen, Dalrymple reported to the directors: 'They know nothing of the captain or the ladies since they parted from them.'

It was only thanks to a pair of chance meetings that the final act was revealed at all. Three weeks after the breakaway, a solitary lascar from the captain's party caught up with Shaw's men at the Bashee River and, questioned by Habberley, related

> that Captain Coxon, Mr Newman, Mr Hayes [the purser], Mr Beale, Mr Harris [fifth mate] with other officers and men and seamen had left Mr and Mrs Logie, Mr and Mrs Hosea and others who were unable to get forward on the same day as we had done.

Habberley obtained corroboration and further detail for this bare outline when he met the *ayahs* at Swellendam after their rescue; but Habberley did not arrive back in London until some months after his fellows. Dalrymple only questioned him after publication of the report, and his testimony was not publicly available until 1786, four years after the wreck, when it came out in an addendum that attracted little notice, perhaps because the most sensational disclosure was a single bald sentence in a thirty-eight-page summary. Dalrymple wrote:

> A lascar told [Habberley] that the captain, Mr Newman and a great many others, had left the ladies the same day they did.

As a Company man, the hydrographer did not linger on matters discreditable to its enterprises, but there is a hint of icy disdain in that summary. The captain and his officers had left the ladies to die, or worse, among natives. The fact that Hosea had paid Coxon £2,000 in passage money had secured him no more protection in the end than was provided to three-year-old Eleanor Dennis, who had been entrusted to the captain's care for the voyage, or young Thomas Chambers.

Despite the four years that elapsed between the wreck and revelation of Coxon's betrayal, it may seem remarkable that there was no public outcry.

Had all this happened even seventy years later, his name would have been dragged through the mud. By then the code of 'Women and Children First' had been enshrined in the heroism of another ship's company. Curiously, that too occurred on the South African coast.

In 1852, an iron paddle steamer, HMS *Birkenhead*, was carrying 494 officers and men to Algoa Bay and the eastern frontier of the Cape where the Eighth Frontier War was in progress. Also on board were fifty-six women and children. On a bright summer's night in February, the *Birkenhead* struck a submerged reef two miles offshore, and started rapidly to break up. Paraded on deck, the soldiers were commanded to observe 'order and silence' as the women and children were embarked in the three serviceable lifeboats. Discipline held, even as the funnel crashed over the side and the bow was torn away. When she started to go down, Captain Robert Salmond told his crew that they could take to the water, but regimental officers – fearing that the lifeboats might be swamped in a wholesale evacuation – ordered the soldiers to stand fast. So they did, shaking hands and saying farewell as the drummer boys, according to legend, rattled out the rhythm that became known as the Birkenhead Drill. One survivor wrote: 'There was not a murmur or a cry among them until the vessel made her final plunge.'

The *Birkenhead* entered Victorian legend. Kipling penned a verse that concluded:

> to stand and be still,
> to the Birkenhead Drill
> is a damn tough bullet to chew.

On the site of the wreck, at Danger Point, a brass plaque was raised that recorded the final balance sheet:

NINE OFFICERS, THREE HUNDRED &
FORTY-NINE OF OTHER RANKS AND
EIGHTY-SEVEN OF THE SHIP'S
COMPANY LOST THEIR LIVES.
EVERY WOMAN AND CHILD WAS SAVED.

Every woman and child saved. The fact that seventy years earlier the master and officers of an English ship had walked away from women and children along the same coastline says a good deal about changes in seafaring. In Coxon's day, transporting civilian passengers was in its infancy, and insofar as there was a British tradition of mercantile shipping, it lay with the laws of profit and survival. Desperate perils brought forth desperate methods, and seamen – whether officers or foremastmen – were no more or less honourable than the society from which they came. A comparison may be drawn with the Indiaman *Halsewell*, driven on to the Devon coast in 1786. In her agonisingly protracted death throes, thirty-three of the forty-nine sailors managed to save themselves, but, left to their own devices, all the passengers were lost, including at least a dozen women. They included the two teenage daughters of Captain Richard Pierce, who chose to die with them and was depicted as a hero in contemporary prints, clutching the girls in his arms as the sea swept over them.

In the case of the *Grosvenor*, information was extremely sketchy, confused and often contradictory. The daily press was in its infancy and no more reliable than the coffee-house gossip with which it competed. One of the earliest newspaper reports stated that Coxon's conduct was 'spoken of as well-collected, patient and brave. He fell on the march on the eighth day.' There was, moreover, no defining moment when all the facts became clear.

It was partly the increasing number of women and children passengers transported by East Indiamen in the following decades that brought about change. By the time of the *Birkenhead*, the rise of the ironclad steamer had created new levels of passenger numbers and safety standards. Any captain conducting himself as Coxon had done would have suffered disgrace, if not worse.

As it was, all might not have gone easily with him had he survived and returned to England. Even by the standards of the time, there was something chilling in the way that Coxon and Beale, the two men who bore responsibility for the disaster in the first place, led the last men away. While contemporary reports tended to dwell on the fate of the women, our age is more likely to be discomforted by the treatment of the children. Tom Chambers had at least been in the care of the Hoseas. Among the others left behind were the three youngsters travelling alone on their way back to be educated in England. Robert Saunders and Mary Wilmot, both seven, had been entrusted to the personal care of the captain in the same way as Eleanor Dennis.

The precise number who went with Coxon is not known, but they were about thirty in all and included the purser, bosun, surgeon and quartermaster. Charles Newman had recovered sufficiently from his stab wound to join them. He may have justified his action to himself on the ground that he had been entrusted by the Company with the investigation of corruption in the Madras presidency and had a duty to get back and report his findings.

Seeing that they were about to be completely abandoned, Hosea and James tried to bribe sailors to stay. James was successful; Hosea was not.

If anyone ought to have been in a position to buy loyalty, it was the former Resident. He alone had escaped from the wreck with some of his wealth intact, in the form of a packet of diamonds worth £7,000 (about £420,000 today). Hosea's riches may well have figured in the bargaining that had begun with the crew the moment the *Grosvenor* went aground; but diamonds alone could no longer secure loyalty for him, probably because they were no longer in his possession.

The handful of lost souls left watching as Coxon's group followed Shaw's over the ridge included, of course, the Hoseas, still accompanied by Mary's *ayah* Hoakim, their daughter Frances, and Tom Chambers. A short distance off were Edward and Sophia James, and the four sailors who had been induced to stay. There too was Lydia Logie, who had shown remarkable fortitude in getting this far in her state. Her husband Alexander was dying, but Lydia's *ayah* Betty had remained faithful and was tending to them both. What had become of the three unaccompanied children at this stage is an open question.

The final dissolution among the passengers took place over the next few days, and was recounted by Betty and Hoakim to Habberley. His stark account of what they told him is worth reproducing in full:

> One was servant to Mrs Hosea, the other to Mrs Logie. From them I obtained the following account of the passengers. Mrs Logie's servant informed us that she had remained with Mrs Logie about five days after the captain, purser, surgeon, third mate and others had left them, that Mr Logie was almost dead when she quitted him, then in company with Mr and Mrs Hosea and a few others, that Colonel and Mrs James had retired from them the next day after the captain did so, likewise that she and the other girl had deserted their mistresses with an intention of joining the lascars, that she had passed Colonel

and Mrs James, and that the colonel was unable to move without assistance. Mrs James wanted her particularly to remain. The colonel had four seamen assisting him.

Although Habberley's prose requires close reading and leaves many questions unanswered, the outline is clear enough. Colonel James and Sophia, assisted by the four sailors, set off after Coxon on 12 August. The Hoseas were left with the Logies and the servants, and presumably the children. The actions of William and Mary point to a kind of numbed paralysis, but after five days, with Alexander Logie on the point of death and no one left to turn to, they too made a pathetic and hopeless attempt to escape, starting forward with Lydia Logie, accompanied by Betty and Hoakim. Finally, the maids, seeing that their mistresses were beyond hope, recognised that their only hope of salvation lay among their own kind and went off with the lascars.

We are left with the pathetic final images of the erstwhile *burra sahibs* abandoned at the last even by their servants: of Edward James, a commander of troops now just a helpless man in his mid-fifties, hobbling along on the arms of seamen and soon to be deserted; of his wife Sophia, pleading with the maids not to leave them; and of the Hoseas, beyond even that feeble show of resistance to fate.

If, at the last, Hosea was indeed in the grip of a kind of mortified trance, it is hardly to be wondered at. Just before leaving Murshidabad for Calcutta, he had written to Sir Robert Chambers: 'I have long since made a resolution never to leave Bengal in an unfavourable season.' In those last days he was not short of opportunity to reflect on the madness that had overwhelmed this visceral instinct. Fear of exposure in the intrigues of Bengal, corrupt enterprise in Oudh – how remote and trivial that all must have seemed. The penniless boy of fifteen had struggled, perhaps ignobly, but dutifully and doggedly, for position and fortune in an unforgiving world, only to be brought here to die at the age of thirty-three. Worse still was his torment at recognising that he had brought about not only his own destruction but also that of the woman whom he had loved, and who had given him what little comfort and contentment he had known. As a drama of a man drawn to the destiny he most dreaded, the death of William Hosea was as bleak as a Jacobean tragedy.

When death came, it may not have corresponded with his worst fears. It came neither by drowning nor murder – both of which he had imagined –

but rather as a gradual failure brought about by exhaustion, starvation and fatalism. From the accounts of the many others who died in the same way on the march, it would not seem to have been a very uncomfortable end – the acceptance of the inevitable, a passage of sleep, extending into shorter and shorter spells of consciousness, so that slowly the swish of the sea and the clatter of cicadas became lost with the fading of bright light and the loss of a warming sun.

The French aviator Antoine de Saint-Exupéry experienced something similar after crashing in the Libyan desert and hallucinating as he felt himself slip towards death:

> I have the feeling that this torrent of visions is sweeping me away to a tranquil dream; so rivers cease their turbulence in the embrace of the sea.

There is a profound gap in our knowledge of what happened to those left with William and Mary. In the case of their daughter Frances, however, it was by no means the end. Still a toddler, the youngest and most defenceless of those on the *Grosvenor*, hers may have been the most extraordinary story of the whole saga.

Nor had the last been heard of another passenger. Alexander Logie probably died before the Hoseas. As for his wife, an account of an incident that would appear to have been witnessed by a maid or a seaman was shortly to reverberate from England to Bengal. This was that Lydia Logie, née Blechynden, a Calcutta lady recently married to the *Grosvenor*'s chief mate, had been seized and carried off by the savages.

Not a great deal more can be said about Coxon and his fellows. None survived. Less youthful and fit than the men with the second mate, they were dispersed early on by the fearsome obstacles that lay ahead. The rivers of which Trout had given due warning exacted their toll. Coxon was among those who succeeded in crossing the Umzimvubu, but by the time they reached the Umtata, the captain was flagging and ill. The last few fit men swam it, leaving him with a handful of stragglers.

A second man who caught up with Shaw's group provided the last glimpse of Coxon. This was George McDonald, a carpenter's mate, who had been among those who swam the Umtata. He related that, the last he saw, Coxon had been heading upstream in search of a place to cross. At that point the captain of the *Grosvenor* vanishes, never to be heard of again. But it would seem that he did not survive for very long, and quite possibly his end came violently. The *ayah* Betty told Habberley that, until being rescued, she had lived with a tribe and that 'she had seen Captain Coxon's coat on one of the natives'. While widespread reports of crewmen being murdered were only conjecture, sources among the Pondo and neighbouring tribes did later indicate that some of the castaways had been killed. From the survivors' reports, the only known victims of attacks were Williams and Taylor, so it is certainly a possibility that Coxon and his companions were murdered. The hot-tempered bosun Robert Rea had lashed out at their antagonists before, and had he done so again it could well have brought a summary conclusion both to his own career and that of his captain.

Beyond such speculation, no further light can be cast on the manner in which the others with Coxon met their deaths – from the officer whose wilful incompetence had carried the Indiaman on to the rocks, Thomas Beale, to the Bengal lawyer, Charles Newman. All that can be said with certainty is that they were among the great majority of *Grosvenor* castaways whose bones were given to the African soil. In the final analysis, of the 140 souls on board the East Indiaman, thirteen escaped, twenty-one drowned (including the lascars who were being repatriated on the *Nicobar*) and 106 died, mainly of starvation, exhaustion or despair, somewhere along that shore.

Whatever anxieties had been raised in Madras and London by Newman's investigation gradually eased as it became evident that his findings on treachery and corruption had died with him.* Another legacy of his career was not so readily subsumed, however. It emerged a few years later.

In about 1785, a farmer on the eastern frontier was approached by a wandering Xhosa who offered him a few silver buttons for sale. Each was engraved with the monogram 'CN'. These objects reached the Cape, where

* Three weeks after the *Grosvenor* sailed from Madras, Macartney – apparently uneasy about what Newman had found – wrote to Hastings claiming that he had resisted the bribes of the Nawab's durbar, which had 'found me incorruptible'. Another subject of Newman's inquiries, the former Governor Sir Thomas Rumbold, who 'shook the pagoda tree' more vigorously than anyone since Clive, was brought to trial before the British Parliament later that year, but was acquitted. In 1784 he was elected MP for Weymouth and, his fortune intact, lived in the manner expected of a nabob until his death in 1791.

they were examined and sent on to Bengal. A colleague of Newman's identified the buttons as having once been attached to the green broadcloth coat worn by the dandy of the Supreme Court when appearing before the bench.

Another relic of the drama took much longer to come to light.

In 1925, an elderly drifter named Johann Bock, formerly a seaman from Germany, found a bright stone on the farm he had leased near the mouth of the Kei River, roughly 150 miles south of where the *Grosvenor* had been wrecked. Over subsequent months similar stones came to light and, discovering that they were diamonds, Bock registered prospecting rights at a local magistrate's office. Other prospectors followed, paying Bock a concession rate to explore, and a Johannesburg mining investor inspected the site. Nobody else found anything, but by the time that police descended on Bock's farm, he had accumulated a cache of 1,038 diamonds. On being questioned, he revealed that all of them had come from the sand of a cattle path beside the Kei, where they were thickly strewn at a depth of about a foot. Bock was brought to court, charged with 'salting' – fraudulently planting the uncut gems for illegal gain. Although protesting his innocence, he was sentenced to three years' hard labour.

The court ignored a key aspect of Bock's defence – the evidence of geological experts that the diamonds were alluvial and could not possibly have originated in South Africa. One mystified expert stated: 'They do not come from any source with which I am conversant.' The logical point of origin, the Diamond Fields of Kimberley, lay 500 miles to the north and produced an entirely different kind of stone. The court also ignored the argument by Bock's lawyer that, rather than a faked find, the nature of the cache indicated an involuntary deposit. The lawyer, one H. F. Sampson, went so far as to propose that the most likely source was a shipwrecked English or Portuguese ship – possibly, he suggested, the *Grosvenor*. This insight is all the more remarkable for the fact that Sampson was unaware at the time that the *Grosvenor* was indeed carrying diamonds.*

* Twenty years later, Sampson came upon the evidence that vindicated him – confirmation that a *Grosvenor* passenger, William Hosea, had had a substantial parcel of diamonds. It was too late to help Bock, who had died soon after his release, and by then the diamonds had mysteriously disappeared. In recent years a campaign has begun to clear Bock's name and his descendants have claimed that they are due compensation for loss of the treasure.

While it cannot be stated categorically that the unfortunate Bock's gems came from the Indiaman, the circumstantial evidence is persuasive. It is unlikely to have been a coincidence that the mouth of the Kei, where Bock came upon the cache, is precisely the spot where Shaw's group met George McDonald, the carpenter's mate who had been with Hosea and Coxon. Habberley urged McDonald to accompany them upriver, but he refused, saying he would try to swim. Habberley thought this curious as the man appeared in no condition to fend for himself:

> . . . we thought it impossible for him to [swim] for when we left him, he was so weak that he could barely stand, and what became of him afterwards we never knew.

If McDonald had the diamonds with him, it begs the question how they were parted from their owner. One interpretation is that, as Coxon was about to abandon him, realising that he would never enjoy their benefit, Hosea gave them to the captain and the seamen with his blessing. The other is that a relationship that began in Calcutta when Coxon saw a chance to exploit a vulnerable man, ended in the same manner, and that as well as being abandoned to die, Hosea had his diamonds stolen from him.

15

'THE VILEST BRUTISH PROSTITUTION'

East India House, London, 22 July 1783

At that imposing entrance the two seamen paused and quailed. The classical structure where carriages clattered up Leadenhall Street to deposit bewigged gentlemen in breeches and stockings was, in the proper sense, London's greatest emporium. Midway between St Paul's and the Tower, it was as significant in its way as either. What St Paul's was to Church and the Tower to Crown, East India House had become to the new god of Trade – headquarters of the self-proclaimed 'Grandest Society of Merchants in the Universe'. Small wonder that the sailors shrank before the portico. John Warmington and Barney Leary, late of the *Grosvenor*, had come to answer for themselves before the Honourable Company.

The first report of the wreck, three months earlier, had given little hint of the sensation to come. In its 21 April issue, the *Morning Herald and Daily Advertiser* stated simply that authentic intelligence had been received of the loss of the East Indiaman *Grosvenor*. It had been a black year for shipping: four East Indiamen lost – three wrecked, including the *Earl of Hertford* on her first voyage, and one taken by the French; but initially it was by no means clear that the wreck of the *Grosvenor* had been a catastrophe. The *Daily Advertiser* reported a gentleman just arrived from the Cape in a fast-sailing packet as saying, 'the crew was saved'. The main concern was said to be for her cargo, with an estimated value of £300,000.

Woman assailed by two 'cannibals', by a French artist, c.1847

It was another of the new coffee-house publications, the *Morning Chronicle and London Advertiser*, that informed readers of the shocking information brought to London from the Cape by Francois Duminy, captain of a Dutch Indiaman. He told the *Advertiser* that, after the *Grosvenor* had been driven on shore,

> the Caffres had come down on the people, carried off the female passengers, and had killed several of the men who had tried to protect them.

The next day the *Herald* and the *London Chronicle* picked up the story, repeating this account verbatim; but the *Advertiser* had the bit between its teeth and topped its sensational exclusive with a hair-raising follow-up:

> The situation of the female passengers who were on the *Grosvenor*, must be the most dreadful that imagination can form, or humanity feel for. The ship was lost on the coast of the Caffres, a country inhabited by the most barbarous and monstrous of the human species. By these Hottentots, they were dragged up into the interior parts of the country, for the purposes of the vilest brutish prostitution, and had the misfortune to see those friends, who were their fellow passengers, sacrificed in their defence.

One lady reader found this image so distressing she wrote to the *Advertiser* that, 'not being able to support the idea of the fate which, it is said, befel the unhappy ladies of the *Grosvenor*, [she] would esteem it benevolent if anyone in possession of authentic information would give it to the world'. The paper, perhaps recognising that its association of 'brutish prostitution' with lady passengers – it was not yet known that they included the wives of a senior Company official, a prominent regimental commander and the Indiaman's chief officer – may have been ill-judged, moderated its tone and on 2 May reported reassuringly:

> A detachment of Dutch and French troops has been sent from the Cape towards the place where the Grosvenor East Indiaman was lost, to procure the release of the unfortunate passengers seized by the Caffres . . . The letters received yesterday from Holland say they were in hopes their endeavours would prove successful.

The *Bristol Journal* of 10 May was even more sanguine:

> We have authority from the best information, and great pleasure, to contradict the report that the ladies had been carried off by the blacks. The ladies and gentlemen who were passengers we are assured are all safe.

The *Journal*'s blithe assurances only added to an already confused picture. Relatives anticipating the return of loved ones from the East could not be entirely certain who had obtained a passage on the *Grosvenor* and who had delayed their departure until the following season. For those like Sarah Brown, who had little doubt that her daughter Mary Hosea was on the ill-fated Indiaman, the wait was agonisingly protracted as spring turned to summer without any further information from the Cape. In part, the silence was due to the voyage time; but there was, in truth, not much new intelligence to relate.

Then, in July, the first official account was received from Daniel Corneille, the Governor of St Helena. Far from reporting the safe retrieval of the passengers, it confirmed the harrowing earlier details. These were duly seized upon by the *Advertiser*, which must have felt itself vindicated. The Caffres, it reported,

> flocked to the coast and, stripping them all, selected from the women the wife of the chief officer whom they carried off. This unfortunate lady was with child at the time. Resistance was made to this act of violence and some lives were lost . . .

This was the first report pointing to the abduction of Lydia Logie. Its original source has never been identified. The *Advertiser* went on to report that at least seven Europeans were thought to be alive near the site of the wreck, although the captain and most of the passengers were dead. This story was published on 10 July.

Around the same date, the first two sailors, Warmington and Leary, arrived at Portsmouth – which was why, with the Company anxious to establish the facts and the public avid for further details, the pair found themselves before East India House at noon on 22 July. The *Advertiser*, having identified the story as 'a subject of public conversation and universal compassion', had a correspondent on hand to follow the latest developments.

It is the fate of the survivor to be doubted, perhaps because nobility and self-sacrifice seem inherently less natural in extremity than deceit and selfishness. The Company was unlikely to have looked kindly on seamen who had deserted gentlefolk, especially when they included such senior officials as Hosea and Newman, and the child of Sir Robert and Lady Chambers. We know that one press report blamed the sailors for the onshore disaster – claiming that 'the jacks got drunk and committed every excess, the consequence was a quarrel betwixt them and the Colpees [*sic*] which soon became general – the innocent as well as the guilty were attacked'. Who knows what the more sceptical minds may have hinted at. A shore on which there were no African savages, only European ones? Brutes who, finding the rich and mighty at their mercy, plundered and murdered them? In any event, there was reason for a close scrutiny of events.

Certainly when they were brought before the Committee of Correspondence – six directors responsible for administration of Company affairs – the two sailors were overawed and probably terrified. Young, illiterate, and perhaps not very bright – Leary was noted only for 'a very robust habit of body' – they gave testimony that was brief and confused. The *Advertiser* noted pointedly the next day that the pair 'were in a hurry relating these particulars'. But after another grilling, this time at the hands of the formidable Dalrymple and an Indiaman captain named Burnet Abercromby, it was clear that they were not dissembling. Their accounts, shamefaced in tone, clumsily told, were nevertheless convincing in corroborative detail, and were confirmed by the evidence of later witnesses.

What first-hand information they could provide about the passengers was not encouraging. Those who had been left behind were said to be 'all near expiring'; but one point was seized upon gratefully: the Caffres 'did not take away any of the ladies, but treated them [all] without distinction very ill'. The women passengers were not identified, but the implication was clear. If they had not been abducted, they must be dead, which was a matter for thanks. There, for the time being, matters rested, pending the arrival of more survivors from the Cape.

Bengal received informal intelligence of the wreck early in August, more than three months after it reached England, in the form of a letter from the

Cape to Calcutta. The writer is unknown, but among the first to read it was Thomas Law, father of the castaway child.

> It is with concern that I have to inform you that the *Grosvenor* Capt Coxon was lost on the coast about the lat of 29S to the eastward of the Cape. Four of the people have come here after a fatiguing march of upwards of three months. A troop of horses is sent to endeavour to relieve the unhappy sufferers all of whom excepting 16 were saved from the wreck. The report says that most of them have perished, and that they carried off the chief officer's wife who was big with child, but let us hope we will hear more favourable accounts.

While the identity of the chief officer's wife was unknown in London, the name of Lydia Logie, née Blechynden, soon spread in Calcutta, where she had been living before the *Grosvenor*'s departure. One of the first to hear about the letter was Margaret Fowke, who had replaced Eliza Fay as a gossipy and acerbic social chronicler. On 11 August Margaret wrote to her brother Francis, the Resident in Benares, in horror at the 'cruel account' of the *Grosvenor* and the fate of 'a Mrs Logy the wife of the chief mate formerly Miss Bletcherly taken by the negroes, tho' well with child . . .'

Margaret had been a friend of Mary Hosea's and was on close terms with Sir Robert and Lady Chambers. Her letters reveal that the Chambers marriage had run into difficulties since the *Grosvenor*'s departure. The lovely Fanny, much younger than her husband, was suspected of an affair with a man named Adair, with whom she had been indiscreet.*

Whether because of their problems or not, news of the wreck was withheld from the couple. Two weeks passed before Sir Robert heard about it inadvertently from a merchant who, fearing for his goods on the *Grosvenor*, mentioned it to him. Sir Robert is said to have fallen, stunned, and gone into convulsions; and 'on coming to himself he begged that Lady Chambers might be kept ignorant of the dreadful report till it was confirmed'.

* On 2 July 1783 Margaret wrote to her brother of Fanny Chambers: 'A young, handsome wife with unsteady principles and immodest vanity has lost her reputation entirely – I hope she has not lost her honour, tho' the candid must allow appearances are greatly against her.'

Fanny Chambers, in fact, already had a strong suspicion that all was not well. The artist Zoffany had just arrived in Bengal, bringing with him a portrait he had executed of her daughter already in England and relating that nothing had been heard at St Helena of the *Grosvenor*, although the *Valentine*, which had sailed later, was already home. Whatever her fears, Fanny would remain in the dark for months. As late as October a friend observed: 'The circumstance of Sir Robert's child being on board the *Grosvenor* is so generally known that I should think there is little danger of its being mentioned in their presence.'

The perils of the journey home had been brought home to one and all by the loss of four ships in a single season. 'At this rate one may as well mount a forlorn hope as go into an Indiaman,' Margaret remarked tartly; but the subject that mesmerised her was what had befallen Lydia Logie. She wrote to her brother on 18 August:

> I make frequent enquiries after the poor people of the *Grosvenor* – but no more letters have yet been received – I hope Mrs Hosea will escape the dreadful fate of Mrs Loguy – Can there be on earth a more desolate situation than hers? – the Dutch have no kind of influence in the part of the country where they were wrecked – she must despair of ever recovering her liberty.

And, before embarking on a journey to Benares: 'Due to the unsettled state of the country, I shall perhaps meet with the fate of Mrs Loguy!'

It was not until February 1784, six months after the first news in Calcutta, that Fanny Chambers was informed that the ship had been wrecked. A bare piece of paper with a brief inscription records perhaps the instant of her discovery. 'Loss of the Grosvenor. My Son, Alas!' On another sheet is a quotation from a letter of condolence that evidently gave her comfort: 'The deep shall give up her dead & the pure in spirit shall see their God!'

But anger and reproach, as well as grief, are evident in her letter, dated 20 March, to Margaret Fowke: 'The many lies my friends have at different times invented add only to the horror of my mind about the fate of the poor unhappy boy – If I had known the worst when everybody else knew it at least I might have tried to compose my mind and bear with resignation what human strength cannot resist. But at present I doubt the truth of every story I hear.'

In London, another grief-stricken mother was meanwhile writing to Fanny herself. Sarah Brown, mother of Mary Hosea and guardian of her children in England, sat down on 2 May to ask Fanny if she would continue to look after the baby, Charlotte, until arrangements could be made for her return. Sarah's deference, and spelling, only add to the poignancy of their common anguish:

> I make no doubt that you must have long since heard of the melancholy feat of the Grosvenor – it is to much for me to describe – it as all most been my death – one moment hope and the next fear. My pease of mind will be lost for ever if I should not see my dear children again as I greatly fear it – I shall be glad to be favoured with a letter to know if Mr Hosea insured for anything in Calcutta or left a will as I should imagine Sir Robert know Mr Hosea's affairs much better than anybody else. I hope that Lady Chambers will excues the libert I take in troublin her.

On 7 April Sir Robert convened a meeting of Hosea's executors to inspect his will. Although diminished by losses in the wreck, the estate was still worth more than £30,000 – enough to provide handsomely for William's heirs, including the four surviving children, Sarah Brown and his own mother.

No further scandals attached to Fanny's name. United in misery, she and Sir Robert erected a plaque to the memory of their son in Calcutta's South Park Cemetery:

To the Memory of Thomas Fitzmaurice Chambers
Born on 28th Oct MDCCLXXVI
Who was shipwrecked in the 'Grosvenor'
And perished on the Coast of Africa in August 1782

In 1799 the couple returned to England. Fanny, however, was haunted by her loss. Years later she was still waking from dreams of seeing Tom at the foot of her bed.

She was not the only grieving relative to suffer nightmares. Lydia Logie's younger brother, Richard Blechynden, had arrived in Calcutta soon after she sailed in the *Grosvenor*. He remained in Bengal for the rest of his life, making a haphazard living as an engineer and journalist, and producing one of the most remarkable records of contemporary life in Calcutta, a diary running to seventy-three volumes, which he began in 1791 and kept for more than thirty years until his death. In the first volume, he wrote:

> December 9, 1791: Putting the date at the head of the page reminds me it was the birthday of my dear sister. It calls to my remembrance with never ceasing grief the melancholy fate of the Grosvenor. O Lord, Thy will be done – whatever *is* is right. But whilst I am thus attempting to reason down my grief my tears are full flowing – inconsistent being.

Every year on that date, Richard would record the anniversary of 'my unfortunate & ever-lamented sister Mrs Logie'. Fully ten years after the wreck he, 'passed a very disagreeable night with shocking dreams about Mrs Logie. Awoke much troubled in my mind.' His grief doubtless arose partly out of the reports of Lydia's abduction, but also from the limbo in which the bereaved were left. Denied certainty, their pain and anger could never quite resolve into the last stage of mourning: acceptance. Always there would be a mystery. Many years later, after the death of her husband, Fanny Chambers wrote briefly of the calamity and how 'the uncertain circumstances of the case left to imagination the most dreadful materials for conjecture'. She, for one, found it easier to come to terms with Tom's death – 'perished on the Coast of Africa', as his plaque had it – than to live with the possibility that he might yet endure, but for ever beyond reach.

Samuel Johnson, Sir Robert's old friend, quite understood. He sent a copy of the Dalrymple report to his confidante, Hester Thrale, urging her to read it and remarking: 'Consider the distress of the parents to whom it would be now a comfort to be sure that he is dead.'

For quite different reasons, the affluent and influential in London were also inclined to overlook the odds of survival among those left behind.

Dalrymple's inquiry was not assisted by the haphazard manner in which the sailors were repatriated. They had been generously treated by the Dutch but, in the continued absence of English ships at the Cape, were obliged to make their way home as best they could. Six of them – Habberley, Hynes, Lewis, Price, Di Lasso and Feancon – boarded a pair of

Danish vessels to work their passage on 5 May. On reaching the English Channel, the boy Price and Lewis were put ashore. The other four were told that they were needed for the final leg to Copenhagen. Even then their trials were not over, for the captain refused to pay their wages until the British ambassador was summoned. Only in mid-September, more than a year after the wreck, did they reach London.

The effect of these uncoordinated arrivals was that Dalrymple questioned only four sailors in compiling his first report, published on 14 August 1783. After Warmington and Leary, Price and Lewis proved comparatively garrulous, the boy, in particular, giving Dalrymple 'a strong impression of precision'; but only much later did he question William Habberley, whose astonishing memory provided a daily chronology and gave a depth of detail that none of the others possessed. The date of this interview is not recorded and it was not published until 1786, as an appendix.

While there could be no hiding the extent of the disaster, Dalrymple's initial report tended to look on the positive side: it had given him much satisfaction, the hydrographer said, 'to see so many efforts of generosity and mutual assistance'. There was reassurance, too, for those distressed by the thought of ladies being manhandled by savages:

> The natives never offered to carry away Mrs Logie or any of the other ladies, nor offered them any injury, except taking their rings or such like.

No inference was drawn about the negligence that had led to the disaster, and though a reference to a 'want of management with the natives' pointed to shortcomings of leadership, at no stage was Coxon criticised directly. No mention was made of the fact that the *Grosvenor*'s departure had been delayed by Lord Macartney in Madras until it had to sail alone, and at an unfavourable time of year. (After hearing of the disaster Margaret Fowke wrote: 'People here exclaim with violence against the madness and folly of sending ships out, out of season.')

It would be glib to accuse Dalrymple of what today would be called a whitewash; such emphasis was standard procedure, a discreet drawing of a veil over matters disagreeable or discreditable. Not for nothing was the Company described by Ned Ward, a poet and wit, as 'a corporation of men with long heads and deep purposes'; and in seeking to allay concern for Lydia Logie and the other ladies Dalrymple may have been guilty of no more than the friends of Fanny Chambers: seeking to shield relatives from unnecessary pain.

But Dalrymple clearly believed that there were women as well as male passengers alive, even at this stage. On 8 August he made an impassioned plea to Sir Henry Fletcher, chairman of the Company's directors, that a new and immediate rescue attempt be launched by the Admiralty:

> I cannot doubt that many lives may yet be preserved amongst the natives . . . I cannot omit recommending that some small vessel should be ordered to range the coast, from the Dutch farms to Delagoa, and as this is a matter of humanity in which the State is equally concerned as the Company, I am led to take notice that the *Swift*, lately come from the West Indies, a small vessel of 50 tons is the fittest that can be imagined for this service . . . Not only humanity but the season require there should be no delay in dispatching this vessel.

Dalrymple's proposal was enthusiastically endorsed by the Company, which requested that the Admiralty make a small craft available, 'as a vessel belonging to His Majesty will go with more authority than any that the Company might hire for that purpose.' And, a cynic might add, with less cost to the Company.

Philip Stephens, Secretary to the Admiralty, duly replied that, 'Their Lordships have ordered the *Swift* brig at Deptford to be fitted out with all possible despatch to proceed in this service.' However, 'all possible despatch' is a wayward term to apply to the Admiralty's sublime indifference to urgency. The Company's request had been made on 27 August; Stephens's reply was dated 22 October; by the time the *Swift*'s commander, a Lieutenant Loveday, received his orders, dated 25 November, three months had passed. Loveday noted that he was to proceed to the Cape, stopping only to collect interpreters before sailing up the coast and landing at 27°s latitude. He made everything ready and awaited permission to sail. And waited. Christmas came and went, and still he waited.

The new year was two months old before another despatch was brought to the *Swift*, still tied up at Deptford. Dated 1 March 1784 – six months since the Company's request – it stated baldly that 'orders to go in quest of the Grosvenor's crew [have] been countermanded'. There was no elaboration. It may have been incompetence, but deliberate obstruction is more likely. In the corridors of the Admiralty, the rescue would appear to have had opponents – officers who resented His Majesty's Navy being sent on fool's errands such as rescuing Company sailors and civilians from foreign shores. Agents of tardiness, they played along with a charade while seeing to it that orders were delayed. Having held up matters to the point that eighteen months had passed since the wreck, they could argue that rescue was no longer feasible.

In doing so, however, they were flying in the face of recent intelligence that some castaways *were* still alive. Among those awaiting news was Hosea's mentor and uncle, Robert Orme, who, in a despatch to Bengal on 12 March 1784, wrote hopefully: 'Captain D'Auvergne who arrived about two months ago from the Cape says there were accounts of more white people inland when he came away.'

Similar information reached Calcutta from another source. On 28 February the *India Gazette* reported that a French ship off the Cape coast had sighted 'some Europeans on the shore, who were waving a flag as a signal for relief; but the weather was too tempestuous to send the boat ashore'.

If the Admiralty had given up, this glimmer of hope still offered good reason for the Company to pick up the challenge; but given the chance to dig into their own pockets to fund a rescue, the same merchants who had so enthusiastically supported the Admiralty's mission balked. No further action was ever taken by the Company.

Just what had happened to Lydia Logie and those left behind at the wreck remained a mystery long after London had found it expedient to brush them out of existence. It would never be entirely resolved; but an intriguing tribute to them, contained in a little volume entitled *Calcutta: Past and Present*, published in 1905, hints at the outcome:

> The story of the *Grosvenor* closed, but, as years passed, again and yet again came rumours of English women being seen in Kaffir kraals, dressed in Kaffir fashion, and refusing to leave their savage surroundings, on the plea that they had become contented mothers of families, and were no longer willing or able to return to their old lives.

> During the Kaffir war of 1835, a curious incident partly raised the veil of doubt and mystery which enwrapped the fate of the lost lady passengers. A tribe of native warriors offered their services as 'brothers' to the English against their own countrymen, the Kaffirs, saying that their tribe, which numbered six hundred souls, were descendants of the English ladies who had been wrecked in the *Grosvenor*.
>
> And when men visit the rugged coast their thoughts rest in pity on the shadowy pathetic figures of those English women who, dead to their former world and all that they held most dear, lived out their lives as wives and mothers among an alien and savage race.

What makes this curiosity remarkable is that the author, Kathleen Blechynden, was the great-granddaughter of Richard Blechynden. Kathleen had pored over the seventy-three volumes of Richard's diary. In their pages she discovered not only the fate of her ancestor Lydia Logie, but also the final untold story, about how Lydia and perhaps five other survivors from the *Grosvenor* had lived on among African people, and come as close to being Africans themselves as white men and women could.

PART THREE

16

AFRICAN CRUSOES

John Bryan, being lame and unable to walk, and Joshua Glover,
a fool, stayed by the wreck . . .
Report on the loss of the Grosvenor, Alexander Dalrymple

Lambasi, 7 August 1782

It was the third day and Bryan had never felt so alone. He had played up the extent of his injury to the officers while telling Hynes that he would take his chances among the natives rather than stay with a doomed company. Now he was less sure. After the tumult and shouting of the wreck, the milling figures on the shore, the soldier gazed around at a gaunt landscape. Solitude was new to him. Whether on campaign in Mysore or in the rough confinement of the Indiaman, he was used to fellowship. Hugging himself against a cool wind coming off the sea, he was shocked by the awful finality of his decision.

Earlier that day Coxon had led the ship's company away to the south. The warriors had gone too, obviously in pursuit, but Bryan was sure that they would be back. Debris from the *Grosvenor* was still eddying around the inlet and snagging on the rocks. With time to himself he began a search, collecting an axe, a knife, rope . . . These he carried across the stream to a forest of milkwoods in the dunes and concealed them in the undergrowth with the last of his salt beef and flour, then dug himself a shelter in the soft sand.

Women and children came the next day and danced at the water's edge. Discovering brightly coloured silks where they had been left by the crew,

Natives of Mosselbaai, engraving, Cornelis de Houtman, 1646

the women ululated and began to drape one another's nakedness, gambolling and darting away with shrieks of laughter, as if to avoid the unfamiliar sensation of the fabric. Bryan watched from the trees, and when they left he felt alone again.

He returned to the inlet and found a flint. That evening, as a gale swept in off the sea, he huddled gratefully around crackling flames, and woke in the morning to find the storm had cast up fresh debris from the wreck, including pewter plates from the great cabin and a copper ewer. These he added to his little trove.

One morning he came out from his shelter to the lagoon where the Tezani and another smaller stream debouched into the sea, and followed each in turn up towards the ridge, looking for fruit among the trees that grew along the banks. The smaller stream gurgled clear and sweet among the rocks, gathering in pools surrounded by reeds. The Tezani was enfolded on either side by tiers of black sandstone that rose sheer and bristled with wild bananas and protea trees. Malachite sunbirds flitted among the branches.

On the sixth day, approaching the inlet, he saw that the warriors had returned. From a vantage point he watched the conical hairstyles bobbing among the rocks as fires were again started and fed with wreckage. When he had prepared himself, Bryan went out to meet them, proffering the axe and pointing to his mouth. He spoke in his own tongue, of his need for shelter as well as food. They replied in their own way, and he noted that some of them wore ladies' jewellery in their hair. He continued talking – about the wreck, his poverty. They listened impassively but without any sign of antagonism.

He took up the axe and set about cleaving a spar. They resumed their search. Later, as they gathered up their iron oddments and started up the ridge, he went with them.

On the evening of 12 August, John Bryan, late of the Madras Infantry, joined another tribe. His background and almost everything else about him are a mystery but, a veteran in his thirties, he lacked neither intuitive shrewdness nor practical skills. In confiding to Hynes that he intended making 'trinkets to amuse the natives, hoping to ingratiate himself with them', he had a real strategy for survival, and his statement that he might as well die among the natives as starve on a march showed an insight that his fellows lacked. None of them was ever to know what became of him, and it was widely assumed that he had died. Of his life with the Pondo, and of their traditions, enough is known for this telling.

The *umzi* was an enclosure of thirty huts, set below the escarpment of the Mkweni River with crop patches running down almost to the water's edge. At the highest point was the *inkundla* – the great house – occupied by an improbable patriarch of spare frame who appeared to be all bone and rheumy eyes. Nothing besides his age distinguished him from the other males: a hide sheath covered their genitals; otherwise they wore only long hide cloaks. But there was no mistaking the deference, even awe, shown to this ancient by the hundred or so inhabitants of his kraal. Over time Bryan perceived that he was living with a large, polygamous family headed by the *inkosi*, Ntlane, and including his four wives, their sons and daughters, and their spouses and offspring.

Other *umzi* dotted hills around the valley, of varying sizes but each with its own *inkosi*. It took Bryan rather longer to discover that the inhabitants were kin, linked to an ancestor named Pondo by a connection as significant to each individual as it was complex. Among the *inkosi* in the vicinity Ntlane had paramountcy, although how he came by it was for Bryan another mystery.

From the escarpment Bryan could see the ocean, for the *umzi* was no more than three miles from where the Indiaman had grounded. The perspective it commanded provided other insights: the blackened hillside explained the lights in the dark seen by *Grosvenor* lookouts; late in the dry season the Pondo burnt off the old grass to promote fresh growth immediately the rains began. He saw, too, that the warriors who had descended on the wreck and then pursued the castaways were not an organised cohort but men of the various family groups scattered around the valley.

For the first few days he shared a hut with two of Ntlane's unmarried sons. It was a cave of mud and thatch, barren apart from a few clay pots and spears, dark during the day and smoke-filled at night from embers in the hearth. The floor, of compacted, polished cattle dung, was ungiving, despite the woven rush mats on which they slept, and he rose in the mornings unrested with smoke-reddened eyes.

Little appeared to be expected of him and little was done by the other men either, once the cattle had been taken from a stockade opposite

Ntlane's hut to be milked and then herded by boys into the hills. The women, on the other hand, set off early to the land with hoes of fire-hardened wood and stayed all day, breaking muddy soil softened by the onset of the rains, and planting maize and pumpkin. By evening they had returned, to rekindle fires and prepare meals that at this time of year were necessarily sparse. Once Bryan was familiar with the agricultural cycle, he realised that the natives' reluctance to feed the castaways had been due largely to the fact that the wreck had occurred at precisely the point at which their resources were most strained. The previous harvest was all but consumed, the cattle were lean and spare.

One morning he went back to his old shelter by the lagoon and retrieved a pewter plate, which he presented to Ntlane. Bryan's reward was to be given an *imizi* of his own. Once he became accustomed to the burnished dung floor, he found it was deliciously cool in the sultry summer months and yet retained the cosy warmth of a hearth fire in the short winter.

Of the younger men he remained wary. Two had women's gold brooches pinned in their hair, another wore a charm of silver monogrammed buttons that Bryan recalled having seen on Charles Newman's coat. So he was careful to conceal the copper ewer when he brought that back to his hut, and – working covertly at night – fashioned it into four bangles. These he gave to Ntlane's wives, with the largest for Mamguntu, the great wife. After that he brought his tools to the *umzi* and worked openly.

He went hunting with the men. A spirit medium smeared them with a potion designed to attract their prey before they set off across the escarpment. The first day they saw antelope at a distance, which they chased unsuccessfully with the dogs. Bryan, no match for his fleet-footed companions, mourned the loss of his old musket. Another day passed in fruitless pursuit. Towards sunset on the third day, with only a little grain left, they crested a ridge. A barrel-like creature the like of which he had never seen before was grazing with its young on the banks of a river below.

Years later Bryan admitted to his friend Poto that had he known their peril he would not have joined the hunters who crept down into the valley, then followed a reed bed that came out within ten yards of the animals. Sprinting out, the men interposed themselves between calf and mother. As she charged, they stood their ground, taking her on their points. In a moment there was blood everywhere, the calf was squealing under the spears, and the barrel-like creature was bellowing and slashing about with her tusks. Had the hippopotamus cow been fully grown they must have found her irresistible, but as more men came, stabbing and hacking, she sank to the sand. A cry went up, a praise to the ancestors.

One hunter died of his wounds that night. Bryan, although among a number with gashes, joined the rest in gorging on the sweet flesh of the calf. Next day they cut the cow into long strips, which were draped on poles and borne home in triumph.

He picked up some of their tongue and started to venture out beyond the valley. Once, exploring the hills north of the wreck, he came to another *umzi* and found Joshua Glover.

It is easy to imagine their joy. Bryan and Glover seem to have come by their salvation in a similar fashion, the latter having salvaged from the wreck a chisel with which he performed useful tasks and carved wooden figures that he gave to children. Yet there is nothing in the admittedly fragmentary accounts of their lives to suggest that they formed any particular bond. The sailor had been regarded by his fellows as a lunatic and was shunned by them as a Jonah. It is likely that some of his more superstitious shipmates blamed him for the wreck, which would help to explain his disappearance with the Pondo soon afterwards. In any event, he too found a place among them. Tribal society was tolerant of eccentricity and although less is known of Glover's subsequent life than Bryan's, he was also remembered.* We may assume that if he and Bryan did not become intimate acquaintances, they continued occasionally to meet.

As the days grew hotter, and fields ripened with pumpkin and sorghum, the tempo of life quickened. During the spring fertility rituals, Bryan noticed the high breasts and long limbs of a girl named Sipho. Later he went to sit by her. One night he followed her and was surprised when his fumbling advances were not repulsed. She began his instruction in *ukumetsha*. Though much gratified, he found her self-control disconcerting, for she would not permit penetration, and as he had previously been

* While the Pondo knew Bryan as the blacksmith, Glover was always described as the carpenter.

acquainted only with garrison women, it took him some time to comprehend that, although adept at this form of external intercourse, Sipho remained a virgin.

Late that first year – it must have been December – the older women wove long grass into baskets tight enough to hold liquid, and harvested maize and sorghum. Grain was ground to the accompaniment of songs, and when all was ready, Ntlane gathered his people and they set off up the valley. In two days of walking Bryan's shoes finally fell to pieces and he was limping on raw feet when they reached a labyrinth of huts and pens sprawling across a low grassy knoll. Many of the sixty-odd clans of the royal house were already at Qawukeni, the Great House of the paramount, and by the time the moon reached its fullest phase, all of Pondo's people were at hand for *inxwala*, the first fruits ceremony, being celebrated by his descendant, Ngqungqushe.

Women deposited their crops, then withdrew to a nearby hilltop to observe. Oxen were slaughtered. Beer was passed round in calabashes, and pipes were filled with a plant that grew wild on the hills. Young men grew boastful while their elders engaged in rumbling debate punctuated by choruses of consensus, and the sweet scent of cannabis wafted on the air and mingled with the smell of roasting flesh.

A circle of male diviners prepared pots of a medicine composed of the fresh grains, herbs and a secret ingredient. First to taste the potion was Ngqungqushe. The warriors followed suit, for now each clan sent forward its young men to make an army for the paramount. Chunks of fatty beef circulated on wooden trays. After the feast, diviners came among the men, scarifying them under the right eye in order that their aim should be true. With the rite complete and the warriors made strong, they awaited only the orders of Ngqungqushe.*

Which of their traditional foes – the Pondomise, the Bomvana or the Tembu – suffered the Pondo onslaught in that summer early in 1783 is lost in legend. Bryan saw them go. He had achieved his initial objective among his adopted people; but it was as more than a maker of trinkets that he

* Ngqungqushe is said in some of the Pondo traditions to have ordered the attacks on the *Grosvenor* castaways, but neither Bryan nor Glover was ever harmed. He appears to have been a chief of no great ability and died a few years later in tribal warfare. He is remembered, however, for having fathered the great Pondo chief Faku.

would be remembered. The harvest of iron from the *Grosvenor* was soon depleted by war and hunting. Some time after that first *inxwala* ceremony, Bryan went back to the wreck.

All in pieces, the Indiaman lay in the inlet, the stern section of her hull no more than thirty yards offshore. It was only severe storms that brought up further treasure now, but by feeling his way around the rocks at the start, then diving below the surface as he gained in confidence, Bryan found the stern at a depth of about fifteen feet. He never did discover the chest of gold mohurs that disgorged its contents on the rocks a few decades later. Of far more value to him, however, were the oblong pigs of ballast that had spilled from the Indiaman's hull and were churning around on the seabed like iron bricks.

With a rudimentary forge and bellows of oxhide, he began to produce assegai heads, then utensils. The next growing season his rough hoes transformed the women's labours, and his renown spread beyond the valley. He was called Umbethi, meaning the Beater, and men brought cattle to barter for his wares. Soon he had his own herd. Then, with the blessing of Ntlane, he moved up the valley. Beside a thicket of wild banana trees he established his own *umzi*, a large hut with a fine, smooth dung floor laid by Sipho and the women, and a circular cattle stockade made by the men.

Not long after that Sipho's father accepted *lobola* of ten cattle for her. She was bathed in the contents of a cow's gall bladder, so that her family should be blessed with cattle, and after a feast on the rest of the animal – to which Umbethi was not admitted – she was delivered by a delegation to the *umzi* of her new husband.

The next year was a bad one in the valley. It started with an accusation of sorcery against a wife of Msingali, one of Ntlane's sons. Umbethi heard about the case, how the child of another woman in the *umzi* had died and she had claimed that Msingali's wife was a *thakathi* – a witch. Ntlane was consulted and rather than have her killed out of hand, he ordered Msingali to send her back to her family; but he was attached to that wife, and instead left the two others and took her a few miles away, where they built a hut. A few months later Msingali visited Umbethi, relating that new accusations against his wife had been made from another *umzi* – that she was responsible for cattle sickness. A few days later news came that men had arrived in the night, set fire to Msingali's hut and beaten him and his wife to death.

When the dry season came again, and the grass turned the colour of biscuit, fires were started in the hills in anticipation of rain. No rain came. At dawn each day Ntlane would limp down to the cattle stockade and gaze silently on his precious creatures. Each day they had to be herded further from the *umzi*, yet they were producing little milk and were as spindly as the *idama* tree. Word came that fighting had broken out over grazing in another valley. Soon afterwards, other *inkosi* came from across the hills to petition Ntlane for rain.

All the Pondo rainmakers had their own methods. An early researcher took down the following account almost a century ago:

> The chief sends a black beast without spot. It is killed and the hide is prepared. A human being is killed and in his skull is put the fat of the beast. The rainmaker goes to live in a hut by himself. He covers himself with the hide and smears the hide with the fat from the human skull. Then a snake comes by night and licks the fat off the hide. It should not be seen by any one except the rainmaker. After that it rains.

The valley came to life with almost the first drops. Green shoots burst above the charred stalks. Great was the acclaim for Ntlane; but the old *inkosi* was saddened by loss, and by his sacrifice. Soon afterwards he died, and was buried within his *umzi*. His eldest son, Geza, became *inkosi* but did not succeed Ntlane as head of the clan because a conclave of the other headmen ordained that another of their number was the rightful mediator with the ancestral spirits.

As Bryan's metamorphosis to Umbethi continued, his skin darkened and his hair grew thick and matted under the sun, the soles of his bare feet were hardened like leather and if he never attained the agility and endurance of his fellows he could still join them in the hunt.

Mostly the days were divided between his cattle and his forge. Sipho tended the fields of maize and sorghum. In the evening he bathed in the river. Sometimes he would return to the *umzi* and drink beer with Poto and the other sons of Ntlane, but more often he was content by his own fire with a pipe of the sweet-smelling herb. The heavens had an aspect of startling clarity at night, and he would lie back on the grass, gazing at the beam-like brightness of Venus, tracing patterns among the stars and mesmerised by the Milky Way.

Castaways have usually attempted to keep track of time, as a link to their former lives and perhaps as a subconscious assurance that they will return to it. Barney Leary kept a notched stick in the march down the coast, until losing it on the thirty-ninth day. Defoe has Robinson Crusoe record the date of his shipwreck on a cross, then score it daily to maintain an annual calendar. At some point, though, Umbethi forgot time, and when the second anniversary of the wreck came, he was in all probability oblivious to it.

Rather than the calendar, he became aware of cycles – of the moon's phases, of the season of grass-burning, of the planting time and of the wet season when black clouds blew in thunderously from the sea. There followed long, sultry days in the valley when he plucked sweet red *matungulu* plums and wallowed in the Mkweni's thick brown waters: at this time the hills were hung with soft mossy foliage, the cows grew fat and the baskets were full of beer and grain. Then once again the grass turned to the colour of sand and a cool breeze coming off the river rustled the dry wild-banana fronds.

Their firstborn was a girl, called Mambethi, or daughter of Umbethi. If there had been any doubt beforehand, there was no question after that of going back. As the years passed, he may have sighted a passing sail on the horizon, must have learnt that Delagoa Bay to the north could be reached with no great hardship. He never tried to go back. Instead, for some years he had the satisfaction of emerging in the morning from his hut, its entrance facing to the east, to feel the dew under his feet and the sun on his face, and to savour a glow of proprietorial pride as he surveyed his herd.*

He had every reason to be grateful to his new people. The manner of his acceptance recalls other early visitors' accounts of the Nguni-speaking tribes – of people tolerant, patient, indulgent and gregarious, 'loving one another with a most remarkable strength of affection', as one put it – rather than the brigands associated with the *Grosvenor* survivors. Whether he assimilated in the fullest sense is another matter.

* Bryan's later life recalls that of an earlier castaway, an old Portuguese who was found by Dutch seamen along this coast in 1689 but refused to leave. They reported: 'He had been circumcised, and had a wife, children, cattle and land, he spoke only the African language, having forgotten everything, his God included.'

Among them he was a phenomenon; but a society in which a man's lineage – his relationship with the ancestors – was so essential to his standing, had some difficulty revealing itself completely to outsiders. For Bryan's part, a pragmatic, rational spirit may have stood in the way of participation in tribal life at its deepest level. Perhaps Glover was a readier vessel for accepting an existence ordained by magic and witchcraft. England was not so distant itself from a belief in witches and their familiars, and the sailor was touched by the fantastic. He never took a wife but gained some renown as a praise-singer and was invariably seen at *inxwala* where he would extol the virtues of the paramount, to much approbation.

As for Bryan, there was another tenet of tribal culture to which he was resistant. While he had the land and cattle of an *inkosi*, he did not proceed like others to procure more wives. For one of his wealth and standing, six was not uncommon; but Sipho was to remain his only mate. She was pregnant with their second child when the invaders came.

The circumstances are unclear. For some years the clans living up the coast, beyond the Umzimkulu River, had been engaged in a process of conquest and subordination that would culminate twenty years later in an illegitimate outcast named Shaka emerging at the head of a centralised kingdom. Already the northern clans of the Zulu were being organised into the disciplined age-group regiments, the *amabutho*, that would sweep down on the Pondo and other smaller clans. At the same time, the Pondo had a history of conflict with their neighbours and the raiders may have come from the same Bomvana group that killed the paramount Ngqungqushe at around this time.

Whoever the raiders were, they came for Umbethi's cattle, and his wife. When the sun went down Sipho had been carried off. He seems to have gone after her, for he made no attempt to rebuild his *umzi* but left the valley and set off with their daughter Mambethi on a wanderers' trail. He never did find his mate. What eventually became of her is not known, but she survived long enough to bear their second child, a son Faku, who in due course returned to the valley.* Some thirty years later, Faku told the

* This Faku is not to be confused with the great Pondo paramount of the same name, the successor to Ngqungqushe, and a leader whose shrewd diplomacy and generalship brought his people through the turmoil of Shaka's era relatively unscathed.

final chapter of his father's story to Henry Fynn, an English adventurer who spent most of his life among the Zulu and Pondo, took a number of native wives and evidently recognised a kindred spirit in the castaway soldier. Fynn wrote in his diary:

> He was in despair on account of the loss of his wife. He resided for a time among the amaXolo tribe, near the Umzimkulu, with his daughter, and built a canoe for exploring the river. He, however, failed to proceed far up because of the beds of rocks that extend across it. Leaving his daughter, he went off in an inland direction, from whence, soon afterwards, news was received by the amaXolo of his death. His daughter was killed in 1823 in the general slaughter of the surrounding peaceful nations by Shaka. Faku is still living, he has a large family and possesses a few cattle.

An earlier, more famous castaway, Alexander Selkirk, marooned on the tiny Pacific island of Juan Fernandez with the company only of cats and goats, endured more than four years of solitude before being rescued in 1709. He returned to England and fame, attracting the notice of Daniel Defoe, who used his story as the basis of his seminal novel. An old sea captain thought Selkirk's case 'may instruct us how much a plain and temperate way of living conduces to the health of the body and the vigour of the mind, both of which we are apt to destroy by excess and plenty, especially of strong liquor'. Selkirk, indeed, lived to regret being rescued, and was given to staring at the sea and lamenting, 'Oh my beloved island! I wish I had never left thee.'

Umbethi died in about 1795, so he had some thirteen years to contemplate the vindication of his decision. A man of desperate fortune – nothing else explains his recruitment to the most wretched corps in the Company's service – he had sought only survival yet had found much more. In crossing the line between his two worlds like few Englishmen, he had wrought a life of freedom and endeavour, and had he returned to London the scribes would doubtless have fallen on him as another Selkirk to weave a thrilling tale from his experiences.

In fact, Bryan and Glover were forgotten, their lives left unchronicled. Journalists, authors and even composers had in the meantime been exercised by a far more outlandish idea than male castaways. Not long after

Bryan's death, the Drury Lane Theatre in London staged a musical drama by the composer Charles Dibdin entitled *Hannah Hewit, the Female Crusoe*. It was the first of a variety of popular entertainments about English ladies lost among tribesmen who dressed in skins and hunted wild animals with spears and clubs.

17

THE QUEST

Calcutta, 23 February 1792

Richard Blechynden awoke at three that morning. This was not unusual. Ten years since his arrival in Calcutta, Blechynden remained one of the city's less successful entrepreneurs, a worrier and a slave to insomnia who rarely slept as late as the dawn firing of the Fort William cannon, even in these relatively comfortable months of what passed for winter in Bengal. He followed his usual routine when roused by his nightmares or the oppression of the air, donning a loose robe and crossing to the desk where his diary lay.

By the time a bearer arrived to dress him, he had completed a particularly exhaustive account of his previous day's endeavours and dashed off some correspondence for Europe, to go by the next Indiaman. Another servant brought his breakfast and the *Calcutta Gazette*. Blechynden glanced at the column of shipping news, an announcement of the first theatrical production of the season, a Greek tragedy, and news of General Abercromby's army in Seringapatam. Then, at the foot of the page, his eye was caught by an item headlined:

THE GROSVENOR INDIAMAN

A chill fell on his heart as he read:

> *The lateſt accounts concerning the Groſvenor Indiaman which was wrecked on the coast of Africa ſome years ago in the 28th degree of*

A Boer trek wagon, by William Burchell, c.1823

Southern latitude, affure us that not the fmallest vestige of her crew or paffengers now exists and that Mrs Logie, the firft mate's wife, who lived with one of the black Princes by whom she had feveral children, was also dead. This unfortunate Lady had the additional misfortune to furvive for a few years all her fhip-mates.

Blechynden's first reaction, as he later recorded, was disbelief. Nine years had passed since the disaster, and while he would never be reconciled to losing Lydia, the reports and the inquiry, which he followed with ferocious intensity, had at least convinced him that her sufferings had not been prolonged. This was desperately important to him. They had been unusually close siblings, brought together in grief by losing their parents when Richard was fifteen. His sister, two years older, became the focus of his affectionate nature and an ideal for womanhood in general – 'a delicate young female, tenderly brought up & of such exquisite sensibility that she might be said to be alive at every pore', as he described her. Blechynden scrutinised the *Gazette* report again, and this time was angered and a little reassured. There was 'no mention by how this account had come – or any reason assigned why this melancholy account was at this length of time brought before the public to wound the feelings of the friends and relatives of those unfortunate persons'. His conclusion was: 'Improbable I may say, *Impossible* as to the latter part.'

For all his protestations, he was so agitated that he could not touch his breakfast. A *syce* was told to bring the phaeton and Blechynden set off to see his friend Edward Tiretta.

Losing their parents was not the only hardship to have befallen Richard and Lydia. A profligate grandfather had squandered the family estate in Kent, and the premature death of their father, a London merchant, would have cast them into a parish workhouse but for a kindly uncle, James Theobald, who provided for their education. Richard studied mathematics and astronomy before going to sea as a midshipman in the *Godfrey*, which was captured by the French in 1780 when he was twenty. His spell as a prisoner must have been quite brief because the following year he sailed as a midshipman again, this time in the *Deptford* East Indiaman, for Calcutta. It seems that he was to join Lydia there in order that they might set up home together, pending the marriage of one or the other.

Lydia had left a year earlier in another Indiaman with marriage very much in mind. Young women with more wit than fortune commonly went to India in search of prosperous and eligible men under a system of assisted passages offered by the Company, dubbed laconically 'the Fishing Fleet'. As it turned out, destiny took a hand in Lydia's plans. No sooner had she embarked on the *Grosvenor*, in June 1780, than the vivacious and handsome young woman passenger came to the attention of the ship's chief mate, Alexander Logie. He courted her over the seven months of the outward passage.

At first glance, it might have seemed an unlikely match. On the one hand Lydia, with the exquisite sensibilities noted by her brother, from a family only recently fallen from gentility; on the other Logie, the former apprentice boy who for the past ten years had been whipping sailors into line from the Caribbean to the Bay of Bengal. But they were suited by need as well as by age – Logie being now twenty-eight and Lydia twenty-three. Lydia wanted a husband and Logie, having every expectation that he would take over command of the ship from Coxon, was a man of prospects. Far more improbable unions had been contracted in the volatile social mixture of Company India. While at sea, the couple came to an understanding.

On landing, Lydia proceeded to Calcutta and was provided with lodgings at the home of William Larkins, the Accountant-General of Bengal, whose wife Mary took in guests. Two other Larkins brothers were Indiamen captains, acquainted with Coxon and Logie, and the drawing room was a forum for officers of the shipping fraternity. Here Lydia stayed for more than six months while the *Grosvenor* was engaged on Company business, until Logie was able to free himself and travel to Calcutta for their marriage.

Three weeks later she boarded the Indiaman again, to sail home with her new husband. Her brother Richard was already bound for India, so in all likelihood their ships crossed in the Bay of Bengal. When the *Deptford* anchored at Kedgeree Roads on 31 May 1782, the *Grosvenor* was just about to sail from Trincomalee. Well over a year was to pass before word reached Richard of the disaster that had befallen his sister.

His friend Edward Tiretta had seen the *Gazette* report as well. A colourful figure, Italian by birth and formerly a fencing master in Paris, Tiretta had landed in Bengal after deserting from a Dutch ship and subsequently contrived an appointment as Surveyor of Roads. Now aged sixty-seven, he held court in a sprawling Calcutta mansion like some oriental potentate – he had just taken a new bride aged fourteen – and was both patron and father figure to Blechynden.

Tiretta tried to reassure him. Of course the report was nonsense. Had not Dalrymple stated quite categorically that the reports of Lydia's seizure by Caffres were false? And there was that letter from the Cape military commander . . . yes, Colonel Gordon . . . had he not said that all the passengers had almost certainly died soon after being cast away? Blechynden acknowledged as much. Even so, he could not shake off 'a great depression of spirits'. After an hour or two, unable to work or think, he returned to his apartment.

His years in Bengal had been marked by all the ups and downs to be expected in a risky business environment, including a few days in prison for debt, and he had experimented with various careers – architect, engineer and newspaper proprietor. By the standards of Calcutta he was unusually high-minded and honourable, esteemed as a man of his word by a circle of friends with whom he dined and drank chilled claret on most evenings. Although presently impecunious, he had rooms in town, a garden house and stables at the lakes where he grew roses and shot snipe, and at least three children by a variety of local *bibis*, for all of whom he had a patent affection. Aged thirty-one, he had just started the diary that he would keep until his death, finding the act of self-expression soothing when he was oppressed or vexed.

He turned to it again now and began scratching away furiously. The uppermost question was whether Lydia might, after all, have long survived.

> Impossible! I say impossible because in the first instance it entirely militates with the evidence. And second that it is beyond the power of belief that in the hardship she must have experienced, [being] at the time of the catastrophe far gone with child and a sick husband, that she should long live with such accumulated evils – shut out entirely from the world, from all she held dear, surrounded by savages, whose language she could not comprehend, whose repast she could not even think of without loathing – without one cleansing ray of hope that she should ever revisit her native land and friends.

Reason with himself as he might, however, there was one phrase that he could not dismiss from his mind. He wrote it down – 'one of the black Princes by whom she had several children' – then appended an exclamation mark, and embarked on a rambling and agonised internal dialogue:

> I will yield for arguments sake so far to the account as to suppose that where the mind's passions do not go hand in hand with the body that fruition can follow – the contrary is so well known to be the case that it is useless to attempt a refutation. Nay, do not our very law Books maintain that where a woman is big with child she *cannot* have been *forced* – and what other name can they give to the horrid connexion to which they allude?

At the heart of Blechynden's anguish was a touching ambiguity. While he knew no more about the supposedly savage Caffres than the next Englishman, he was uncommonly free of either social or racial prejudice in the circle with which he was familiar. He dined with Asians and took an interest in their society, and was painfully aware of the discrimination that his own children, who were illegitimate as well as Eurasian, were likely to encounter when he sent them to be schooled in England. He had, of course, experienced frequent 'connexions' himself with Bengali women, and kept company with one couple to whom he referred elliptically as Othello and Desdemona, evidently seeing nothing 'horrid' in that. But Lydia, delicate and tenderly brought up . . . Lydia, a concubine among naked brutes from a primitive tribe – that was another matter.

In almost ten years he had not wept for her. That night he thrashed about, tormented, until: 'I know not what might have been the event had not a plentiful flood of tears come to my relief.' Respite was short-lived. The nightmares resumed.

The wreck helped to rebuild ties between what had been, in effect, enemy capitals. Warren Hastings was sufficiently moved by Dutch efforts to save the castaways that he sent Governor Van Plettenburg a diamond ring that cost the Company £1,437 10s, inscribed with a quotation from Virgil: *Ab hoste docere* – It is right to be taught, even by an enemy. The ring was carried to the Cape, with a message expressing the hope that the recent restoration of peace in Europe meant that British ships would soon be able to receive again the hospitality for which the 'tavern of the seas' was renowned.*

Van Plettenburg, however, was troubled. Louis Pisani, the Italian member of the rescue expedition, was protesting publicly that Muller's decision to turn back had been a terrible mistake and, having just received 'a vague report of some Europeans now living among the Caffrees', the Governor was forced to acknowledge that Pisani might be right. He replied in these terms to Hastings, vowing that if the account should be confirmed another party would be despatched 'for the purpose of delivering all such as may be discovered'.

The reappearance in Cape Town, after a series of journeys through Caffraria, of François Le Vaillant, the French traveller, ornithologist and artist, gave rise to new speculation. Le Vaillant related that he had heard of a shipwreck and of women survivors being 'cruelly reserved' by the Caffres. Among the tribes living along the Great Fish River he saw metal trinkets that he suspected had come from the castaways. He wrote in his celebrated volumes of *Travels*:

> The idea of these miserable people haunted me everywhere; and I could not help reflecting on the melancholy situation of the poor women, condemned to drag out their existence amidst the torment and horror of despair.

Le Vaillant's sympathies were passed on to Colonel Robert Gordon, commander of the Cape garrison, a Dutchman of Scots descent. Gordon, too, had explored beyond the colony's boundaries, mapping the region visited by Le Vaillant, and although unable to break away from his duties at the bastioned Castle down at the edge of Table Bay, he identified with the plight of those he called the *stranders* and resolved to do what he could.

Other echoes were meanwhile being heard along the colony's frontier. From farmers in eastern districts, the Cape authorities started receiving accounts of whites living among natives up the coast. One particular

* Hastings returned to England three years later, where the malevolent Philip Francis finally obtained his revenge, successfully manipulating the political forces in Parliament so that Hastings was impeached and brought to trial. Proceedings dragged on for seven years before he was acquitted.

report, which landed on Van Plettenburg's desk in March 1784, described a visit to a farmer named Stephanus Scheepers in the distant mountain region of the Winterhoek, two days' journey north of Algoa Bay, by a delegation of 'Kaffers and Gonakwas', who 'bore witness that the English people were still alive'. Twice the Governor issued orders to the field commander of the Camdebo district, David van der Merwe, to organise a new rescue expedition. Twice the missions were abandoned, because of disputes among the farmers and a shortage of resources.

Then, late in 1785, the process was given new momentum when Lord Macartney visited the Cape. On his way home from Madras, Macartney may have been among those whose regret at the *Grosvenor* tragedy had been tempered by the disappearance of Charles Newman's evidence of corruption in his presidency. He certainly retained a keen interest in the East Indiaman and her human cargo and, as the most senior British envoy since the restoration of peace, raised the subject with Gordon. Macartney reported in his diary on 18 October:

> Lt Col Gordon a very well informed & Ingenious man . . . Told me the Grosvenor was lost only 8 or 10 days South distance from De Lagoa – & that if the people had gone a little within the Country they would have got safe . . . Believes most of the people perished – perhaps one lady not dead.

Gordon's instincts were soon tested. A month after Macartney's visit, he was ordered to take a detachment up the coast to investigate suspicions that the crew of a British vessel, the *Pigot*, had made an unauthorised landing about 300 miles up the coast at Cape St Francis. He set out in November and was away almost five months. He pushed his orders to the limit and beyond, venturing at least 150 miles beyond his supposed destination, through the region where William Habberley had resided with the Xhosa, and nearly to the Great Fish River, where Taylor and Williams had met their deaths. Here Gordon interrogated local tribesmen, and was deeply moved by one story in particular. He related it later to another prominent visitor to the Cape.

On a wet day in 1788, His Majesty's armed vessel *Bounty* dropped anchor in Table Bay. The *Bounty*'s commander, a protégé of Cook's named William Bligh, was under orders to proceed to the Pacific and take on breadfruit for the West Indies slave plantations. While his ship provisioned for the next stage of his voyage, he called at the Castle, where he met Gordon. His story so gripped Bligh that he recorded it in detail:

> He said that in his travels to the Caffre country, he had met with a native who described to him that there was a white woman among his countrymen, who had a child, and that she frequently embraced the child, and cried most violently. This was all he could understand; and, being then on his return home, with his health much impaired by fatigue, the only thing he could do was to make a friend of the native, by presents and promise of reward, on condition that he would take a letter to this woman, and bring him back an answer.
>
> Accordingly, he wrote letters in English, French and Dutch, desiring that some sign or mark might be returned, either by writing with a burnt stick or by any means that she should be able to devise, to satisfy him that she was there; and that on receiving such token from her, every effort should be made to ensure her safety and escape. But the Caffre, although apparently delighted with the commission which he had undertaken, never returned, nor has the colonel ever heard anything more of him.*

A mother and child. The description pointed to Lydia Logie and her baby, unborn at the time of the wreck. It might equally have applied to Mary Hosea, last seen with her two-year-old daughter Frances. But then the sources reporting to Gordon sometimes told different stories. At some stage he met another Xhosa who told him that there was not one woman, but two. Gordon related this to another visitor, a young Frenchman named Perneau.

Six years after the wreck, in other words, there was a substantial body of confused but nevertheless broadly consistent evidence that cried out for further investigation, an expedition that would go all the way to the site and resolve the mystery one way or another; but the new Governor, Cornelis Van de Graaff, was preoccupied by renewed frontier tensions with the Xhosa.

* Bligh remained fascinated by the story. Eighteen months later, on his way back to Europe after the mutiny that made his name notorious, he stopped again and, on asking the latest news of the *Grosvenor*, was told of a recent account received by a farmer 'from some Kaffirs that at a kraal or village in their country there were white women'.

Gordon was a decent and sensitive man. While convinced by now that there were survivors, he saw no purpose, as he told Bligh, in raising the hopes of those whose loss was still raw until the facts were established one way or another. At around the same time, he received a letter from James Theobald in London, introducing himself as the uncle of Lydia Logie, and with an enclosure addressed to her. Theobald explained that he had heard Lydia might still be alive and asked Gordon to have the message taken up the coast by a bearer. Having written just such a letter himself and heard no more, Gordon did what he thought was for the best: he returned the letter 'with the positive assurance of all the *Grosvenor Stranders* being dead'. It was received with relief by Theobald, who passed it on to his nephew, Richard Blechynden.

Blechynden kept Gordon's letter. He used it as a kind of talisman against his visions of Lydia. More difficult to explain are his reasons for hanging in his rooms a dramatic picture of the sinking Indiaman, in all probability the aquatint by Robert Pollard, after an original oil by Robert Smirke, which was published two years after the wreck and became the best-known image of the *Grosvenor*.* But if it is difficult to comprehend why he kept at hand this harrowing reminder of the disaster, there can be no doubt that Blechynden's distress was genuine. In the months after publication of the *Gazette* report, there are frequent references to Lydia in the diaries:

> 9 December, 1792: This day always makes me melancholy. It is the anniversary of the birthday of my unfortunate & ever lamented Sister Mrs Logie!
>
> 16 December, 1792: Passed a very disagreeable night. Had shocking dreams about Mrs Logie. Awoke much troubled in my mind.

Years went by, but Blechynden's peace of mind remained fragile. Soon after he heard about Gordon's suicide in 1795, precipitated by the British

* In this vividly melodramatic piece, the three white women are clearly portrayed. Lydia is shown clutching at a masterful figure in an officer's tricorn hat directing the rescue, evidently her husband Alexander Logie. Among other identifiable figures, Mary Hosea is shown swooning in William's arms with Frances, while Sophia James's arms are raised imploringly to heaven.

occupation of the Cape – 'I am very sorry for this . . . I am much indebted to him for the endeavours he took to trace out my poor dear sister Mrs Logie,' he wrote – an uncannily coincidental meeting with Perneau, the Frenchman who had spoken to Gordon before his death, brought all these events together and shook Blechynden deeply:

> 10 November, 1796: Perneau called on me to visit. I hate visits. [His] attention was attracted by the print of the loss of the Grosvenor and he pretended with all the levity of a Frenchman that there were two ladies in existence among the Caffres in 1788 – that Colonel Gordon told him this. How this man can fib when I myself have a letter from Colonel Gordon to my uncle in which he opines him they are all dead! It however served to sink my spirits.

While Richard continued to assert with an air of defiant certainty that Lydia had died soon after the wreck, in his heart he feared that the persistence of the stories from the Cape marked them as true. Nightmares plagued him for years, and every year, on 9 December, he would start his diary with the same melancholy reflection. The last entry in 1810, a few years before his death, is typical and reads: 'My poor lost Sister's Birthday!'

When finally the expedition was launched, it came not at the instigation of a reluctant Governor but on the initiative of a handful of conscience-stricken colonists. On 24 August 1790 a commando of thirteen burghers mustered at the Kaffir Kuils River, a picturesque spot about 170 miles due east of Cape Town. It included no fewer than five members of the first rescue attempt, including Stephanus Scheepers, the Winterhoek farmer who had been troubled since being visited by the Xhosa delegation six years earlier. Also there was Heligert Muller, who had had plenty of opportunity to reflect on his mistakes as commander of the first expedition. This time, however, the party was commanded by Jan Holthausen, and it would succeed in reaching its destination, more than 620 miles away.

They rode, following the line of the coast but holding to a course between thirty and forty miles inland, avoiding the magnificent but awkward Outeniqua mountains and Tsitsikama forest, instead making fast progress on the bleached plains of the Karoo scrubland as they swung along in the saddle for up to ten hours a day. Lessons had been learned, and when, after four weeks, they crossed the Great Fish River, the column consisted of just ten wagons.

They lived off the land – and well, too, using long-barrelled *roers* to provide daily feasts of eland, buffalo and hippopotamus. Bontebok and wildebeest darted across the plains, and birds dazzled from acacia thorn trees (Holthausen recorded the first sighting by a European of the distinctive crowned crane). And they shot elephants for ivory – twenty in all. One of their number, a grizzled wanderer named Tjaart van der Walt, was impaled and trampled to death by the largest of these creatures; and Holthausen's son, a youth name Jan, fell into a staked pit set by the Xhosa to trap animals and died of infected wounds. Amid these fragments of tragedy, drama and adventure in a grand space, their trek anticipated a greater saga to come. Holthausen might have been on a quest, but he was pioneering territory that Boer dissidents would follow a generation later when they rejected English rule and rode away beyond the Cape in the exodus known as the Great Trek. Crossing the Amatola mountains into the Xhosa country, the land-hungry eyes of the farmers noted what their scribe, Jacob van Reenen, described as 'beautiful countryside interspersed with little perennial streams, all of which are suitable for irrigation, and which possesses everything necessary for good and fine farms, broken grassland excellent for cattle . . . a great deal of game'.

The Xhosa were welcoming. Chief Ndlambe of the Rarabe, warring with the neighbouring Gqunukhwebe, wished the searchers a safe journey and provided guides so that they might avoid his foe. On 14 October Holthausen crossed the broad, lovely Qora River into the land of the Tembu, distributing gifts and receiving in return interpreters and guides. Two months after setting out, they reached the Umtakatyi, the point at which the first expedition had turned back. They were nearing the site of the wreck.

Two days later, at a Bomvana kraal, Holthausen received electrifying news. Nearby stood 'a kraal of Christian bastaards descended from people from a ship wrecked there'.

Early on 4 November the riders came down from a ridge to a settlement of about a hundred thatch huts set above the Umgazana River. Smoke from a dozen fires was rising through the trees as the inhabitants came out. Their features and complexions were not of pure Africans, but of 'whites and also from yellow slaves and Bengalese'.

There also, in the clearing, were three white women.

'They were deeply moved to see people of their race,' Van Reenen wrote. And, it was said, a cry of rejoicing went up from this strange tribe at the sight of white men on horseback: 'Our fathers are come . . .'

18

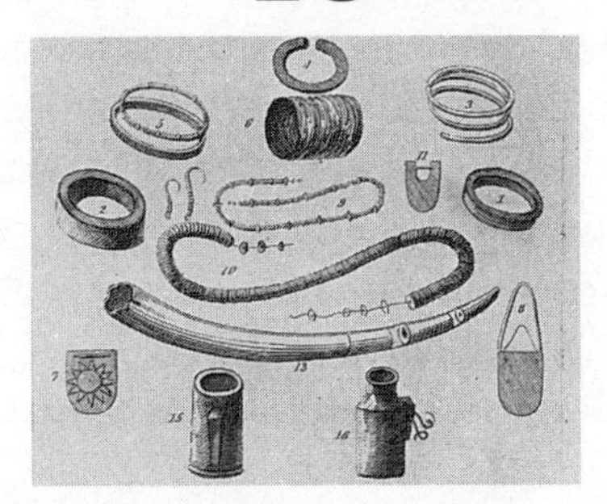

'OUR FATHERS ARE GONE'

Ntafufu River, 14 August 1782

For Lydia Logie, Mary Hosea and Sophia James, the shock of betrayal must have been worst. After the terror of shipwreck had come recognition of a world order turned upside down – where the means of authority were lost and black brigands held sway, where a sailor was better fitted for survival than a gentleman and where their own husbands were as helpless as they. Perhaps this realisation softened the next blow. There was, after all, a kind of brutal logic to the breakaway by the seamen under Shaw. But the women must still have clung to a last desperate faith in the figure who had regimented their existence since that unimaginably far-off time when they had sailed from India. Nothing could have prepared them for the moment when the moral universe collapsed entirely, and Coxon and other men of their own class walked away.

For four months the women had been thrown together almost constantly: Lydia, young, handsome, gregarious; Mary, sweet but frail and anxious; and Sophia, matronly and probably childless. Whatever the state of their relations in the great cabin – whether amity, icy politeness or mutual detestation – it was unlikely to have been indifference. Since the wreck, however, each had been thrown back on her husband. We see Lydia nursing the chief mate as he lay dying, Mary united with William in a state of rigid mortification. Sophia and Edward James, despite being older than the others, had been struggling on gamely and the Army man

Ornaments and weapons, by John Campbell, c.1816

had one last effort within him. The day after Coxon left, Edward and Sophia followed with the four seamen they had induced to stay. It was a vain effort. The James's were to be seen once more only, and the last reported view of Sophia, pleading for help as they were overtaken, offers little indication that the sufferings of either were much prolonged.

That left eleven people at the Ntafufu River – the most vulnerable group, still barely twelve miles from the site of the wreck: the Logies, the Hoseas and their daughter Frances, the boys Tom Chambers and Robert Saunders, the girls Mary Wilmot and Eleanor Dennis, and the *ayahs* Betty and Hoakim.

Like so many of the landscapes crossed by the castaways, it is a place both beguiling and forbidding. From the hill where they were abandoned, one looks north up the coast – across a lagoon formed by the narrowed river mouth to a line where golden dunes meet the white-flecked swell. Around the lagoon a natural drama is in perpetual cycle, partly below the surface, where fish are drawn to feed on the myriad creatures sustained by red and black mangroves, and partly in a grand display above, where fish eagles and giant kingfishers circle and swoop for their prey. Beyond, the land might be a reclining body, the long, smooth green hills curving away like limbs in either direction and, tucked away like tufts of hair in the clefts of valleys, thick forests of milkwood and stinkwood. A handful of modern-day castaways have been lured here, living in cottages hidden away among wild fig trees, but no road comes to the broad river mouth. Reachable only on foot or by water, it retains a sense of mystery that works powerfully on an imagination reaching out for lost souls.

Logie was their last hope, and they spent five days there in the hope that he might yet recover. They sheltered among the milkwoods. They prayed. In drowsy moments their spirits fled back to Calcutta, to airings on the maidan, dinners at Fort William and, above everything, the notional world of order. All the while Lydia watched her husband of just eight months slowly sinking, and felt the new life growing within her.

On 17 August, with their provisions nearly exhausted and the chief mate either dead or on the point of death, they left him. Lydia's *ayah* Betty was later to relate that she and the other *ayah*, Hoakim, went forward with the Hoseas 'and a few others'. This latter reference must be to the children, as there was no one else left.

The evidence for what followed is fragmentary. Nor are there the stories attaching to individuals, as in the case of 'the blacksmith' and 'the carpenter', that make it possible to put names to figures who come into view yet remain tantalisingly elusive. The sources that pick up their trail present a patchwork piece made up of a mixture of threads, some of which run in contradictory patterns or create a texture that does not quite sit with the whole. Nevertheless, it amounts to a compelling refutation of the reports that none of the *Grosvenor* females survived. English society saw theirs as the fate that was worse than death and out of kindness wished them dead; but tribal history, attested to by commoners and chiefs, links the Lambasi site to a central historical event in which white women and children came from the sea and stayed. What follows is necessarily speculative while being consistent with this evidence.

The Hoseas did not last much longer. Neither was resilient enough to have struggled further against the cumulative horrors they had endured. It would appear, however, that little Frances may not have died with them. A toddler, the youngest of all those on the ship, she is one of those discernible in the patchwork. Let us leave her for the time being with her parents, after they collapsed for the last time, on or about 18 August.

In the absence of information about the two remaining boys, Tom Chambers and Robert Saunders, it would seem that they had become separated or fallen; but Lydia carried on with the *ayahs* and Mary Wilmot and Eleanor Dennis. Allowing for slow progress, they would have reached the Umzimvubu within a day, no more than two. The fearsome river had caused each group so far to fragment, and here the last band did as well. Whether at the Umzimvubu, or near to it, Betty and Hoakim left Lydia, as they later explained, 'with an intention of joining the lascars'.

Before they did so, however, it would appear they observed the encounter that gave rise to reports that Lydia had been abducted. The story was contained in a despatch from Daniel Corneille, the Governor of St Helena, and although the source was never identified, it must have been one or both of the *ayahs*. Dalrymple, of course, found that none of the women was seized or ill-treated, and as a result it was concluded that the whole story was fallacious. But if Lydia was not taken against her will, she may still have gone willingly. Abandoned by everyone else and driven by instinct to preserve her unborn child, she was ready to accept any sort of help – and especially if it came from people similar to her own kind.

No more than ten miles away, just beyond the Umzimvubu, lay a settlement unique in southern Africa, of a people known as the amaTshomane who were descended from shipwreck victims. Their *inkosi* was one Sango. His wife, the matriarch of their clan, was named Gquma. She was white and she was English. As we shall see, she had been cast away here as a child about forty years earlier.

Around 22 August, perhaps alerted to the presence of another white woman in their vicinity, the amaTshomane came upon Lydia. When she went off with them it was not as a captive, but as a refugee. Mary Wilmot and Eleanor Dennis went too. In the circumstances it would have been quite natural for such an episode to be misinterpreted or misreported, whether by the *ayahs*, one of the rescued sailors to whom they related it, or the Cape authorities who passed it on to Corneille at St Helena. It must be acknowledged that Habberley, the best informed of the survivors, made no mention of Lydia's fate, but he may not have heard about it or, more probably, stayed silent out of discretion.

At that point, for the time being, Lydia and the girls disappeared; but they emerged occasionally from the haze of travellers' tales, sightings and speculation reaching the Cape over the next few years. One of these tales, it may be recalled, convinced Colonel Gordon of the need for another rescue – the account he heard in Caffraria of 'a white woman who had a child, and that she frequently embraced the child and cried most violently'.

And so, eight years later, the second burgher commando set out from the Cape.

The stir created by its return in June 1791 with news of three castaway women living 600 miles up the coast was accompanied by disappointment. Jacob van Reenen, the party's chronicler, wrote that their mission 'to discover whether any of the English women of the ship *Grosvenor* were still alive', had resulted in failure: 'We found no one there, and one can rest assured that nobody from that ship is still alive.'

His account was none the less riveting for that. Of coming to the seafarers' tribe, the amaTshomane, along the Umgazana River on 4 November, he wrote:

> We found three old women who said they were sisters, wrecked there and saved when children; but [they] could not say of what nation they were, as they were too young at the time. We offered to take the old women and their children back with us on their return, which, so it seemed to us, they were very willing to do.

At this point the rescuers had yet to reach their objective and it was another two weeks, over the most difficult final fifty miles, before they came to Lambasi. On 15 November, eight years and three months after the *Grosvenor* struck, a party from the Cape finally reached the wreck site – to find 'nothing except a few pieces of cannon, ballast iron and lead . . . two small pieces of spermaceti candle . . . and some broken white English porcelain'. Of castaways they found no sign and, after looking around the site for a few hours, they left. Van Reenen's confident claim that nobody had survived was taken as the final word on the subject – even though Bryan and Glover were living less than a day's journey away.

They returned to the tribe of the white women on 26 November. Van Reenen wrote:

> I now wanted to take the old women with me. For this they had great inclination and wished very much to live among Christians; but they wanted to take with them their entire progeny, which amounted to fully four hundred, saying that they preferred to stay with their children and grandchildren, rather than to live parted. I promised to report to the Cape Government in order that they might be fetched thence ... They were deeply moved when we left them.

Unequivocal, and powerful, this account would seem to set the matter to rest. Three elderly sisters, unable to recall even where they came from, shipwrecked many years earlier: such a description ruled out anyone from the *Grosvenor*. On examination, it becomes less clear-cut. One of the trio was undoubtedly the Englishwoman, Gquma; but never is it suggested in the oral histories attaching to her name that she had sisters and, given the great body of testimony portraying her as a solitary matriarch who came alone from the sea as a child, that is hard to explain. It would be unwise to make too much of the discrepancy. Still, two additional females would chime with some of the earlier reports of the *Grosvenor* women received at the Cape by Colonel Gordon. The identification of the three as sisters came through interpreters and may well have meant no more than that they were of the same race.

This is not to suggest that the trio included Lydia Logie. In all probability she had died, perhaps quite recently. The report seen by her brother in the *Calcutta Gazette* seven months later, assuring readers of the death of 'Mrs Logie, the first mate's wife, who lived with one of the black Princes by whom she had several children', suggests that this was information discovered by the rescuers.

What had passed after Lydia joined the amaTshomane can only be imagined. Over the years she had perhaps come to terms with her destiny, and the woman who used to weep over her child, over her lost life, had learnt to tan hide for clothing to replace her shredded garments, had tilled her ground with wooden tools, breaking down the hard-caked chunks of red soil to smaller lumps, then crumbling it between calloused fingers, sowing her seed, and awaiting the rain and the appearance of the tiny green sprouts. She had collected firewood from thickets increasingly distant from the kraal, bundled it and borne it home to the hearth. It would not be honest to endow this pastoral with an idyllic quality for, in truth, while the *Grosvenor* brought two destitute men, a soldier and a sailor, to a life that was almost certainly better than the one they had left, it cannot be pretended that it did the same for an educated young woman of her time. Cumulative strains had taken a toll of her spirit and her strength, and she had died short of her thirty-second birthday.

It is tempting to reflect on her life as wife of 'one of the black Princes', but wiser to resist, for though it is reasonable to suppose that in a society which celebrated motherhood a young and fertile woman would in time have been drawn to assimilate in the full sense, we can know nothing of how this came about or who her black prince was. Of what became of her various children, by a Scottish mariner and an Nguni chief, it must be admitted that nothing more can be said either.

Van Reenen made no mention of Lydia, but his report is lacking in detail and vague in so many respects that it cannot be taken altogether at face value. His assertion that no one from the *Grosvenor* survived was clearly mistaken, for the rescuers had failed to find Bryan and Glover. They had also failed to find at least two other females from the Indiaman, for whose continued survival there is further evidence.

An earlier writer was sceptical of Van Reenen's report. Writing in the *South African Magazine* in 1902, Ernest Schwarz, an academic and author, thought the claim that the women were all dead, 'too optimistic, however kind and judicious it may have been when their near relatives were still living'. Schwarz went on: 'It should not be dismissed as impossible that they may have found a refuge among the tribe of the white women, and that when Van Reenen came along, they either kept out the way of their own accord, or were hidden . . . In time the women might also have become reconciled to their fate, watching their young progeny with a mother's fondness.'

Forty years later, a daughter of the white woman Gquma provided a missionary named William Shaw with evidence that if females from the *Grosvenor* were not actually at the kraal when Van Reenen's party arrived, they were in the vicinity. In his diary entry for 29 June 1829, Shaw related meeting this 'strong, lively old woman with truly European features':

> She distinctly recollected the wreck of the Grosvenor, and informed us that it occurred near the large river Zimvooboo. They came out of the ship, she said, like as if a whole nation were coming. She confirmed the account of their separating into parties, and also that those

who left the coast and went to the interior, were murdered by the Amapondo, when the father of Faku was chief;* the female, however, as well as some female children, were spared, and she informs us that there are many of their descendants among the Amapondo.

This reference to a female points again to the survival of Lydia Logie. Here too is evidence of the later lives of Mary Wilmot and Eleanor Dennis. For children, with less psychological baggage, assimilating had been easier. By the time of Van Reenen's coming Mary was aged sixteen and Eleanor twelve. The distant past must have appeared dream-like and probably disturbing. It had been replaced by a world that was ordered, sufficient, enfolding. Sharing tasks and duties bred in young women a deep affinity, a delight in dance and song, and a blessed capacity for laughter. Although not rich in cattle, the amaTshomane were adept at agriculture. Van Reenen described the kraal on the west bank of the Umgazana as surrounded with 'large and beautiful gardens which they had planted with kaffer-corn, mealies, sugar-cane, potatoes, bananas, black beans'. Mary and Eleanor may have seen the white men and felt a strange confusion, but the appearance of the riders is unlikely to have lured two adolescent girls back to the past. If Mary still recalled something of her previous family, her earlier home, her first language, it is unlikely that Eleanor did.

Once again an opportunity to resolve the matter once and for all was lost: Van Reenen had promised Gquma that the women would be fetched to the Cape with their families. They never were. The Governor's Council, informed about the half-caste tribe, 'decided that it would be inexpedient, even were it possible, to bring so many uncivilised people to the Cape'. If this attitude betrayed a lack of empathy, the Council may still have been right in deciding that it was best not to disturb the women further, but to leave them with their families, among their adopted people.

A silence fell over the land of the amaTshomane. Years passed, but no more was heard of what one observer called 'this interesting people' until 1803, when Henry Lichtenstein, a young German doctor, accompanied an official Cape delegation to the Xhosa. From them Lichtenstein was fascinated to hear

* i.e. Ngqungqushe.

> of an extraordinary people, far to the north, that have no resemblance to the Caffres, who do not speak their language or follow their customs. Hitherto no one has visited or seen these people, but according to report, the colour of their hair is yellow, which they do up in locks, and wind round the head. Such an account does not seem deserving of much attention, and appears to be wholly fabulous. But probably Europeans may here be meant, who have from time to time landed upon various parts of the coast.

Control of the Cape passed to the British, giving momentum to white expansion over the interior. Still that turbulent corner of the south-east coast continued to obstruct pathfinders. A new phase was heralded by the end of the Napoleonic Wars, and the release into Britain's growing empire of a generation of fortune-seekers. Francis Farewell was a Royal Navy man in the Kidd tradition, a buccaneering former lieutenant who ventured up the coast to seek his fortune in the land of the Zulu ruler Shaka. In 1823 Farewell came upon

> the wreck of the Grosvenor East Indiaman. A carpenter and armourer had lived at this place until lately. There were also two women who had lived on the spot for some time, but upon an irruption of the tribes from the westward, all the tribes that then inhabited that part of the coast were killed, when these women fled, hid themselves in the bush, and were then starved to death.

That is all. No dates, no detail. The carpenter and the armourer were, of course, Glover and Bryan, even if Farewell's estimation of time was well out (Bryan had been dead for more than twenty years). Otherwise we are back in the realm of speculation. The most plausible interpretation of Farewell's findings must write a desolate final chapter to the story of Mary Wilmot and Eleanor Dennis: that in the inter-tribal conflicts common among the Nguni even before Shaka's time they fell victim in a raid, probably by the Tembu, on the amaTshomane.

By the time of their deaths Mary and Eleanor had spent perhaps twenty years among their adopted people. They had never learned to read or acquired any of the accomplishments of other young well-to-do girls whose education they had been sent back to England to share, whether playing the pianoforte, embroidering or writing verse. They had heard the rustle of a breeze passing through a withered maize field before the rains came, had seen the flutter of a paradise flycatcher on the wing and tasted warm milk and wild honey. The manner of their deaths is sufficient caution against any tendency to romanticise their lives. Still, they had survived and accepted, and it is quite possible that in the ethnic fusion that remains startlingly evident among some inhabitants of the Wild Coast – of Bantu pastoralists and European and Oriental seafarers – traces of the two Anglo-Indian girls endure to this day.*

There would seem to have been still one more survivor. A strand from the Pondo traditions gives another haunting account of a female from the *Grosvenor*.

In 1905 James Stuart, a travelling magistrate who roamed across south-east Africa collecting oral history, was introduced to a man who, he noticed, spoke Zulu with a Pondo inflexion. Mahaya ka Nongqabana gave Stuart an account of Shaka's raids on the Pondo in the 1820s, which had led to the migration of his people, then explained that he was descended from a white woman from a ship 'wrecked at Lambasi near the Msikaba river'. Mahaya went on to relate the story of his ancestor:

> Men went to gather mussels and found a white girl and tended her. They reported this. 'We saw a white person with long hair, a wanderer or waif.' They said she had come out of an *uqwembe* [a wooden meat tray] not knowing what a ship was. The chief then told them to go and catch her on the beach. The girl cried. They escorted her back to the chief. . . . She lived on fowl's eggs chiefly. She then saw no harm was intended and was happy. The chief then looked out for an *umnumzana* [a clan head] who had much property. She was married off to Mbukwe and made a wife. She first bore Mxokwane, a boy, then Mntengwane, then a girl, Nqolisa. This European girl was afterwards searched for by her friends.

* One other account that speaks of two women survivors needs to be treated with caution. In 1796 an American ship, the *Hercules*, was run ashore near the Great Fish River by her captain Benjamin Stout. In his published narrative, he wrote of having questioned the natives who pointed out the *Grosvenor* wreck site and related how a chief 'insisted on taking two of the white ladies to his kraal . . . the captain and his people resisted and were destroyed.' Stout reported that although one of the women had died, the other still lived and had several children. But as the *Hercules* was lost well over 200 miles south of the *Grosvenor*, the whole story sounds apocryphal.

The identity of the girl is a mystery, but another of Stuart's informants takes the story on a wild leap. This was a grizzled old Pondoland character named William Bazley, a trader who had become fascinated with the *Grosvenor* and had made his own inquiries. He told Stuart it had become difficult to trace descendants of the castaways, but that forty years earlier he had met someone who he believed had actually been on the ship. She was

> a very old white woman living exactly as a native between Springvale and Highflats between 1860 and 1870, she being then about 86 years of age and speaking only Zulu . . . [Bazley] got full accounts of her having been saved from drowning and then concealed by natives. The relief party that came failed to find any of the [*Grosvenor*] survivors in consequence of natives being loath to deliver up wives so cheaply secured.

This elderly woman, according to Bazley, was Frances Hosea.

A wild leap indeed, then, but just plausible. The dates fit. When Bazley saw her, the old woman was living eighty miles north of the wreck. Although she spoke Zulu, that does not exclude the possibility that she had lived among the Pondo until Shaka's raids and, like other members of smaller tribes, been absorbed by a Zulu-speaking clan. It would be the most remarkable episode of the whole saga if Frances, born to an East India Company grandee in Bengal and aged two when she was shipwrecked, should have been taken in by an African tribe before being caught up in the cataclysm that gave rise to the Zulu kingdom.

There remains the troubling question raised by Van Reenen: who were the two other women he found living with Gquma and her tribe? Clearly Mary and Eleanor were too young; but is it just possible that the pair were not as elderly as he indicated – that they were from a more recent shipwreck, and that, having assimilated with natives, they were appalled at being discovered and begged that their secret should be preserved? Is it possible that they were Mary Hosea and Sophia James – the former now aged about forty, prematurely aged, the latter in her mid-fifties? On any objective assessment of the evidence the answer must be no, but then the story of the *Grosvenor* women is beyond the test of history. It has acquired the quality of legend.

19

GQUMA'S TRIBE

Eastern Cape frontier, 1820–35

Ingredients of shipwreck, mystery and the sufferings of gentry made the *Grosvenor* a natural subject for popular literature, art and drama. Carter's best-selling *Narrative* was widely used as a source of information, just as his original artwork was copied by artists such as Morland and Smirke. It bears repeating, however, that foremost in the public interest was that matter of the women and what they may, or may not, have endured. While Lydia, Mary and Sophia had not been the first European women to fall into the hands of 'savages', captivity had always involved deliverance and, as the years went by, it became clear that this time there would be no rescue. The complete disappearance of the *Grosvenor* women left unanswered the question raised in the first place, so that variations on the original fable – that their husbands had been murdered and they forced to become the wives of chiefs – continued to crop up well over a century later.

Their story inspired at least two novels and a musical drama – Dibdin's *Hannah Hewit, or the Female Crusoe* – as well as a good deal of fanciful journalism and some awesomely dire verse. In the fog of contradictory reports the line between fact and fantasy had become blurred, fostering a protean quality in new accounts. One purportedly factual narrative in a publication called *Chambers Repository* identified the trio of women passengers as 'the daughters of Colonel Campbell', thereby achieving the

George Cato's picture of Gquma's grandson

distinction of introducing to the *Grosvenor* characters from an entirely fictional creation – Jane Austen's *Emma*. Captain Frederick Marryat, author of seafaring adventure tales such as *Mr Midshipman Easy*, at least used real passengers' names in his novel *The Mission*.*

Such curiosities aside, the story of the *Grosvenor* women has a wider place in literary tradition. For the preceding two centuries the British had been engaging more closely with the outside world, simultaneously beguiled by its wonders and repelled by its strangeness, but rarely in charge of their own destinies. Since the beginning of the seventeenth century thousands of Britons, the vast majority of them seamen and soldiers, had found themselves taken captive from isolated settlements in North Africa and North America and at the mercy of people who were neither European nor Christian. As Linda Colley has written of the era: 'Britons *could* be slaves – and were.' Many were ransomed, some escaped, to return home and find that their experiences had become the stuff first of pamphlets and ballads, then of a new publishing phenomenon. Captivity narratives were the earliest best-sellers, relating the experiences of men enslaved by Barbary corsairs or taken hostage by American Indians. These parables of rescue by the Grace of God found an echo in another literary landmark. Before casting Robinson Crusoe away on a desert island, Defoe had him held a prisoner by Moors.

Female captives were, for obvious reasons, more rare but correspondingly more intriguing. One of the first was Mary Rowlandson, a Somerset woman whose narrative of three months as a prisoner of Wampanoag and other New England Indians was published in Massachusetts and London in 1682. Narratives concerning other settler captives of Native Americans enjoyed a huge vogue in Britain after 1750. These too tended to be tales of faith and redemption, but sentiment was by no means hostile to the

* Marryat's story concerns Sir Charles Wilmot, nearing the end of his life in the Berkshire countryside and deeply troubled by rumours that his castaway daughter, 'Elizabeth Wilmot', who has travelled on the *Grosvenor* with a Colonel and Mrs James, remains alive among the natives. His nephew, as a service to the old man, sets out on a mission to Africa, where he establishes that Elizabeth had in fact perished with the rest. He makes all haste back to Berkshire to tell Sir Charles 'that he has no grandchildren living the life of a heathen', upon which assurance the grateful old man, joining his hands above the bed-clothes, exclaims: 'Gracious Lord, I thank thee that this weight has been removed from my mind,' before expiring.

Indians, who were often viewed as fine, free spirits, a judgment with which even some of their victims concurred.

A change in the narrative emphasis was signalled by another woman. Elizabeth Marsh, the daughter of a naval official in Gibraltar, was held captive by Moroccan pirates for a few months in 1756, and thirteen years later published an account of her experiences that hinted at a certain romantic attachment with her princely captor, 'an elegant figure . . . finely shaped, of good complexion', who invited her to share his Marrakesh palace. Scholars such as Colley have suggested that this sexual chemistry was embellished, if not manufactured, for commercial purposes – Marsh's earlier drafts reflected a more traditional pattern of Christian faith in the face of Islamic persecution – in what was to be a durable prototype for romantic fiction. Reassuringly, in Marsh's case as with her successors, virtue invariably proved resilient in the face of the amorous sheikh. Coincidentally, the opera *Die Entfuhrung aus dem Serail* received its première in Vienna in the year of the *Grosvenor*'s last voyage, so Mozart's comic masterpiece about a pert English maiden named Blonde escaping from a sultan's harem was being launched just as the wreck spawned another shift in the captivity narrative.

In the *Grosvenor*, gentlewomen are visible for the first time as victims of an unmistakably 'other' sexual predator. This new genre has been described by one writer as pandering 'to that White male desire at once to relish and deplore, vicariously share and publicly condemn, the rape of White female innocence', and in truth it is hard to read the early newspaper reports without recognising a certain savage glee in the description of women being subjected to the 'vilest brutish prostitution'. Whatever the truth of their fate, the women would always be associated with sexual captivity. A preface to a new 1802 edition of Carter's *Narrative* failed to dispel this notion, despite noting that readers, 'long harassed with the belief that they had been doomed to worse than death among the natives', could take comfort from Van Reenen's findings.

'Doomed to worse than death among the natives' – the phrase speaks from another age with all its baggage of racial dominance, exclusivity and dread. In South Africa, where the *Grosvenor* long served whites as an illustration of the likely fate of those left to the mercy of Africans, it was to have a special potency. When the first officially sponsored band of English settlers set out for the Cape in 1820, many considered them mad as well as doomed: a George Cruikshank cartoon of the day showed them alighting to be devoured by cannibals or ravening beasts.

The reality was not all that different. Among the settlers was John Cantilivres Chase, a young man lured with his wife from London, only to be deposited on a frontier in a state of almost constant war with the Xhosa. Chase and his fellow settlers were part of a human buffer zone in the Eastern Cape set up by the new British administration. He spent five years farming along the Great Fish River, where the nabobs Williams and Taylor met their deaths, and at the end had little to show for it besides the hard-line views that he brought to his subsequent political career in the Cape legislative assembly and a knowledge of the *Grosvenor* that produced the following bit of doggerel about the women, called 'Our Fathers are Come':

The long long look'd for day, the dawn
I have dream'd of many a night,
Hath broken on this blessed morn
With its visions of delight
And ev'ry cherished fleeting form
Is now palpable to sight;

Haste! Let us leave this hated shore, where I must aye retain,
My memory of sorrow, and my sense of sin and shame.
For our long expected freedom, our day of joy's begun,
And we shall reach our lovely land, for at length Our Father's Come.

Why art thou wailing at my breast,
My Babe? And thou my eldest-born,
My boy of guilt, yet happiness,
For thou soothest me when forlorn,
Why art thou plucking at my dress?
Art thou wishing to be gone?

Ah No! I read the reason and it chills my heart to stone.
That thy native clime my children hath charms for thee alone,
And I must seek my sepulchre beneath your southern sun,
And I cannot flee this fated land, although Our Father's Come.

Another of the settlers had also drunk deeply of the *Grosvenor* story. William Shaw was a missionary, the pastor in charge of the volatile frontier district, and a man of energy and humanity. Conceiving a plan for a chain of missions to the native peoples reaching up the coast, through the Zulu country as far as Delagoa Bay, Shaw and his fellow Wesleyans went forth. And so the story of Gquma was revealed to them.

In 1827, the brethren at Wesley House in London received a letter from their most far-flung outpost, Butterworth, in the heart of the Xhosa country. Shaw reported on an encounter with a white drifter who said that no more than two days' journey away 'there is now residing a Caffre with a numerous family who is descended from one of the unhappy sufferers of the Grosvenor East Indiaman wrecked about 50 years ago. This female consented to marry a Caffre chief by whom she had a son who now succeeds his father; and from reverence to his mother's memory he is strongly attached to Englishmen.'

The brethren could recognise a sign from God, a summons to save the souls of people descended from Christian kindred. The fact that the chief had 'begged that a missionary be sent to his tribe' appeared no more than confirmation of a Divine purpose. Shaw's conclusions clinched the matter: 'It will really be a most surprising occurrence if the wreck of that ship which produced such sympathetic feeling for the poor sufferers should prove the means of opening the way for a Christian mission. Let us follow into the regions where the Lord is very evidently leading us.'

The man chosen to report back on this promising field of endeavour was William Shrewsbury. A blunt, pugnacious fellow from Kent, he had found the deafness of the Xhosa to the Word exasperating, but his expectations were raised by what he saw as he rode north. The Xhosa disdained to eat fish, but these natives were gathering mussels; in such a slender shred Shrewsbury was able to discern evidence 'of the *Grosvenor* and its unfortunate crew'. The landscape was magnificent. Nature seemed to have barricaded the region and penetration by wagons was impossible: 'Deep ravines, the sea, and rivers on each side – it appears to be marked out as a place of defence.'

On 27 August, two hours' ride west of the Umtata, Shrewsbury reached a kraal and was ushered into the presence of an elderly man – 'a complete Caffer in his habit and manners [but] of European countenance and features'. This striking figure had an aquiline nose, long hair and blue eyes. His name was Dapa.

> He is nearly seventy years of age. His mother died at a very advanced age, twelve or fourteen years ago. She had three sons and one daughter, of whom Dapa and his sister alone remain. On being introduced to him as his mother's countryman, he took hold of me with both hands and was almost frantic with joy. But his ignorance was so great that I could not learn his mother's English name, nor the name of the vessel in which she was wrecked. All he knew was that she was white, she was an English woman, that she had been shipwrecked, that she had been married to his father according to custom, and would never afterwards leave, and that she died and was buried in such a place.

The Wesleyans poring over Shrewsbury's account must have paused at this. Although he had avoided concluding that the old chief was not connected with the *Grosvenor*, it was obvious that if he was aged seventy, Dapa could not be descended from anyone shipwrecked a mere forty-five years earlier. Yet the fact remained that his mother had been English and that she had somehow occupied a pivotal place in the life of this tawny tribe of some 700 souls, the amaTshomane, who presented themselves as a heaven-sent bridge between Christianity and heathendom. For if one thing was clear from Shrewsbury's report it was the enthusiasm of the old chief to host a mission: 'Of the Christian religion he seems never to have heard a word. But his desire to have a Christian missionary exceeds everything I ever saw . . . They said "Oh, let him make haste and come and we will do everything he shall tell us to do. The country is before him."'

Though the brethren were not to know it, such keenness had more to do with the increasingly volatile political environment than with any instinctive response to the Gospel. Since 1824, the Zulu king Shaka had been responsible for a widening circle of warfare across the region, and the whites who had come among smaller chiefdoms calling themselves teachers were seen as representing a powerful outside agency that might be enlisted as an ally. Before a missionary could be appointed to the amaTshomane, however, Zulu *impis* overran the territory up to the Umtata, scattering all before them, including Dapa's little tribe. Not for another year did matters stabilise sufficiently for Shrewsbury to write: 'Praise the Lord! Dapa has a missionary appointed . . . The task of saving souls can begin.'

It was not that easy. No sooner had he arrived than the missionary William Shepstone found himself at the centre of a squabble between Dapa and his uncle Qanda over where the mission should be located. As he wrote home in bewilderment, each claimed a right of pre-eminence based on his association with 'the white queen':

> Qanda urges: 'Your mother was married to my brother; she returned to my care in her old age and by my kraal she was buried; and as the mission will spring out of her ashes, here must the missionary dwell.' He further appeals to the fact that he found Dapa's mother when she was wrecked on the coast.
>
> Dapa replies: 'The institution must be mine; I called for the missionary and he comes at my request.'
>
> 'But' rejoins the other, 'we are the counsellors of your father. Though you are descended from the Great Woman and are the chief, and an old man, you are nevertheless our child.

Eventually, a neutral site was chosen high on a hillside about two miles west of the wide Umtata and called Morley, a cool spot where the sun fell dappling through the surrounding trees. In May 1829 Shepstone preached his first sermon and, in his account of the occasion to Wesley House, paid dutiful observance to those whose misfortunes had provided this opportunity: 'It is truly affecting to see so many of the descendants of those white women, completely immersed in all the depths of heathen superstition.' Over the next few years, Shepstone and his successor Samuel Palmer were to piece together the connection between 'those white women' and 'the white queen'.

The white child had been aged about seven when she was found crying on the beach by a Bomvana clan whose *inkosi* was Tshomane. She had said only one word: 'Bess.' This was taken to be her name, and as such she was known when she was spoken of to Europeans; but the name given to her was Gquma, meaning Roar of the Sea.* The year was around 1750.

Of her childhood years nothing is known but as she approached puberty her marriage prospects were despaired of, for it was said: 'What chief would marry a frog, a thing that comes out of the water?' But she did find a chief. Tshomane himself took her into his *umzi*, and although it is not clear whether she actually became his wife, after his death she married his son and successor, Sango. From a frog, she was turned into a princess.

She bore Sango three sons, Mlawu, Gela and Dapa, and a daughter who was named Bessie after her. As the great wife of an *inkosi* – it would appear that contrary to custom she was Sango's only spouse – she was honoured with the title *inkosozane*. Sango, moreover, 'was more than ordinarily attached to her and therefore constituted her head of his household, which gave her great power and influence'.

She was held in no less esteem by the meek and lowly. One said: 'When our eyes saw Gquma, the hungry were always fed.' Such is the substance of oral history, and if it has a whiff of idealised memory, it is still consistent with another depiction of her as a much-celebrated matriarch:

> She used to dress in native costume, twisting or plaiting her hair into cords which extended to her waist, and covered or rubbed over with red clay. It was on account of her remarkable beauty that even to this day the people when reciting her eulogies use the expression, '*Izinkabi zikaDawa*', ie the oxen of the white lady.

Her husband's death is not recorded. Their son Mlawu was designated his successor, but he died young and his eldest son, Cetani, was nominated. Something of a power struggle ensued in which Gquma played a crucial part. As in many conservative patriarchal systems, the coastal tribes were comfortable with powerful women, and she would appear to have become the guiding figure behind the emergence of Dapa as chief. Signs of this rivalry were still visible when the missionaries arrived to witness Dapa and Qanda disputing her legacy.

* The combination of the letters 'g' and 'q' indicates the characteristic fricative click of Xhosa, so Gquma is rendered Cl'ooma. According to some versions of the story she was not alone when found, being accompanied by two or three men said to be her brothers and a dark woman, an Indian maid. The men married and had numerous descendants but played no significant part in the future of the tribe.

At the time of the *Grosvenor* wreck Gquma was aged about fifty, and when Van Reenen arrived nine years later, she remained the dominant personality of her people. She 'lived to a good old age and went down to the grave full of days', being buried with all her trinkets in around 1815, near the Umgazana River. To the last, Van Reenen and his companions were the only whites ever to meet her, and despite the power of that description – 'the three old women in the kraals of the *bastaards* ... were deeply moved when we arrived to see people of their race, and likewise when we left them' – his account is frustratingly unrevealing about this fascinating figure.

The missionaries arrived too late to make up for Van Reenen's omissions, but they established these few facts of Gquma's life, as well as her connection with females from the *Grosvenor* – although some of the amaTshomane were reluctant to discuss the wreck. When Dapa was questioned, he said that he recalled it; but on being pressed his answers became 'confused and unsatisfactory'. His nephew, Cetani, was more forthcoming, confirming that the tribe had indeed absorbed other white females:

> Two seem either to have married persons of inferior rank, or to have been wives of an inferior order, for very little is now known concerning them or their offspring. When cast ashore, the females were all young.

This clear allusion to Mary Wilmot and Eleanor Dennis offers an explanation for the relative silence of the oral traditions about them: that in a society dominated by the figure of Gquma, they were minor personalities.

Gquma's daughter Bessie added another small but important piece to the jigsaw. Bessie – who, like her brother Dapa, had a distinctly European cast to her features – had burst into tears the first time she saw whites, saying they looked like her mother. She it was who, on being visited by Shaw, said that 'she distinctly recollected the wreck of the Grosvenor' and whites who 'came out of the ship as if a whole nation'. Some, she related, had been murdered – a reason perhaps for a discreet silence being maintained over the episode; but, as we have seen, she went on to say that 'the female as well as some female children were spared' and many of their descendants remained alive.

*

For all the optimism with which it was launched and the loveliness of its situation, Morley sorely disappointed the Wesleyans. In its eight-year existence it was once engulfed in flames as tribal warfare again spilled across the countryside and once hit by famine. More significantly, it failed to win souls.

The increasingly frail Dapa visited rarely, and it became plainer that his enthusiasm to receive a missionary had been a political strategy. The brethren remained fond of the old chief, although Palmer confessed that he was deeply distressed to have 'the son of an Englishwoman ask me for rain'. He tellingly spelt out the gulf of misunderstanding between missionary and African: 'When I directed him to pray to God for it he replied "Why does God not come and show himself and then I could ask him much better?"'

In his dotage, Dapa was invited to the mission school and told how delighted his mother's family in England would be that the 200 or so children were learning to read; privately the missionaries acknowledged that 'it all appeared a mystery to him'. They kept their hopes up to the end, relating of Dapa's last visit that he 'endeavoured in the best way he could with his quivering lips and faltering voice to sing the Doxology to the Trinity'.

Dapa died in about 1835 and was buried at Morley under Christian rite, so there was at least one small gravestone to show for its existence before the station was abandoned that same year. It was Palmer who closed the school door for the last time. He had expected the descendants of Europeans to be more receptive, but in the end the Word had met with the same bafflement as shown by the majority of Africans. His account of a conversation with Bessie provides a further touching insight into this failure of understanding:

> When I directed her to pray to God she asked 'Where does God live? How can I pray to him when I don't know where he is?' I enquired if her mother never talked to her about God and as tho' ashamed of her mother's negligence she said 'I was too young when my mother died to recollect.'
>
> I replied, that cannot be as your son was a young man at the time of your mother's death. Finding that I knew this, she said 'Why did she not? I am her child and God is a person my mother knew. I think

> she had so much to do with the law (politics) that she forgot God. You must call her up again. Why did God let her die?'
>
> Oh! How painful to behold one so old and the daughter of a European thus as dark as midnight!

Bessie herself seems to have died around 1840. Visual evidence of her family's existence might have died with her but for an encounter near Lambasi in 1853. A Natal pioneer named George Cato was visiting the site of the *Grosvenor* wreck when he came upon a man aged between fifty and sixty with European features. Cato arranged for him to be taken to Durban in order to be photographed. Although his name was never established, he said that he was the grandson of a white woman named Betsy, a child when she was cast away. It would seem therefore that he was Gqubile, a son of Bessie and grandson of Gquma.

Any attempt to establish Gquma's identity must start with the ship in which she was a passenger. Almost fifty years ago, Professor Percival Kirby invited researchers to follow up his theory that she had been on an Indiaman wrecked between 1720 and 1750; and, further, that some indications of her being accompanied by an *ayah* showed they were homeward bound from India.

A search of the Company's shipping records produces one vessel that fits these criteria: the *Normanton,* an Indiaman of 490 tons, commanded by Captain Reginald Keyes, sailed from Madras on 18 January 1740 on her homeward voyage and simply disappeared.

If the search is widened to include outward-bound East Indiamen, another vessel comes into view. On 30 January 1748 the *Dolphin,* under Captain George Newton, sailed from the Downs in Kent for the Coromandel Coast and Bengal. The Company's register of lost ships records her fate tersely: 'Not heard of again.'

Either the *Normanton* or the *Dolphin* could have been carrying the little girl, but an element of sailors' lore points to the latter. It may be recalled that this narrative began with another East Indiaman wreck, that of the *Dodington* on Bird Island in Algoa Bay in 1755. In the few minutes left to him before he was swept to his death, Captain James Samson, in trying to account for what had happened to his ship, told the chief mate, 'that this must be the rock the *Dolphin* was lost upon, and no one spar'd to tell their fate'. It is stretching the bounds of credibility too far to suggest that two

Indiamen came to grief on precisely the same uncharted island, but Samson's words indicate mariners had reason to believe that the *Dolphin* had been lost somewhere off the coast of south-east Africa. She had, it would seem, arrived safely at her Atlantic port, in the Canary or Cape Verde islands, before proceeding around the Cape of Good Hope and vanishing.

The lists of passengers for both the *Normanton* and the *Dolphin* were lost with their logs and searches of other records to establish the names of those on board have been unavailing. Without such information it must be concluded that Gquma's European identity is now beyond discovery.

Pondo tradition has always held to another improbable coincidence – that Gquma was shipwrecked at Lambasi, exactly the same spot as the *Grosvenor*. This sounds like the kind of conflation to which oral history is understandably prone, given that both events cast up white strangers. The amaTshomane kraal was located beyond the formidable natural barrier of the Umzimvubu, and I would suggest that Bess's ship was actually wrecked about 50 miles south of the *Grosvenor*. Some Pondo accounts speak of other individuals coming from the sea at the same time as well: these stories are inconsistent and contradictory – one, for example, suggests that Bess was accompanied by her father, another that she had a maid, hence the suggestion of an *ayah*, yet another that there were three young men – sailors perhaps – who were called Bati, Jekwa and Hati, and who also joined her tribe.*

Gquma's people started to break up in the mid-nineteenth century, after an attack by another coastal clan. One section retained the name amaTshomane and settled near the Umtata. The other moved west to the Bashee where they were long known as the abeLungu, or 'the whites', before they drifted apart and assimilated with other tribes. However, such was Gquma's reputation among the Nguni-speaking people that three generations later her female descendants continued to be sought as brides for chiefs. In the royal lines of the Pondo and Bomvana they were especially favoured. One tribal elder told a government commission in 1881

* Another mixed-race people linked with shipwreck castaways made their home in the vicinity of the Umgazi and were known as the amaMholo; they were darker-skinned and appear to have been descended from lascars and other Asian people, including slaves escaped from the Cape, such as Trout.

that this was 'because these people are regarded as wise and friendly to the white people'. As a result, the European features and pale skins noted in the past century by anthropologists to be commonly found among the Pondo in particular, remain evident in individuals along the coast to this day.

Some of Gquma's descendants achieved a wider prestige. One of Dapa's daughters, for example, Nonibe, married Mdushane, a son of the great Xhosa chief Ndlambe, and used her influence to protect white missionaries and traders caught up in the conflict of 1835, usually known as the Sixth Frontier War.

Another descendant, Nosepesi, a daughter of Dapa's son Cawo, married the Tembu king Ngangelizwe. What makes this particularly remarkable is that in the process this woman, a great-granddaughter of Gquma, joined the bloodline that produced Nelson Mandela.

This is not to suggest a direct connection between the South African statesman and an English child castaway. The section of the Tembu royal house to which Nelson Rolihlahla Mandela is affiliated comes from his grandfather, Mandela, while the paramount's line is descended from the original Mandela's brother, Mthikrakra. Nosepesi, in short, joined a different line of the royal house. Moreover, although she married Mthikrakra's son, Ngangelizwe, she was not the great wife who produced the next king, Dalindyebo. However, on the early death of the latter, his son, Jongintaba, became regent, and offered to act as guardian to the future South African President when he was orphaned at the age of nine. So after the young Mandela moved from his first home at Qunu to the Tembu great place, where he spent his teen years in the 1930s, with companions from other sections of the royal house, ploughing, shepherding and, as he recorded in his memoirs, downing birds with a slingshot, he would have had about him descendants of the little girl lost here almost two centuries earlier.

20

'WHEN THE LONG TRICK'S OVER'

I must go down to the seas again, to the vagrant gypsy life,
To the gull's way and the whale's way where the wind's like a whetted knife;
And all I ask is a merry yarn from a laughing fellow-rover
And quiet sleep and a sweet dream when the long trick's over.

From 'Sea Fever', by John Masefield

London, 1783–c.1820

On returning to London, the surviving seamen all received a gratuity from the Company of £3 12s, the equivalent of four months' wages. For penniless men, long without grog or bawds, this was a tidy sum, for which the taverns and brothels of Wapping would have been the natural outlet. It was not, however, sufficient to start a new life and most of the men had no option but to return to the sea. Epic events lay ahead in British seafaring, and one is bound to wonder whether, when Nelson's fleet engaged the French in the 1790s, some of the old *Grosvenor* hands were there, willingly or not.

John Hynes, that man of Limerick whose first experience of the sea had been in the *Grosvenor*, having joined Coxon's crew at Dublin in 1779 after a mass desertion, was soon back in the ratlines. On Christmas Eve 1785, now an experienced hand, rated able, he signed on the *Manship*, an Indiaman of 812 tons making her maiden voyage to Bengal. The *Manship*'s captain, Charles Gregorie, was a capable officer and the biggest fuss in the six-month journey before they sighted the Indian coast was caused by the

Saturday Night at Sea, cartoon by George Cruikshank

seaman who was caught 'trying to sodomise two of the Company's young recruits' and forced to run a gauntlet of knotted ropes.

Hynes had meanwhile been sought out by one of the ship's passengers, one George Carter, an artist bound for Bengal. Like everyone else, Carter had been gripped by the *Grosvenor* drama and was intrigued to hear that one of the survivors was on board. Introducing himself, Carter first drew Hynes into his confidence and then, for the remainder of the voyage, occupied the long, empty hours when the sailor was off duty by questioning him about those events. Later, in his cabin, Carter would write up his notes and sketch the scenes described by Hynes. As he related later, to test the sailor's veracity he would go back on an incident described earlier, and 'found that the sad impression seemed so deeply engraven on his mind that he invariably told the same artless tale'. Carter also raised the subject at the dinner table and questioned Captain Gregorie about the options that had faced John Coxon. The consensus among the officers was that the *Grosvenor*'s commander had blundered at almost every step in a way that was 'not to be accounted for'.

Just as they approached Balasore Roads, south of Calcutta, at the end of what appeared to have been an entirely uneventful voyage, the *Manship* struck a sandbank and stuck fast. The tide was high, a fresh gale blew up, and as the Indiaman shook from stem to stern it suddenly appeared that a further disaster was unfolding. She was 'beating with such violence', Carter recalled, 'that every moment she was expected to go to pieces and the masts to tumble about our ears, when every soul would in all probability have perished'. The *Manship* was a stout vessel, however – another six voyages lay ahead of her – and within an hour she had worn free. Asked by Carter how he felt, Hynes said he had been convinced that this time his number really was up and that even if he had reached the shore, 'he must inevitably have perished on the fangs of a tyger'.

The crew was to spend five months in India and at some point, while on shore leave, Hynes was astonished to be reunited with one of his old shipmates, another survivor from the *Grosvenor*, Barney Leary. How the young ox of the Indiaman came to be in Calcutta is a matter of speculation. He had not been heard of since his mumbling appearance before Dalrymple's inquiry three years earlier, but he must have signed on to another Indiaman, only perhaps to find a regime not to his liking. Here he was, in any event, in a foreign port, seeking a passage home. Hynes was able to reassure him that Gregorie ran a tight but fair ship, and when the *Manship* sailed from Kedgeree Roads on 12 October 1786, she was carrying not just one former *Grosvenor* hand, but two.

Her passage home was the kind of voyage that old sailors would talk about with fondness after a lifetime at sea. The season was fine, the white clouds scudding across the lonely sea and the sky. Not a single unruly event marked the *Manship*'s course as she arched against the wind in a south-westerly direction across the Indian Ocean with 'the wheel's kick and the wind's song and the white sail's shaking'. Day after day, Gregorie made the same unadorned entry in the log: 'Pleasant weather.' He wrote these words on 1 February as she entered the latitude 31° 15′s. When the *Manship* passed Lambasi over the horizon the following day, Hynes and Leary were in all probability unaware of it.

They arrived back in England on 5 May. Leary's wages for the voyage from Calcutta were £8 15s 11d. Having made the full round trip, Hynes was paid off in the sum of £21 5s 6d. That was a substantial amount and, although no more is heard of either man after that, it may be hoped that Hynes, at least, had seen enough of the world and the dangers in it to carry his experiences off to a contemplative life in Limerick.

Carter, of course, followed them back to England the following year and turned his hand to the best-selling *Narrative of the Loss of the Grosvenor*, published in 1791. He was gracious enough to acknowledge on the title-page that his account had been . . .

COMPILED FROM THE EXAMINATION OF
JOHN HYNES, one of the Unfortunate Survivors

. . . though whether the sailor received any more tangible reward for his contribution is not recorded.

Of the other survivors, we may surmise that Francisco di Lasso returned to his native Genoa and Francisco Feancon to Venice. Of Robert Price, the captain's servant, and Thomas Lewis, nothing can be said. Like the spirits of their dead shipmates, they simply vanished.

John Warmington, the bosun's mate, returned to his native Cornwall. Alone among the survivors, Warmington had a wife to go home to, having wed Elizabeth Roberts in their village, St Columb Minor, a few months before joining the *Grosvenor*. Warmington, the oldest and most experienced of the survivors, had been desperate enough to propose cannibalism as a last resort on the march, the effects of which would appear to have done lasting harm to his health. He lived only three years longer, dying short of his thirty-fourth birthday.

Jeremiah Evans, a doughty fellow and one fiercely loyal to his mates – he had joined the first rescue party to search for survivors and complained bitterly when Muller turned back before reaching the wreck – was yet completely unwarlike. (It will be recalled that he told the boy Price he feared being pressed into the Navy.) Having been enchanted by the coastal country beyond the Tsitsikama forest, he applied successfully to the Dutch authorities for permission to stay at the Cape and was made a grant of land along the Krom River, near Cape St Francis. Here he farmed for some years but not for the remainder of his life, for at some point he returned to England. He did in any event avoid a violent end with Nelson's Navy, dying aged forty-six at Stanford le Hope, Essex, in 1810, five years after the Battle of Trafalgar.

On his arrival in London, William Habberley duly visited the house in Walthamstow owned by John Williams. His widow, Sarah, was no doubt moved to hear from the young seaman how he had guided her husband and her brother, George Taylor, almost to safety before the onslaught of the Xhosa. According to her descendants, she never recovered from that double loss, but she had been left an extremely wealthy woman, with an estate of £20,000 from her husband's will alone, as well as a large collection of china and oriental curiosities from his travels, and it does not seem unduly cynical to suggest that Habberley felt he was entitled to some recognition for his pains in the nabobs' service. He may not have been Sarah's only caller from the *Grosvenor*, nor the only one to go away with some consideration, for the family recalled that 'sailors used to come down to Walthamstow to give accounts of what they remembered' of those events.

Whatever his reward, William remained in need of employment and, although a young man of bright confidence and some education, all he knew was the sea. For lack of any other facts it may be concluded that he went back to it, but as he does not appear on the register of Indiamen officers, he would seem to have plied his trade on other routes. He may even have joined the Navy. Nothing is heard of him for fifteen years and so lengthy a gap would be consistent with either a seafaring life or another career in foreign parts.

When, in 1797, he reappeared, it was in Bethnal Green, a rather less salubrious part of London than his shabbily respectable former home of Finsbury. On an early spring day in April he attended the christening at the Church of St Matthew of his first child by Elizabeth Galloway – a daughter, Sophia. The fact that they were not married did nothing to deter the couple from having a second child – a son, William – born at home in Stepney the following year. At this point William thought it only proper to make a respectable woman of Elizabeth and on 23 November 1800 they were married at St Dunstan's.

William was forty at the time, Elizabeth twenty-five. She was from Wapping, an ill-favoured area frequented by sailors, notorious for harlotry and the execution of men found guilty of high crimes at sea. But if Elizabeth had narrowly escaped a career as what Peter Ackroyd refers to as one of the 'sailors' women, inured to immorality from childhood, rotten with disease', she and Habberley were nevertheless to enjoy a comparatively long, stable and above all fertile marriage. They had eight children in all – two girls and six boys – the last, George, being born in 1811.

Some time around this date, perhaps encouraged by other old seamen who had heard his tales in the taverns of London's docklands, William began a memoir. (The period is known because the paper on which he wrote was watermarked 1809.) Using his testimony to Dalrymple as a framework, he sat down to produce a retrospective journal, which he entitled *Loss of the Grosvenor Indiaman*. Even after Carter's *Narrative* there remained a public appetite for the subject and there can be little doubt that Habberley intended his own work for a wider audience.

It remains a powerful document. For all his clumsy prose, his tendency to dwell on the mundane while being parsimonious with detail about the greater human drama of which he was a part, Habberley's is the only first-hand narrative of the saga from the time that the *Grosvenor* sailed from Madras to his arrival in London eighteen months later. Within its 225 pages are a vivid account of the wreck and moving details of his life among tribal people. One may picture him, a patriarch surrounded by children beside the fire on a winter's night, his seafaring days done and old age approaching, recalling a far-off time and a sun-kissed African shore that had been both brutal and benign to an English youth.

At times he appeared to be almost consciously imitating *Robinson Crusoe*. Precisely the same fears enunciated by Defoe's hero, 'that I should be devoured by wild beasts, murdered by savages or starved to death for want of food', are those that recur throughout Habberley's journal. He would also have been an unusual survivor if he had not embellished his experiences but, as the reader may recognise from the many extracts used in the present narrative, his tone was phlegmatic and where exaggeration occurred it was generally in overstating the frequency of the episodes involving wild beasts or savages, rather than embroidering the substance of what occurred. There is corroborative evidence for almost everything he described, apart from one crucial event.

Habberley was the only witness to the deaths of the nabobs. The young seaman had pinned hopes of a life-changing reward on bringing them home and one is bound to wonder whether he embellished his account of this episode. Human nature being what it is, it would not be surprising, or even very discreditable, if – Williams and Taylor having perished, like so many others, of privation – Habberley fabricated a band of murderous Xhosa in order to cast himself in a particularly creditable light and redeem his reward. That said, the Fish River cited by him as the site of the attack was indeed an area of high tension at the time, and the scene where he wrote of taking shelter in the dunes with George Taylor is just as he described it, so there is no particular reason to doubt his story.

In many respects, Habberley was an improbable hero. Unlike Crusoe, he was under no illusion of being in charge of his own destiny. Crusoe's native, when he appears on the scene, is a compliant inferior, eager to learn from the man he calls 'Master'. Habberley's natives were always in charge, whether as his tormentors or the means of his salvation. Habberley himself is invariably on the back foot, grateful just to survive another day, wary of the next.

In effect, Habberley created a captivity narrative of his own, one quite unsung. His vicissitudes, a wanderer beset by events, persecuted on all sides until, a solitary fugitive, he comes upon a society willing to accept him, recall not Crusoe but Jonathan Swift's Gulliver. Like Gulliver – Linda

Colley's model in her study of the forgotten captives of early Empire – Habberley had ventured abroad but won 'no conquests, or riches, or easy complacencies: only terror, vulnerability, and repeated captivities'; but whereas Gulliver is the eternal victim, in turn a slave and a sideshow spectacle among his captors, Habberley shared enough of ordinary life among the Xhosa to recognise their common humanity and to report faithfully what he had found.

When he died is not known, but he fathered the last of his children when he was fifty-one, which itself was not a bad age for a seamen of his time, so he lived for at least thirty years after the wreck that had accounted for so many of his shipmates. He certainly predeceased Elizabeth, who died aged sixty-three at Shoreditch in 1837.

William did not find a publisher and his exploits were forgotten, even by his descendants. His handwritten journal, *Loss of the Grosvenor Indiaman*, a quarto volume in cardboard covers, attracted no further attention until it came to light on the shelves of a London antiquarian book dealer in 1940. It was acquired by Richard Currie, a South African collector, who presented it to the Durban Museum. Fortunately, it came to the attention of Professor Percival Kirby, who arranged its publication in 1953. But for this foresight, Habberley's record would be not only unknown but lost to the world. In the course of researching this book, I visited the Durban Museum and asked to see it. The staff were unable to find it in the vaults. Records showed that it had been put on display in 1987 but had not been noted since. Further searches were unavailing and it must be concluded that this little-known but valuable narrative has been mislaid or stolen.

Of course, all the castaways were in the end captives – not of hostage-takers or ransom-seekers, but of the shore on which they were wrecked and which allowed just thirteen out of 140 of them to escape. Even Gquma and the other women, offered a return to their own past, evidently recognised that, having become a part of Africa themselves, there could be no going back.

The story began with the Hoseas, so it is apt that it should end with them. When William and Mary left Calcutta in haste with Frances and Tom Chambers, they left their newborn baby Charlotte in the care of

Tom's parents, Sir Robert and Fanny Chambers. 'The little Hosea', as Charlotte was called, remained with them for some years and is glimpsed in the pages of correspondence, for example accompanying them on a visit to Benares. Sir Robert and Fanny returned to Europe in 1799, where he died in Paris four years later. Fanny, still a beautiful woman, survived him by thirty-six years. Shortly before her death, in 1839, aged eighty-one, she catalogued and published his Sanskrit manuscript collection with a personal memoir that recalled their shared grief at the death of their eldest son Tom in the loss of the *Grosvenor*, still 'too well remembered by many families'. Their last connection with 'the little Hosea' seems to have been arranging for her to be sent back to England shortly before she turned eight, for in February 1790 Captain John Dempster of the Indiaman *Rose* wrote to Lady Chambers from St Helena: 'Your dear little Charlotte is on shore with me & in the most perfect health. She has slept in my cabin the whole voyage.'

Some years later a Bengali aristocrat named Mirza abu Taleb Khan embarked on a tour of Europe, visiting acquaintances from Calcutta and taking in the sights, of which he wrote an account, later translated into English. He was a frequent caller at the London home of Sir Theophilus Metcalfe, an old nabob and director of the Company, being drawn there by a young woman of 'angelic qualities'. On a summer's evening in 1798, abu Taleb visited Sir Theophilus and his family at their country residence near Windsor, and as they sat outside under an oak tree drinking tea, his eyes fell again on this lovely girl. When Lady Metcalfe remarked that the tree beneath which they sat was not very tall for one of its species, the Bengali was moved to declaim that he would outreach the tree if he could only spend as much time in Miss Hosea's company as it did. This gallantry produced much laughter and applause.

Charlotte Hosea had recently turned sixteen. Her godfather, Sir Theophilus, had stood at her hastily organised christening on 2 February 1782, the day before her parents had left Calcutta on their fatal journey. Her future after being orphaned had been uncertain, abu Taleb wrote, until Sir Theophilus 'afforded her an asylum in his house'. The patronage of such a man – as well as being a director of the Company Sir Theophilus had fathered a future Governor General of India – would secure Charlotte the comforts of privilege, access to the best circles and, in time, a good marriage. Before leaving Bengal, Mary Hosea had declared with more truth than she knew that to be separated from her children would be the death of her, but whatever their mistakes in those mad, desperate weeks early in 1782, she and William had decided for the best in leaving their baby daughter behind. Charlotte, at least, had escaped the captive shore.

EPILOGUE

I visited the Wild Coast three times in the course of writing this book, starting with a walk in the castaways' footsteps and ending with a final visit to the wreck site on the occasion of an aptly ferocious storm. In the first instance, I was hoping that studying the location would help to explain the survivors' actions for, in the nature of such accounts, they were sparing with detail and especially niggardly in describing terrain. As it happened, it was not simply the landscape that came to my assistance, but the seasons, the elemental nature of the place, its flora and fauna, its inhabitants – in short, its very spirit.

Walking the coast, I had thought, would be a stiff but fairly straightforward hike. While I knew better than to imagine a stroll along a long, sunny stretch of beach, my expectations did not go beyond rocky headlands, a few steep inclines, the occasional detour. Skirting the sea was an agreeably simple concept. Fortunately, my companion Alan had walked the Wild Coast previously and disabused me, but once we started it quickly became apparent that even knowing the place did not preclude mistakes. The sea was frequently lost to view and, after scrambling through forests and clambering down gorges, there were occasions when Alan too had difficulty regaining his bearings. Always there were the rivers; many were shallow enough to wade, but some had to be swum with rucksacks floated on makeshift rafts, and some – the Umzimvubu, the Umsikaba – could only be

The inlet where the stern section of the *Grosvenor* was washed in, carrying with it the passengers and most of the crew crossed after boatmen ghosted out from the far bank and ferried us over. Repeatedly I was humbled to find how easy it would have been for anyone lost here – exhausted, demoralised – simply to lie down and die. While it would be mistaken to characterise the castaways' march as a survival epic, the fact that so few reached the Cape speaks for itself.

Not every aspect of the most fearsome section – the forty or fifty miles on either side of the Umzimvubu – was intimidating. One golden afternoon, at the Umkambati, we turned inland and after a few hundred yards came upon a place of magic, a large pool at the foot of a waterfall, surrounded by a bank of sheer red sandstone and surmounted by forest. We stripped and swam, then climbed among the rocks to a cave where, it was reputed, a modern-day fugitive had spent years scavenging and hiding from the law until, his transgression forgotten, he was able to return unnoticed to society. Naked and basking on the rocks, I could imagine no more idyllic place of exile.

But the mood of the landscape could shift as swiftly as the light. I returned to Lambasi whenever I could, as if deeper association with the place might bring me closer to the spirits of the castaways. One balmy blue day early in September, when the wind switched abruptly from the north-east to the south-west and a black mountain bearing thunderbolts surged out of the Indian Ocean in a matter of minutes, obliterating the landscape in a storm of such force that roads along the coast were washed away and towns left stranded for days, it became again a terrifying place.

I wandered the rocks on to which the *Grosvenor* had been swept by the waves, where the Hoseas and the rest had clambered to safety, drenched and stunned by their miraculous deliverance. Absurdly, I found myself repeatedly scanning the place – for was that not the *precise* spot where the broken Indiaman grounded? – as if in hope that concentration could bring the figures to life before my eyes. Instead, the sea's mocking timelessness made them more distant, so it became possible to imagine that the wreck had not happened at all and that that scene, of waves boiling ceaselessly over the rocks, was all there had ever been. I climbed the hills behind, where the Tezani wove its trail among forests that had offered shelter to John Bryan, and was beguiled again. It was after the sun had disappeared, when its last glow had drained away and the endless Indian Ocean had been replaced by the endless Milky Way, and the green slopes by the phantasmagoric flickerings of glow-worms, that the imagination began to work. Then I would start a fire, not so much for warmth as for the pulse of an element that I might control, and so create an illusion of power against all that is unseen, mysterious and frightening.

Here, too, I found the relics of the final part of the *Grosvenor*'s story.

Beside the Tezani, where the seamen slept on the night of the wreck, a handful of cottages mark the pinprick on the map known today as Port Grosvenor. They are used by fishermen, who come as much for the solitude as the sport and who make their way down by four-wheel drive from Lusikisiki, a country town and seat of Mpondombini Sigcau, King of the Eastern Pondo. A fifteen-minute walk along the coast from the cottages lies the rusting carcass of a steam winch. Nearby is another oddity, a tunnel that peters out about fifty feet down towards the sea. They are all that remain of a treasure hunt as madcap as it was misconceived, a tawdry postscript to the great drama that spawned it.

It began innocently enough with a Norfolk man named Sidney Turner, the skipper of a small coaster, who put in at Lambasi in 1880. The site had not been disturbed since Bryan used to comb it for steel and copper, and the seas had done their work. Walking among the rocks, Turner came upon an assortment of wreckage. No less than nine ship's cannon had been dredged up from the seabed, along with pigs of ballast, broken porcelain, crockery and personal oddments such as shoe buckles. Turner found coins as well – star pagodas and gold mohurs – and on his arrival in Durban the press pricked up its ears. The *Natal Mercantile Advertiser* reported that the *Grosvenor* had 'had much treasure in gold on board'. This seed, so casually found and tossed on the ground, would yield a mighty crop of speculative ventures.

Turner sailed back to Lambasi, to which he gave the name Port Grosvenor, with a large quantity of dynamite. A ridge of rocks running down to the sea – identifiable as the 'cliff' portrayed by artists – was blasted to pieces in the hope that it would somehow reveal real treasure; but if the landscape was transformed, Turner's fortunes were not.

A hint of things to come was glimpsed in a venture launched soon after Turner left the scene scattered with rubble. Alfred Raleigh, an enterprising Natal fraudster, used a treasure chart, a personal hypnotist and a child medium to persuade personal investors to put up money to find the *Grosvenor* gold. At seances, the mesmerised medium announced that he could see boxes of gold and kegs of silver. How this escapade might have developed can only be imagined, as Raleigh's explorations at Port Grosvenor were interrupted by envoys from the Pondo paramount, who said the place was sacred and ordered him to clear off.

On the strength of a few gold coins, however, the *Grosvenor* was now established in the public mind as a 'treasure ship'. In 1905 a consortium of Johannesburg businessmen launched the first salvage operation, the Grosvenor Recovery Syndicate, to win 'all the treasure whether in bullion, precious stones, bar gold or silver bars' in the Indiaman. Over the next six years, this syndicate and its successor, the Grosvenor Treasure Recovery Syndicate, attempted without success to locate the wreck. A steam winch was transported to the site, where it proceeded to rust, and a dredger was hired, which ran aground. By 1911 not so much as a trace of the Indiaman's hull had been produced as evidence to warrant further expenditure.

It made no difference. Over the next fifty years investors were to be repeatedly fleeced through a series of bogus investment schemes marked on the one hand by breathtaking audacity and on the other by an astonishing willingness to be gulled. Although venture after venture brought only failure and ruin, credulity continued to work hand in glove with cupidity. Only swindlers ever turned a profit out of the *Grosvenor*.

This lemming-like instinct was fostered by the remoteness of the site. Fanciful reports could be issued in Johannesburg about the progress being made at that distant spot, with little risk that investors would go to the lengths required for a personal inspection. The spectacular fraud of the Grosvenor Bullion Syndicate, launched in 1921 by a man named Martin Luther Webster, demonstrated this in emphatic fashion. Webster produced an archive of documents, purportedly from the India Office, including a bill of lading and extracts from Captain Coxon's log. The fact that these might have been expected to be at the bottom of the sea did not deter would-be shareholders impressed by Coxon's note, seemingly urging investment from beyond the grave and citing nineteen boxes of precious stones 'stored in the strong room beneath my cabin', along with more than 2,000 bars of gold and silver 'in the bottom of the lazaretto'. The treasure, said to be worth £1,714,710 in 1782 was impressive enough; but it was nothing to the mind-boggling method proposed to retrieve the trove. Claiming that 'it would be a waste of money to attempt it from the surface', Webster anounced triumphantly that a tunnel would be bored below the seabed, to come up inside the submerged hull.

Those who hastened to subscribe for the 700,000 shares at a shilling each came from around the world and included Sir Arthur Conan Doyle, creator of Sherlock Holmes and no stranger to woolly fairy tales. Encouraging reports came in thick and fast: the tunnel had advanced 180 feet; it was within 150 feet of the hull. Share values rocketed. Then silence. After a year all Webster could produce was a small piece of timber, supposedly from the hull. Examination showed that it was not even oak.

The press's role in this sorry tale was an inglorious one, reflecting a consistent willingness to publish uncritically each new fatuous claim for the sake of a good yarn. At this stage, however, the *Rand Daily Mail* sensed a rat and sent an investigator to visit the site. He was scathing, reporting that the 'tunnel' turned out to be little more than a hole in the ground. That ought to have sunk the venture, but just then a sensational story, planted in a rival publication, announced that the *Grosvenor* had been carrying 'two of the Golden Peacocks looted from Delhi . . . worked in the most priceless stones'. These objects, worth £5 million, had been 'imbedded in concrete, placed in brass-bound chests and smuggled into the hold of the ship by some important official on board'. A new myth had been floated, and was soon breezing along under full sail: nothing less than the Peacock Throne of the Great Moghuls was lying off Pondoland. (Sadly, the throne no longer existed, having been broken up by the Persian conqueror Nadir Shah after he sacked Delhi in 1739.) Only in the 1960s, when the last band of tricksters was arrested – they had produced a map engraved on copper by none other than John Bryan, 'which indicates the exact position of the *Grosvenor*' – did the penny finally drop among gullible speculators.*

* The most intriguing and sophisticated tactic used by the various fraudsters attracted to the *Grosvenor* involved a letter on cream paper, supposedly written by Captain Coxon to the directors of the Company stating: 'The list of bars should read 720 gold bars – not 270 as in my official list. The balance 1400 silver bar[s] and nine boxes of precious stones and the specie is correct.' The letter was placed in Sir Joseph Banks's copy of Dalrymple's report, now in the British Library, and was shown to me by a librarian. Of all the strands of evidence proving the letter to be a fraud, the clearest is at the head: 'Capetown 29 August 1782' – in other words, just twenty-five days after the wreck and around the time that Coxon was last seen at the Umtata river.

Still the *Grosvenor* withheld her secrets. When eventually the truth was established, it was not by financiers but by enthusiasts.

Early in 1982, a Cape Town diver named Steve Valentine was called by a friend excited at finding a gold coin on the rocks at Port Grosvenor. Modern scuba equipment had opened up a new playground for divers in South Africa, its coastline bristling with hundreds of wrecks from the mid-sixteenth century, and Valentine, aware like others of the *Grosvenor* legends, was interested in older vessels. On inspecting the site, it became clear to him that the heaviness of the sea meant diving would be limited to brief seasons when the winds were not in play, and even then difficult – 'A treacherous site, roughest of the wrecks I've worked on,' he recalled. In all the confusion engendered by the treasure hunt, just where the *Grosvenor* actually went down had become widely disputed, so that any of a number of rocky bays north of the Tezani was thought to be a possibility; no less an authority on the wreck than Percival Kirby insisted that the river mouth itself was the place. Instead, Valentine opted for an inlet about 600 yards to the north and littered with boulders that he thought might constitute what was left of the cliff after Turner's attentions. Almost immediately, metaphorically speaking, he struck gold.

For the uninitiated, diving for wrecks may conjure up images of a wooden hull resting on a sandy bed, open chests spilling coins, ghostly sails wafting with the current and the odd shark for dramatic effect. The only thing Valentine could see below the sea's surface was a blizzard of churning sand and bubbles; but within a few feet of the shoreline and at a depth of no more than fifteen feet, he found lumps of matter that felt at first like rock but were curiously friable. This was a substance known as concretion, consisting of iron ballast adhering with sand and salt to shipboard detritus. He was right on top of the wreck. Virtually no wood from the hull remained, but the seabed was carpeted with a layer of concretion.

On his first day at the site, he brought to the surface material that, when separated, revealed star pagodas and ducats. More intriguing was what appeared to be the remains of a silver buckle engraved with the initials 'CN'. Although not immediately aware of the full significance of this object, Valentine returned to Cape Town almost certain that he had located the *Grosvenor*. On going back to the texts he became convinced: there on the passenger list was the name of Charles Newman.

Following up the discovery was never going to be simple. Apart from the distance and remoteness of the site, Valentine's initial misgivings about the riskiness of diving so close to a turbulent shore were well founded: conditions were safe on no more than twenty to forty days of the year. It was not until 1999, five years after Nelson Mandela was elected President of South Africa, that a systematic exploration of the spot began. A Hungarian group named Octopus was granted a permit to excavate the seabed under the eye of government-appointed archaeologists and Valentine's company, Argo. Over two months of calm weather a team of divers raised large quantities of conglomerate.

The artefacts brought to light and removed to the East London Museum to be catalogued and displayed, confirmed what Valentine had long believed: that he had come upon the passengers' quarters in the Indiaman's stern. What they revealed was a moment of on-board domesticity frozen in time: sewing pins, needles, the remains of an ivory fan used by one of the ladies. Other finds would open another window on the great cabin: a brass handbasin, a cut-throat razor, brushes, teaspoons, buttons, part of a protractor by Bennett of London, and an enamel-faced gold watch in an exquisitely worked case, inscribed 'Jules Le Roy, Paris'. Although there were coins galore – hundreds of the lovely little gold pagodas, chunky silver rupees, ducats, reals, pieces of eight, and a Charles II silver crown of 1679 – real riches were another matter. The seabed was to reward historians, not treasure-seekers.

No one doubted that they had exhumed the grave of the *Grosvenor*; but there was still one defining moment, when the final piece of evidence fell into place.

On 19 August a lump of conglomerate weighing about 3 kilograms was brought up and laid on the rocks. The surface was chipped away, exposing a small blackened brass plate that had once been fixed to the lid of a wooden trunk. Carefully the deposits accumulated over 217 years were cleaned away, and there revealed was the name 'Colonel Edw'd James'.

If discovery of this constantly alluring coastline brought its own rewards, I had to admit failure in another respect. In following the castaways' route, I had hoped it would be possible to trace some of their descendants. Once or twice it appeared that a discovery was in the offing. King Mpondombini was enthusiastic, when I visited to explain my purpose, and said he thought it feasible; the *Grosvenor* was intrinsic to the history of his people, he said, and families linked with it ought to be locatable. But his efforts, and my own searches along the way, did not produce anything resembling proof. Physical variations have long been evident among the Pondo – on the one hand, the characteristics typical of other Nguni-speaking peoples; on the other, aquiline features and lighter complexions inherited from generations of castaways. Some of those I met were certainly descended from seafarers of old. A young woman named Sigcamo, dark-skinned but with a startlingly European cast to her features, affirmed that it was part of her family tradition that their ancestors had come from the sea, but more than that she could not say. Usually, the connection was with Englishmen who arrived here in the nineteenth century; the names of the adventurers Cane and King are still common.

I was disappointed but not greatly surprised: the tide had brought too many layers of humanity to the Wild Coast for anyone to be specific about one particular shipwreck more than 200 years ago.

Still, one encounter had about it a distant echo of those times. At the village of Mbotji, once the home of the fugitive Trout, I met a Dutchman named Hans who had washed up here on two wheels. He told of his arrival in Pondoland ten years earlier after cycling the length of Africa, of how he had spotted a house – rare in these parts – and dismounted to rest under a tree. After some time an elderly gentleman had come out of the house to inquire about him and, on hearing his story, invited him to lunch. The old man, it turned out, was King Mpondombini and Hans was to spend the next five years at Qawukeni, or the Great Place, helping out around the house. He remained a regular visitor but had assimilated more widely with Pondo life. A modern castaway himself, he had acquired a little shanty by the sea and taken a wife. The place was alive with *umfaans*, children who dropped in at all times of the day.

That night, a few of us cooked meat over an open fire. Beers were sent for from the store. Children ate grilled chicken legs; adults sipped from the cool cans. Hans and his neighbours asked the purpose of my visit and were intrigued to hear that many years before a ship had been wrecked just a few miles up the coast. So, sitting under the stars of an African night, I told them what I knew of the story of the *Grosvenor*.

ACKNOWLEDGEMENTS

This book is a product of the help contributed by many people over an unusually broad spectrum, from those discreet, selfless and all-too-often unsung handmaidens of researchers everywhere, the librarians and keepers of archives, to those who helped in innumerable practical ways while I travelled in Pondoland and the Cape.

The bulk of the material relating to the *Grosvenor* and those who sailed on her in 1782 is contained in the Oriental and India Office Collections at the British Library, and for the aids to researching its contents devised by Anthony Farrington, the former head, and for the invariably enthusiastic and courteous assistance of Hedley Sutton and the staff, I am enormously grateful. In South Africa, Diana Madden of the Brenthurst Library was a source of priceless help in tracing documents across that country; her colleague, Carol Leigh, provided a valuable lead. I am also grateful for the assistance of Cathy Erasmus and Marius Basson at the Harold Strange Library in Johannesburg, Kathy Brooks at Museum Africa, Gill Vernon at the East London Museum, Kate Abbott and Carol Archibald at the Department of Historical Papers at Wits University, and Lalou Melzer at the William Fehr Collection in Cape Town.

Alan Moloney walked the Wild Coast with me and Rob Brogan provided help at a crucial stage during my travels. Mpondombini Sigcau, Paramount Chief of the Eastern Pondos, and Hans Lindeis took a constructive interest. I must also thank for their assistance David McLennan of Select Books in Cape Town and Anthea van Wieringen; and for their hospitality, John Costello, Christine Jacobsen and Manny Milner at the Outspan Inn, Port St Johns, and Mike and Wendy Lyall in Johannesburg. In unravelling recent salvage developments, I was assisted by Jonathan Sharfman, Steve Valentine, John Gribble and Jaco Boshoff.

This is the fourth book on which Tom Fort has given me generously of his editorial advice and it owes much to him as do the three that have gone before, which is to say a great deal. For guidance on their specialist subjects I would like to thank Jean Sutton, Peter Robb and Brian Lavery.

Kate Darian-Smith of Melbourne University kindly introduced me to captivity narratives. Valuable information was provided by Gerald Johnson Fox, Edwin Habberley and Rodney Warmington on their ancestors. Gerald Fox took a particular interest and generously provided the portraits of Lydia Logie and Richard Blechynden.

For a stimulating conversation about the subject of the book I am obliged to Jane Bradish-Elames. But that it was brought thus far was made possible by the efforts of my literary agent, Caroline Dawnay, and Peter Matson in New York. As editors, Julian Loose and Star Lawrence brought to the manuscript the kind of creative advice and eagle eye that writers pray for, and which improved the result immeasurably. My sincere thanks to them, and to Angus Cargill, Kate Ward and the whole team at Faber.

SOURCES

The material on which this book is based falls into four main categories: contemporary publications dealing directly with the wreck; unpublished records and correspondence; published work, mainly covering the period or containing references to the issues and individuals involved; and my own personal observations and interviews.

Anyone familiar with the subject will know how much of the *Grosvenor* source material was brought to light by Percival R. Kirby. A professor (of music) at Johannesburg's Witwatersrand University until his retirement in 1952, Kirby had a wide range of interests and devoted the remaining years of an industrious life to studying the East Indiaman and making widely available, through the Van Riebeeck Society in Cape Town, records long out of print. The most important were published by the society in his *A Source Book on the Wreck of the Grosvenor* (1953), a trove that was open to use by other researchers for seven years before his own study, *The True Story of the Grosvenor East Indiaman*, was published in 1960. It is hard to imagine any researcher acting in the same way today. Furthermore, while the originals of the material that he gathered can still be seen in specialist collections, in one instance Kirby's *Source Book* saved a source that would otherwise now be lost. During the course of my research it turned out that the *Journal of William Habberley*, a handwritten quarto manuscript running to 225 pages, had been mislaid by the Durban Museum, to which it had been presented in 1940. Had Kirby not seen to its preservation, my own book would have lacked a vital ingredient. For this, and much else, I would like to acknowledge my indebtedness to a great researcher.

As anyone who has read *The True Story of the Grosvenor East Indiaman* will recognise, however, our perspectives as well as our conclusions differ in many respects, notably on the conduct of Captain John Coxon. Kirby, moreover, devoted a third of his book to the hunt for the wholly mythical *Grosvenor* treasure – with the aim of discrediting once and for all the syndicate fraudsters who preyed on investors for much of the twentieth century. While it is an intriguing subject, I thought an extended treatment of this rather tawdry tale did not belong in the present book and it had, in any event, to a large extent been overtaken by recent finds. For his part, Kirby touched but lightly on the careers of those who came to grief in Pondoland in 1782, the society in England and Bengal from which they were drawn, and the culture with which they came into conflict. The Oriental and India Office Collection of the British Library holds material that illuminates the lives of William Hosea and Charles Newman, along with the careers of John Coxon and his officers, and that brings to life Bengal and Calcutta society in the eighteenth century. I have also had the benefit of an extended opportunity to observe the site and the terrain covered by the castaways.

Archives and unpublished sources

OIOC Oriental and India Office Collection, British Library
MSS Manuscripts Collection, British Library
MA Museum Africa, Johannesburg
DHP Department of Historial Papers, Wits University, Johannesburg
SOAS Wesleyan Methodist Missionary Society Collection at the School for Oriental and African Studies, University of London
HSL Harold Strange Library at Johannesburg Public Library
AM Albany Museum, Grahamstown
BL Brenthurst Library, Johannesburg

Key publications on the *Grosvenor*

CA Carter, George, *A Narrative of the Loss of the Grosvenor East Indiaman*, reprint of the 1791 edition, Van Riebeeck Society, Cape Town 1927.
In addition to Carter's account, this volume contains the journal kept by Jacob van Reenen on the second rescue expedition of 1790–1.

SB Kirby, Percival, *A Source Book on the Wreck of the Grosvenor*, Van Riebeeck Society, Cape Town 1953.
The main contents are Alexander Dalrymple's 'Account of the Loss of the *Grosvenor* Indiaman', his 'Appendix with the Evidence of William Hubberly' [*sic*], published in 1783 and 1786, Habberley's Journal, and the report of Muller's first rescue expedition.

Other published sources

Ackroyd, Peter, *London, The Biography*, London 2000.

Allen, Geoffrey and David, *Clive's Lost Treasure*, London 1978.

Bird, John, *The Annals of Natal 1495 to 1845*, 2 vols., Cape Town 1965.

Blechynden, Kathleen, *Calcutta Past and Present*, London 1905.

Bligh, William, *A Book of the Bounty* (ed. George Mackaness), London 1938.

Boswell, James, *The Life of Samuel Johnson* (abridged Penguin edition), London 1979.

Busteed, H. E., *Echoes from Old Calcutta*, 4th edition, London 1908.

Carey, W. H., *Good Old Days of Honourable John Company*, 2 vols., Calcutta 1906.

Chapman, F., *Architectura Navalis Mercatoris*, Magdeburg 1957.

Chapman, R. W. (ed.), *The Letters of Samuel Johnson*, 3 vols., Oxford 1952.

Chatterton, E. Keble, *The Old East Indiamen*, London 1933.

Chilvers, Hedley A., *The Seven Lost Trails of Africa*, London 1930.

Colley, Linda, *Captives, Britain, Empire and the World 1600–1850*, London 2002.

Cotton, H. E. A., *Calcutta Old and New*, Calcutta 1907.

Cornwallis Harris, W., *Portraits of the Game and Wild Animals of Southern Africa*, reprint of 1852 edition, Cape Town 1967.

Dash, Mike, *Batavia's Graveyard*, London 2002.

Davenport, T. R. H., *South Africa, A Modern History*, London 1991.

Edwards, Philip (ed.), *The Journals of Captain Cook*, Penguin edition, London 1999.

Elphick, Richard & Giliomee Hermann (eds.), *The Shaping of South African Society 1652–1840*, Cape Town 1979.

Farrington, Anthony, *Trading Places, The East India Company 1600–1834*, London 2002.

Fay, Eliza, *Original Letters from India (1779–1815)*, London 1925.

Feiling, Keith, *Warren Hastings*, London 1954.

Hammond, Dorothy & Jablow, Alta, *The Africa That Never Was*, New York 1970.

Harvey, Robert, *Clive, the Life and Death of a British Emperor*, London 1998.

Hough, Richard, *Captain James Cook, A Biography*, London 1994.

Hunter, Monica, *Reaction to Conquest, Effects of Contact with Europeans on the Pondo of South Africa*, London 1936.

Kay, Stephen, *Travels and Researches in Kaffraria*, 1838.

Keay, John, *The Honourable Company, A History of the English East India Company*, London 1991.

King, Dean, *A Sea of Words, A Lexicon and Companion*, New York 1995.

Kirby, Percival R., *The True Story of the Grosvenor*, London 1960.

Kirby, Percival R., *Jacob van Reenen and the Grosvenor Expedition of 1790–91*, Johannesburg 1958.

Lavery, Brian, *Nelson's Navy*, London 1988.

Le Vaillant, François, *Travels into the Interior Parts of Africa*, 2 vols., reprint of 1790 edition, London 1972.

Leslie, Edward, *Desperate Journeys, Abandoned Souls*, London 1988.

Lichtenstein, M. H. C., *Travels in Southern Africa 1803–1806*, 2 vols., reprint of 1815 edition, Cape Town 1930.

Little, K. L., *Negroes in Britain*, London 1947.
Macaulay, Thomas, *Essay on Warren Hastings*, London 1923.
Mackaness, George (ed.), *A Book of the Bounty, Selections from Bligh's Writings*, London 1938.
Mackeurtan, Graham, *The Cradle Days of Natal (1497–1845)*, London 1930.
Mahony, P. J. B., *Africa Pilot*, vol. III, published by the Hydrographer of the Navy, 1980.
Majumdar, Purna, *The Musnud of Murshidabad (1704–1904)*, Murshidabad, 1905.
Miller, Russell, *The East Indiamen*, Virginia 1980.
Mirza Abu Taleb Khan, *Travels in Asia, Africa and Europe* (translated by Charles Stewart), London 1814.
Moodie, Donald, *The Record*, reprint of 1838 edition, Cape Town 1960.
Morris, James, *Heaven's Command*, London 1979.
Mostert, Noel, *Frontiers*, London 1992.
Owen, W. F., *Narrative of a Voyage to Explore the Shores of Africa*, London 1833.
Palgrave, Keith Coates, *Trees of Southern Africa*, Cape Town 1977.
Parkinson, C. Northcote, *Trade in the Eastern Seas*, Cambridge 1937.
Philbrick, Nathaniel, *In the Heart of the Sea*, London 2000.
Picard, Liza, *Dr Johnson's London*, London 2000.
Richardson, Ralph, *George Morland, Painter*, London 1895.
Richmond, Sir Herbert, *The Navy in India 1763–83*, London 1931.
Robinson, A. M. L., *The Letters of Lady Anne Barnard to Henry Dundas*, Cape Town 1973.
Rodger, N. A. M., *The Wooden World, An Anatomy of the Georgian Navy*, London 1988.
Schama, Simon, *Landscape and Memory*, London 1995.
Schapera, I. (ed.), *The Bantu-Speaking Tribes of South Africa*, Cape Town 1956.
Sobel, Dava, *Longitude*, London 1996.
Soga, J. Henderson, *The South-Eastern Bantu*, Johannesburg 1930.
Souhami, Diana, *Selkirk's Island*, London 2001.
Spencer, Alfred (ed.), *Memoirs of William Hickey*, 4 vols., London 1919.
Sutton, Jean, *Lords of the East*, London 2000.
Theal, G. McCall, *Records of South Eastern Africa*, vols. I & VIII, London 1898.
Thompson, George, *Travels and Adventure in Southern Africa*, 2 vols, London 1827.
Truswell, J. F., *The Geological Evolution of South Africa*, Cape Town 1977.
Turner, Malcolm, *Shipwrecks and Salvage in South Africa*, Cape Town 1988.
Walker, Eric, *A History of Southern Africa*, London 1957.
Walvin, James, *Black Ivory, A History of British Slavery*, London 1992.
Webb C. & Wright, J. (eds.), *The James Stuart Archive*, vols. 1–4, Durban 1976–86.
Wild, Antony, *The East India Company*, London 1999.

Articles and papers

Gribble, John, 'The Doddington Gold Coins', a paper presented at the World Archaeological Congress in Cape Town, 1999.
Kirby, Percival, 'Gquma, Mdepa and the Amatshomane', *African Studies*, vol. 13, 1954.

Rankin, Stuart, 'Shipbuilding in Rotherhithe – an Historical Introduction', privately published.
Robb, Peter, 'Clash of Cultures? An Englishman in Calcutta in the 1790s', lecture at School for Oriental and African Studies, London, 1998.
Sampson, H. F., 'Diamonds from the *Grosvenor*', *African Studies*, vol. 3, 1947.
Sharfman, Jonathan, 'The *Grosvenor* Project: First Fieldwork Season', *Massa Digest*, Cape Town 1999.
Wilson, Monica, 'Early History of Transkei and Ciskei', *African Studies*, vol. 18, 1959.

NOTES

Prologue

The contemporary narratives dealing with the *Dodington* wreck include *A Journal of the Proceedings of the Dodington East Indiaman*, by the third mate, William Webb, and *An Authentic Narrative of the Loss of the Dodington, Indiaman*, by the chief mate, Evan Jones. Both are exceptionally rare and were reprinted in a periodical, the *Indian Antiquary*, vols. XXIX (1900), XXX (1901) and XXXI (1902). *Clive's Lost Treasure*, by Geoffrey and David Allen, London 1978, reprints some of this material and relates an operation to salvage relics from the Indiaman. In 1997, about 1,200 gold coins, supposedly from Clive's treasure, were put up for auction in London, but withdrawn on a challenge from South Africa's National Monuments Council, which had granted no salvage permit. The issues raised by treasure and salvage from vessels such as the *Dodington* and the *Grosvenor* are covered in a paper by John Gribble, 'The Dodington Gold Coins', delivered at the World Archaeological Congress in Cape Town in 1999.

1 'A Man of High Character'

3 For descriptions of Murshidabad, the old capital of Bengal, the river and palace, see Hickey, vol. 3, pp. 277–9, and Majumdar.

4 'Pray keep our going home a secret . . .' Hosea to Lady Chambers, 9 November 1781, MA. Museum Africa in Johannesburg holds a small but valuable collection of letters between the Hosea and Chambers families.

5 'whence he sent forth peals so loud . . .' Boswell, p. 173.
'a girl of sixteen, exquisitely beautiful . . .' Chapman, *Letters*, vol. 1, p. 397.
Lady Chambers's record as a model for Reynolds is in Busteed, p. 146.

7 'The noble appearance of the river . . .' Hickey's love for Calcutta might seem somewhat masochistic, given its notorious climate, but was shared by many early residents. Other good descriptions are to be found in Busteed.

8 For prevailing passenger fares, see Chatterton, p. 231. Details of Coxon's difficulties and the Grosvenor's service are in Bengal Public Council, Z/P/551, OIOC.

9 Details of the fares and privilege space paid by Hosea to Coxon are in Fay, pp. 209–10, and Hosea's will, the original of which is at Museum Africa.
The family history of Taylor and Williams was related in a letter to Percival Kirby by a descendant, Elma Hailey, 30 May 1961. Kirby papers, HSL.

10 '. . . to solicit an order to Captain Hall . . .' Bengal Public Council, Z/P/551, OIOC.
Information about the Blechynden family and Lydia's residence in Calcutta are gathered from the Blechynden diaries at the British Library, Add. 45578–45663,

MSS. That she had arrived on the *Grosvenor*'s outward voyage is confirmed in the correspondence of Margaret Fowke, OIOC.

11 'We live a kind of stupid life here . . .' Mary Hosea to Lady Chambers, 7 May 1781, MA.
'How many women . . .' Mary Hosea to Lady Chambers, 5 March 1781, MA.
'How hard is the lot . . .' Ibid.
'one of the most amiable women I ever knew . . .' Fay, p. 209.

12 For English adventurers and sensualists in Bengal see Morris, p. 73.
Eating and drinking in Calcutta, and Bengal society, are extravagantly dealt with by Hickey and Mrs Fay.

13 For the attrition among Company servants see Parkinson, p. 71–2.

14 The East India Company has been the subject of numerous histories. The most recent are Keay, Wild and Farrington.

15 William Hosea's correspondence with his uncle Robert Orme is illustrative of much more than just the ups and downs of his own career; it provides a fascinating insight into the none-too-subtle ways of patronage and influence in their age. Hosea's fear as a young man of offending his powerful and unpleasant relative was almost palpable. As Hosea's own authority grew, so that of Orme waned and their roles were reversed, with the latter more often than not in the position of petitioning his nephew and benefiting from his remittances. These letters are in the India Office Collection at the British Library: 'I can never enough acknowledge . . .' Eu/Orme OV 43, 19 March 1768, OIOC.
Hosea's letters to his colleagues, illuminative of Company administration, are found in Eu/Orme OV 167: 'You will greatly oblige me . . .' 7 July 1773; 'The confidence my superiors . . .' 6 July 1773; 'Conceived in terms of such severity . . .' 2 August 1773; 'I throw myself . . .' 17 Sept 1773, OIOC.
'the most lucrative office in the Company's service . . .' Hickey, vol. 3, p. 236.

16 'The continuance of your patronage . . .' Eu/Orme OV 167, 24 November 1773, IOC.
'a man of high character . . .' Fay, p. 209.
The plot is well attested. Hosea was careful to conceal his involvement in anti-Hastings intrigues, but hinted at it in a number of letters to Orme and Chambers. The letter to Chambers survives only in a copy in the Kirby papers, HSL, but another held at Museum Africa, dated 30 December 1779, alludes to intrigues as well: 'I have made [Capt Carnac] acquainted with the purport of your note. He will be able to give much useful information and you may with safety mention him as a young man of fidelity.' Hosea's lengthy last letter to Chambers, of April 1782, destroyed in a fire at the University of the Witwatersrand in 1930 after being transcribed, mentions Carnac and 'commissions' entrusted to Hosea. At this point the transcriber noted that six lines had been scratched through, possibly by Hosea but more probably by the recipient Chambers.

17 'I am vastly rejoiced . . .' Hosea to Lady Chambers, 12 December 1780, MA.
'He will try you.' Eu/Orme OV 202, 20 August 1780, OIOC.
'I have long since made a resolution . . .' Hosea to Lady Chambers, 9 November 1781, MA.

18 The original of Hosea's will is in the collection at Museum Africa.

'All is now bustle . . .' Fay, p. 211.
'concerns of my family . . .' Eu/Orme OV 167, 29 January 1782, OIOC.
'seventeen years service . . .' E/4/39, OIOC.

19 'It seemed cruel for a mother . . .' Fay, p. 212.
'I had flattered myself . . .' Mary Hosea to Lady Chambers, 16 February 1782, MA.
'Your beloved boy is well . . .' Ibid.
'Oh my dear girl, what a happyness . . .' Sarah Brown to Mary Hosea, 1 November 1781, MA.

2 Lord Macartney's Displeasure

20 Coxon's trials at the hands of the Madras board, along with correspondence between Charles Newman and the board, are held at the British Library under Madras Public Proceedings, P/240/ 54, OIOC.

21 'the *Grosvenor* not yet being despatched . . .' Ibid. Coxon to board, 12 February 1782.
For details of the *Grosvenor*'s cargo see *A Source Book*, p. 8–9.
For the seasons of sailing, see Parkinson, pp. 98–9 and 111–13.

22 '. . . Captain Coxon be directed . . .' P/240/54, 27 February 1782, OIOC.

23 'made a fine fortune by his profession'. Hickey, vol. 2, p. 192.
'the stature of a nymph . . .' Busteed, p. 231.
For details of George Grand's action against Philip Francis see the entertaining transcript in Busteed, p. 241–59.

24 'Without in the smallest degree insinuating . . .' Ibid., p. 263. Busteed's irony notwithstanding, the case added to a growing body of evidence pointing to corruption by Chambers that brought him to the verge of recall by Parliament.

25 The machinations of the Arcot Interest are described in Keay, pp. 408 and 418.
'are supposed to have unwarrantably . . .' Newman's letter of appointment in Bengal Public Consultations P/2/46, 13 September 1781. Also Bengal letters received E/4/39, OIOC.
'handsomely flattered me . . .' Ibid. Newman to Madras board, 1 February 1782.
'for refusing to turn informer'. Ibid. Newman to board, 13 February 1782.

26 'notoriously spoken of in the settlement . . .' Ibid. Newman to board, 1 February 1782.
'the general style of your letter . . .' Ibid. Freeman to Newman, 19 February 1782.
'I can not, nor will others . . .' Ibid. Newman to board, 13 March 1782.
'Do the Board seriously expect . . .' Ibid.
'disrespectful and improper'. Ibid. Board to Newman, undated. There were no further communications. Newman's findings were lost and attempts to get to the bottom of the Arcot Interest's treachery died with him.

27 Coxon's statement, dated 27 March 1782, is also in Madras Public Proceedings, OIOC.

28 The record of Colonel James's marriage to Sophia Crockett is in the OIOC, along with the scanty records of his military service; details of d'Espinette and de L'Isle in the Kirby papers.

30 The events of the Hoseas' voyage in the *Yarmouth*, and their subsequent race to reach the *Grosvenor* after she sailed, were related in a letter from William to Sir Robert Chambers dated 9 April 1782. This lengthy letter, written over ten days, was destroyed in a fire at the University of the Witwatersrand in 1930 but had fortunately been transcribed, in which form it survives in the Department of Historical Papers.

'he had resisted many solicitations'. Ibid. The cynical might think that Coxon's advice was intended to ensure that Hosea missed his passage so that his quarters could be sold to the highest-bidding passengers.

31 'the fleet was at a considerable distance . . .' Ibid.

'I gave them money and promised large rewards . . .' Ibid.

3 Island of Oak

33 For the history of the East Indiamen, see *Trade in the Eastern Seas*, by C. Northcote Parkinson, *Lords of the East*, by Jean Sutton, and *The Old East Indiamen*, by E. Keble Chatterton.

36 'Here we are after innumerable escapes . . .' Hosea to Chambers, 9 April 1782, MA.

'more like hospital ships than men-of-war'. Richmond, p. 214.

37 The Battle of Providien is described in Richmond, pp. 216–23.

'and the ship greatly damaged . . .' Habberley's account in SB, p. 60.

38 'several of his captains had failed him badly'. Richmond, p. 225.

39 'The habit of buying and selling goods . . .' Parkinson, p. 196.

'a plain man'. Hosea to Chambers, 9 April 1782, MA.

The normal apprenticeship of Indiamen officers is described by Parkinson, pp. 193–4, and conditions of service, p. 219. In assessing Coxon's abilities, I differ in almost every respect with Kirby, who described him as 'a thoroughly competent and experienced seaman'.

40 Details of Coxon's will and his dealings with Sherburne are in the Kirby papers, HSL.

41 The record of Coxon's overlapping service with Alexander Logie, Thomas Beale and David Drummond can be found in L/Mar/C/651, a List of Commanders with their respective rank in the Company's service, and L/Mar/C/652, a Description of Commanders and Mates Examined for the year 1774, both in OIOC.

42 Details of desertions and unrest on the *Grosvenor* and all other information about her first voyage are taken from Coxon's log, held as L/Mar/B/495F in OIOC.

43 'I was desir'd to attend the Council . . .' Ibid.

'Punished Adamson with two dozen lashes . . .' Ibid.

44 Details of the cadets' complaint against Beale were found in the Kirby papers, HSL.

Life in Trincomalee is described by Hickey, vol. 2, p. 207.

The seamen's pay is given in the *Grosvenor*'s impress book, OIOC. For conditions of service on English ships, see both Sutton and Rodger.

45 'A magnificent debauch – sup, bathe . . .' Picard, p. 211.

46 'The multitude of these men are wholly illiterate . . .' Rodger, p. 118.
Information about individual sailors on the *Grosvenor* was gathered from a number of sources, including Dalrymple's 'Account' and descendants contacted by the author.

48 For lascars, see Parkinson, p. 215.

49 Shaw's record is given in L/Mar/C/652, OIOC.

50 Conditions in passengers' quarters are described in Parkinson, pp. 238–9 and 264–8, and by Hickey.
'The diversity of characters . . .' Chatterton, p 226–7.

51 'We have no news of our dear Charlotte . . .' Hosea to Chambers, 9 April 1782, MA.
'a neat well-furnished little room'. Parkinson, p. 238–9.

52 'God bless you. Kiss my infant . . .' Mary Hosea to Lady Chambers, 30 March 1782, MA.

4 A Light in the Dark

53 'Any thing is welcome . . .' Macaulay essay on Warren Hastings, p. 13.

54 Survivors told Dalrymple that they had encountered no vessels beside the *Swallow*.

55 'really speaks prodigiously'. Hosea to Chambers, 9 April 1782, MA.
'The woman, of whom I entertained some suspicion . . .' Fay, p. 104.
Details of the *zemindar*'s suit against Hosea are in Bengal Public Consultations, P/2/42, 15 February 1781, OIOC.

56 '. . . the cries of the sailors . . .' Parkinson, p. 224.

57 'a rude kind of plenty'. Ibid., p. 289.

58 'an example of sobriety and decorum . . .' Chatterton, p. 226.
'All the furniture being removed out of the cuddy . . .' Fay, p. 231.

59 The log of the *Chapman* is L/Mar/B/218A at the OIOC.

60 'A more uncomfortable passage . . .' Fay, p. 218.
Mrs Fay's relationship with the 'tyrannical' John Lewis opens up an intriguing line for the imagination, but while her opinions of him are plain, his meticulous, copperplate hand in the ship's log gives no hint of how he coped with his formidable passenger. The log is L/Mar/B/452/G in the OIOC.
'Longitude observed . . .' Ibid. There is no indication of how Lewis came to so precise a calculation in the era before ships' chronometers.
'. . . the *East* coast of Africa . . .' Fay, p. 219.

61 'the *very ship* . . . unfortunate in missing.' Ibid., p. 221.
Details of the voyage after the gale on 27 July are taken from Dalrymple's 'Account' and Habberley's Journal in the *Source Book*.

62 'drank jovially to our absent friends'. SB, p. 62.

63 Coxon's estimation of their distance from the coast is cited by Dalrymple, SB, p. 32.
'The loss of such a number of lives . . .' Contained in *The Indian Antiquary*, October 1901, p. 296. Again I differ with Kirby, who went to considerable lengths to exonerate Coxon and placed the entire blame for the wreck at Beale's door.

64 'something similar to the Northern Lights', and 'fires kindled by natives'. SB, p. 61.
'gave orders to let the ship remain . . .' and 'cautioned him to keep a good look out . . .' Ibid.

65 'Mr Beale said that he . . .' Ibid. Lewis made a similar statement to Dalrymple, SB, p. 33.
'Instead of paying any attention to their information . . .' CA, p. 2.

66 The final minutes are described by Habberley, SB, p. 62.

5 'Nothing but Confusion and Dismay'

As this chapter is a synthesis of the information provided by the survivors to Dalrymple, and in Habberley's journal and Carter's *Narrative*, I have not cited detailed references.

67 'Nothing but confusion and dismay prevailed . . .' SB, p. 62.
'Despair was painted on every countenance . . .' CA, p. 3.

68 'Our situation was most dreadful . . .' SB, p. 62.

69 'The captain and passengers offered great rewards . . .' Ibid., p. 64.

71 'The greatest part . . . gave themselves up for lost . . .' Ibid., p. 65.
'everybody considered Mr Beale highly blamable'. Ibid., p64

72 'The door into the great cabin was soon torn off . . .' Hickey, vol. 3, pp. 19–22.
'No more would venture . . .' SB, p. 65.

73 'The sea having nothing [to stop it] . . .' Ibid., p. 66.
'All hands now began to do the best they could for themselves.' CA, p. 7.

74 'We expected now the part of the wreck we were on to go to pieces . . .' SB, p. 66.
'representing to us the almost impossibility . . .' Ibid.

6 The Caliban Shore

79 The original oil of *African Hospitality* is held at Museum Africa in Johannesburg, but no longer on display. There is no indication how it came into the museum's possession other than a note that it was in the collection of Sir Harold Parkinson.

81 'They went quite naked . . .' CA, p. 38.
'. . . our dreadful situation not apparently affecting them . . .' SB, p. 67.

85 'Her anxiety [is] great'. Fay, p. 212.

86 'Plenty of timber from the wreck . . .' SB, p. 34.
'A pipe of wine, a barrel of arrack . . .' SB, p. 68.

87 'In great part, their calamities seem to have arisen . . .' SB, p. 31.

87 For Cook's voyages and his feud with Dalrymple, see Hough.

89 The history of British slavery is told in Walvin's *Black Ivory*, the *Zong* episode in pp.16–20. For contemporary attitudes to Africans see also Hammond and Little.

90 'pointed [to the north-east] . . .' SB, p. 35. Previous castaways on this shore, being Portuguese, had started up the coast to Delagoa Bay rather than heading south to the Cape.
'woolly-headed and quite black.' CA, p. 11.

91 'They seemed to consider everything as belonging to them.' SB, p. 68.
'. . . excited in the minds of our people . . .' CA, p. 11.
'This is certainly a very melancholy circumstance . . .' Eu/Orme/OV 167, Hosea to Orme, 29 February 1773, OIOC.

92 Dalrymple noted that the castaways had 'five or six cutlasses', SB, p. 35.
'. . . who endeavoured to wrest them from us . . .'; 'not out of any fear of the natives . . .' and 'everything we found made of metal . . .' SB, p. 68.

93 'Many sailors and lascars . . .' Ibid.

7 Pondo's People

By comparison with the Zulu and Xhosa, whose histories are especially picturesque and dramatic, the Pondo were neglected by early artists and chroniclers and nothing much has changed since. The standard work on Pondo history is Monica Hunter's highly regarded *Reaction to Conquest*, but that was published almost seventy years ago. See also her later study (published under her married name, Wilson) 'Early History of the Transkei and Ciskei' in *African Studies*, vol. 18, 1959. Pondo folklore is retold in J. Henderson Soga's *The South-Eastern Bantu*. For a wider sweep of oral history of the Nguni-speaking tribes, see the magnificent record of traditions collected by James Stuart and published in five volumes by the University of Natal as *The James Stuart Archive*.

94 'There used to be a folktale . . .' Stuart, vol. 1, p. 291.

97 'poor in cattle and therefore extremely rapacious'. SB p. 177.
'. . . go naked and without any iron or copper . . .' Moodie, p. 430–31.

98 The great majority of earlier castaways on the south-east coast of Africa were Portuguese. Their stories, notably those of the *São Joao*, lost near Port Edward in 1552, are told in Theal's *Records*. For a comprehensive overview of shipping losses, see Turner's *Shipwrecks and Salvage in South Africa*.
'There appeared upon a headland . . .' Theal, vol. I, p. 223.

99 '[They] became bolder on seeing us unarmed . . .' Ibid., p. 224.
'We took our arms . . .' Ibid., p. 225.

100 'many natives came out of the woods . . .' Theal, vol. VIII, p. 204.
'When the natives drew near . . .' Ibid., p. 206.

101 '. . . did the first execution with a good shot . . .' Ibid., p. 208.

102 'The Kaffirs were astonished . . .' Ibid., p. 221.
'A sailor named Manuel d'Andrade gradually retreated . . .' Ibid., p. 225.

103 'The men are very lean and upright . . .' Ibid., p. 204–5.

8 A Fatal Dread

104 'They were of course no utility to us.' SB, p. 68.
'Probably the most of us must [have been] drowned . . .' In the *Endeavour Journal of Joseph Banks*, London, 1962, vol. 2, p. 77.
105 '[There was] particularly one boar . . .' SB, p. 34.
106 'lest the natives . . . might destroy [us] all'. CA, p. 11.
Habberley, Lewis and Hynes all mention Coxon's address to the crew. The captain's estimate that they would reach the Dutch in ten to seventeen days was related by Lewis; Habberley recalled it as sixteen days.
107 'for those who had escaped unhurt . . .' SB, p. 70.
'He represented that as he had . . . been their commanding officer . . .' CA, p. 12.
Coxon's estimation of their position is given in CA, p. 12, Dalrymple's in SB, p. 31. The hydrographer asserted quite wrongly: 'It could not possibly be in above 31°S latitude as Lewis and Warmington report.'
109 '. . . to get some pewter and lead from the wreck . . .' CA, p. 13.
110 'We were surrounded by a great number of the natives . . .' SB, p. 71.
111 'We were surrounded by some hundreds . . .' Ibid., p. 71.
112 'The buckles, buttons etc. we freely parted with . . .' Ibid.
'The chief then stepped forwards . . .' SB, p. 72.
113 Trout is described in all the narratives as a Malay, but most Cape slaves were Javanese.
'We had many nations to pass . . .' CA, p. 15.
114 '. . . carefully concealed it from . . . the company . . .' SB, p. 72.

9 'Never After Together Again'

116 'One of them came up and cut the captain . . .' SB, p. 74–5.
'The native endeavoured by signs and entreaty . . .' SB, p. 37.
Hynes's version of the battle is in CA, p. 18, that of Lewis and Habberley in SB, pp. 37 and 74.
'might easily have destroyed us all . . .' SB, p. 74.
117 'We made signs for them to leave us . . .' Ibid.
'After this affray . . .' Ibid.
118 'What a situation this for ladies . . . delicately brought up . . .' CA, p. 19.
119 Coxon's refusal to allow parley with the natives is in SB, pp. 77 and 38.
120 'The Malay was a rogue . . .' Ibid., p. 36.
'to go on and not . . . let all their things be taken from them . . .' Ibid., p. 38.
'What the feelings of the ladies must be . . .' CA, p. 23.
121 'As everyone made the best of their way according to their strength . . .' SB, p. 76.
'they saw at a distance the ladies etc. coming over a hill'. Ibid., p. 38.
122 'The ladies waded over the river breast high . . .' Ibid., p. 39.
'They had shared the difficulties and distresses . . .' CA, p. 25.
'Every person was desirous of making the best of their way . . .' SB, p. 77.

'Some of the people set out, straggling . . .' Ibid., p. 39.

123 The list of those left with Coxon was compiled by Dalrymple, SB pp. 39–40.

124 '. . . induced by the great promises made them . . .' CA, p. 24.

10 Faultlines

125 Two kinds of Arcadia: Schama, p. 517.

126 'Often it seemed to us as if there were fleets at sea . . .' Theal, vol. VIII, p. 210. Schama is again illuminating on forests as habitats of the English psyche, pp. 135–74. The definitive work on southern Africa's trees is Palgrave.

127 'great alarm at the dreadful noise of the beasts'. Scattered throughout Habberley's journal are references to 'the wild beasts with which we were greatly terrified . . .' SB, p. 86.

128 'agility which the inhabitants of Africa are well known to exhibit . . .' See also CA, p. 38: 'They are extremely swift of foot.'

129 'On the fourth day they came to a high mountain . . .' CA pp. 35–6. This was evidently Mount Thesiger on the northern bank of the Umzimvubu.
'it being covered so thick with underwood . . .' SB, p. 78.
The rivers in the text can be named with reasonable certainty, partly as they were rendered by the seamen (for example, Zimvooboo for Umzimvubu) and partly from their descriptions and the intervals at which they were encountered.

130 'many efforts of generosity and mutual assistance'. Ibid., p. 30.

131 Blair remained with Talbot according to Carter, CA, p. 42, but all the other sources are agreed that Talbot was left alone. Lewis related that the captain insisted that for Blair to stay was 'no manner of service'. SB, p. 41.
'Messrs Shaw . . . and self, having agreed to use ours in common . . .' SB, p. 80.

132 'They drove a fine young bullock to us . . .' Ibid., pp. 81–2.

133 The composition of the two parties is given by Dalrymple, SB pp. 41–3.

11 Habberley's Mission

135 Habberley family history provided to the author by Edwin Habberley. There has previously been some confusion over William's origin, as a British consul who met him in Copenhagen related that he came from Aberdeen, but Habberley made clear to one of the rescuers that he was from London. His characteristics are self-evident; he himself expressed disapproval of the more reposeful Lewis.

136 'Our hunger compelled us to devour them.' SB, p. 83.

137 'Elated with having obtained . . .' CA, p. 48.
'But being greatly deceived in their strength . . .' SB, p. 85.

138 'I swam them over one at a time . . .' Ibid., p. 88.
'Friday, 13 September: In the morning we persevered along the beach . . .' Ibid., p. 90.

139 'Mr Shaw, second officer of the *Grosvenor*, died . . .' Ibid., p. 91. Habberley's refer-

ence to having sailed with Shaw to the West Indies in 1778 chimes with the second mate's record of service, evidence of the Journal's authenticity.

140 'About twenty of them surrounded us . . .' Ibid., p. 91.

141 'Wednesday, 9 October. This morning Stockdale was no better . . .' Ibid., p. 98.

142 'Saturday, 12 October. We at daylight crossed the river . . .' Ibid., p. 100.
'This dog we were rejoiced in meeting with . . .' Ibid., p. 102.

143 'Some of them made motions and talked much . . .' Ibid., p. 105.

144 'Not a night since the ship was lost could equal this . . .' Ibid., p. 107.

12 'A Sacred Charge'

145 'the most beautiful and affecting I know associated with a shipwreck'. Dickens's essay, 'The Long Voyage'.

146 'Master Law was first carried by William Thomson . . .' SB, p. 43.

148 'I cannot help lamenting that persons in so perilous a situation . . .' CA, p. 54.

149 'The evidence of the survivors at this stage . . .' Kirby, *True Story*, p. 87.
'. . . treated the individuals that fell singly among them . . .' SB, p. 31.

150 'So apprehensive were the natives of the strangers . . .' CA, p. 72.
'contained in a small basket . . .' Ibid., p. 58.
'The natives, however, no sooner saw . . .' Ibid., p. 49.

151 'borne the inconveniences of so long a journey . . .' Ibid., p. 47.
'chiefly endeavoured to alleviate that fatigue . . .' Ibid., p. 54.

152 'in as just and striking a manner . . .' Ibid., p. 93.

153 [conduct] 'so humane and generous will most assuredly atone . . .' Ibid., p. 54.
'God knows all he does for the poor baby . . .' Dickens, 'The Long Voyage'.

154 'when any could not furnish himself with a draught of urine . . .' CA, p. 97.
'May the Devil cut my right hand off . . .' Ibid., p. 98.
The *Peggy* episode, and the even better-known story of cannibalism at sea involving the crew of the whaleship *Essex*, are told in Nathaniel Philbrick's *In the Heart of the Sea*.

155 'they buried him and said prayers over him . . .' SB, p. 48.
The men's state of abject starvation, and the fact that cannibalism had been proposed on at least one occasion already, adds a slightly suggestive hint to Carter's description of the 'flesh of a young seal which they found close to the steward's grave . . .' CA p. 104.
'Immediately he ran to him as fast as he could . . .' Ibid.

156 '. . . the joy that instantly beamed forth in every breast . . .' CA, p. 110.

13 Caliban Transformed

157 The description of the nabobs, characteristic of the author's style, is in Morris, p. 8.

158 'In despair of any relief, I saw nothing but death before me . . .' Defoe, *Robinson Crusoe*, p. 73 (Penguin Popular Classics edition).

'I gave myself up to grief, unheard and unpitied . . .' SB, p. 110.

159 'So I went and, carefully picking it up . . .' SB, p. 111.
'He sat down, and made motions for me to do the same . . .' Ibid.

160 For Dutch settlement and a history of the frontier wars, see Mostert's *Frontiers*.
'much troubled in my bowels'. SB, p. 112.

161 '. . . the natives had always behaved extremely well to him . . .' Ibid., p. 116. The experiences of Lewis, and of the Italians Bianco and Paro, are so at variance with those described by most of the seamen that it may be suggested some of their mistreatment was exaggerated. At the same time, Habberley's description of treatment both harsh and kind has the ring of authenticity.

162 'Some of my friends hinted to my adversary . . .' Ibid., pp. 117–8.

163 'The women, who are likewise well proportioned . . .' CA, p. 38.
Hlobonga technique is described in Stuart, vol. 4, pp. 299–300 by Ndukwana ka Mbengwana: 'A girl is not penetrated. She crosses her legs and tightens them as she feels the man is about to spend, and the man spends on her thighs. If the man has ejaculated incorrectly, she will point it out at the time in case she becomes pregnant.'
'that he would sooner live and die where he was . . . .' SB, pp. 116–17.

164 'I could not help from shedding a tear . . .' Ibid., p. 119.

165 'a body of men on horseback with fire-arms . . .' Ibid.
The raising of the Muller expedition, and its report, are contained in *A Source Book*, pp. 152–91.

166 'The weather was fine, the house being on the side of a hill . . .' SB, p. 121.

168 'All the people from the ship had passed along the beach . . .' SB, p. 179.
'. . . as they had not waited to learn whether any of the shipwrecked people were still there . . .' Kirby, *The Van Reenen Expedition*, p. 13.

169 The names of the lascars are contained in a note in the Kirby papers, HSL.

14 The Fate of William Hosea

170 Dalrymple noted that Coxon was 'out of heart'. One early newspaper report described the captain's conduct as 'well-collected, patient and brave', but this was unsourced and no statement by any of the seamen redounds to his credit, and the evidence against him is damning. Kirby's assessment is generous, to say the least, perversely so in the case of a judgment that the captain abandoned his passengers 'doubtless in order to try to obtain the help that he imagined would not be procured by the sailors if and when they got to safety' (*True Story*, p. 93). I can only surmise that Kirby's avowed friendship with Commander Alfred Coxon RN, a great-great-grandson of the captain, whose 'constant interest and willing cooperation' he acknowledged, clouded his judgment on this question.
'beautiful and delicate women . . .' CA, pp. 30–31.

171 '. . . that Captain Coxon, Mr Newman . . .' SB, p. 87.

172 There are numerous accounts of the *Birkenhead* disaster. See Mostert, pp. 1138–41, for example.

173 'spoken of as well-collected, patient and brave . . .' The *Morning Post and Daily Advertiser*, 26 July 1783.

174 'One was servant to Mrs Hosea . . .' SB, p. 126. Interestingly, Dalrymple took no note of Habberley's account of his conversation with the *ayahs*, which is found only in his Journal.

175 'I have long since made a resolution never to leave . . .' Hosea to Lady Chambers, 9 November 1781, MA.

176 'I have the feeling that this torrent of visions . . .' Leslie, p. 370.

177 'she had seen Captain Coxon's coat . . .' SB, p. 126. Among the sources who said sailors had been murdered was Gquma's daughter, Bessie. See chapter 19.
The recovery of Charles Newman's buttons is described in Kirby, *The Van Reenen Expedition*, pp. 26–7.

178 The story of Johann Bock was related in an article, 'Diamonds from the *Grosvenor*', in *Africana Notes and News* by H. F. Sampson, the lawyer who defended the old prospector at his trial. Recent developments have been reported in the East London *Dispatch*, e.g. of 19 November 2002.

179 '. . . we thought it impossible for him to [swim] . . .' SB, p. 95.

15 'The Vilest Brutish Prostitution'

180 The appearance of Warmington and Leary before the Company's directors was reported in the *Morning Chronicle and London Advertiser* of 23 July 1783.

181 '. . . the Caffres had come down on the people, carried off the female passengers . . .' The *Morning Chronicle and London Advertiser*, 23 April 1783.
'The situation of the female passengers . . .' Ibid., 25 April 1783.
'not being able to support the idea of the fate . . .' Ibid., 28 April 1783.
'A detachment of Dutch and French troops . . .' Ibid., 2 May 1783.

182 '. . . flocked to the coast and, stripping them all . . .' Ibid., 10 July 1783.

183 'the jacks got drunk and committed every excess . . .' *Calcutta Gazette*, 23 February 1792.

184 'It is with concern that I have to inform you . . .' Unsigned and unaddressed note among *Grosvenor* papers, MA.
'. . . a Mrs Logy the wife of the former chief mate . . .' Fowke letters in Mss/Eur/E4 K24 in OIOC. This letter, of 11 August 1783, is based on the report read by Thomas Law.
'on coming to himself begged that Lady Chambers might be kept ignorant . . .' Ibid. Margaret to Francis Fowke, 18 August 1783.

185 'The circumstance of Sir Robert's child being on board the *Grosvenor* . . .' Ibid. S. Stephenson to Margaret Fowke, 22 October 1783.
'At this rate one may as well mount a forlorn hope as go into an Indiaman.' Ibid. Margaret to Francis, 13 August 1783.
'I make frequent enquiries . . .' Ibid., 16 August 1783.
'Due to the unsettled state of the country . . .' Ibid., 20 August 1783.

'Loss of the Grosvenor . . .' and 'The deep shall give up her dead . . .' Fragments in MA. It has been suggested that these items were written by Hosea's mother, but they are in the hand of Lady Chambers. A number of letters and notes from the Chambers family were passed to this repository by the Africana collector, John Gubbins, although how he acquired them is unknown.
'The many lies my friends have at different times invented . . .' Chambers' letters in Mss/Eur/E5 K26, Lady Chambers to Margaret Fowke, 20 March 1783, OIOC.

186 'I make no doubt that you must have long since heard . . .' Sarah Brown to Lady Chambers, 2 May 1784, MA.
The inscription to Thomas Chambers is taken from Kathleen Blechynden, p. 178.

187 The seventy-three volumes of Blechynden's diaries are held in the Manuscripts Collection, the British Library, Add. 45578–45663. This entry from Add. 45581, MSS.
'passed a very disagreeable night . . .' Add. 45585, 16 December 1792, MSS.
'the uncertain circumstances of the case left to imagination . . .' Contained in the brief memoir by Lady Chambers in her Catalogue of the Sanskrit Manuscripts collected by her husband in the British Library.
'Consider the distress of the parents . . .' Chapman, *Letters*, vol. 3, p. 90.

188 'The natives never offered to carry away Mrs Logie . . .' SB, p. 39.

189 'I cannot doubt that many lives may yet be preserved . . .' Ibid. p. 31.
'as a vessel belonging to His Majesty . . .' Ibid., pp. 18–19.
'orders to go in quest of the Grosvenor's crew . . .' SB, p. 22.

190 'Captain D'Auvergne who arrived about two months ago . . .' Orme to Sir William Jones, Eu/Orme/OV 214, OIOC.
'The story of the *Grosvenor* closed . . .' Blechynden, pp. 181–2. Kathleen's phlegmatic acceptance that her great-grandfather's sister had assimilated with 'savages' was unusual for a memsahib of the Victorian age, but may have been conditioned by the fact that she was herself of mixed Anglo-Indian descent, being a product of Richard's union with his *bibi*, referred to in his diary as 'Sally'.

16 African Crusoes

I have resorted to some speculation here. The accounts of Bryan and Glover's lives among the Pondo are based on the few fragmentary references in the accounts by Fynn and Farewell, a reading of Pondo life and culture based on the writings of Monica Wilson (née Hunter) and personal observation. For the desperate life of an English footsoldier in India see Colley, pp. 269–307.

202 'The chief sends a black beast without spot . . .' Hunter, pp. 80–1.

203 'loving one another with a most remarkable strength of affection'. Moodie, p. 431.
The account of the Portuguese seaman found by the Dutch is in Moodie, p. 431.

204 Fynn confirms that Bryan had just the one wife.

205 'He was in despair on account of the loss of his wife . . .' Fynn, pp. 112–13.
For Selkirk's life as a castaway, see Souhami.

17 The Quest

207 Details of Richard Blechynden's life are gleaned from his diary in the Manuscripts Collection at the British Library – Add. 45578–45663 – and 'Clash of Cultures? An Englishman in Calcutta in the 1790s', a lecture by Peter Robb, Professor of the History of India at the University of London, on 12 March 1998.
'*The lateſt accounts concerning the Groſvenor Indiaman . . .*' *Calcutta Gazette*, No 417.
208 'a delicate young female, tenderly brought up . . .' Add. 45582, MSS.
'no mention by how this account had come . . .' and 'Improbable I may say . . .' Ibid.
210 'Impossible! . . .' and 'I will yield for arguments sake . . .' Ibid.
212 'The idea of these miserable people haunted me . . .' Le Vaillant, vol. 2, p. 208.
213 The delegation of 'Kaffers and Gonakwas' is mentioned in Kirby, *The Van Reenen Expedition*, p. 16.
'Lt Col Gordon a very well informed & ingenious man . . .' is part of a Macartney diary fragment held by the Department of Historical Papers at the University of the Witwatersrand.
214 'He said that in his travels . . .' Mackaness (ed.), pp. 29–30.
215 'with the positive assurance of the *Grosvenor Stranders* being dead'. Add. 45582, 23 February 1792, MSS.
The picture of the *Grosvenor* is mentioned in Add. 45599, 10 November 1796, MSS.
The December entries are contained in Add. 45585, MSS.
216 'I am very sorry for this . . .' Add. 45596, 2 January 1796, MSS.
'10 November, 1796: Perneau called on me to visit . . .' Add. 45599, MSS.
The background to the second rescue expedition is comprehensively described in Kirby's *Jacob van Reenen and the Grosvenor Expedition of 1790–1791*.
217 '. . . a kraal of Christian bastaards . . .' Ibid., p. 101.
218 'They were deeply moved to see people of their race.' Ibid., p. 106.
'Our fathers are come . . .' Thompson, vol. 1, p. 353. Peter Lombard, a member of the party, told Thompson in 1822 of this cry of rejoicing by the 'mullato tribe'.

18 'Our Fathers Are Come'

219 Accounts of the women being deserted were provided by the lascar and *ayahs*.
222 Corneille's report was relayed, as we have seen, in the British press.
For Gquma and the amaTshomane, see following chapter.
223 'We found no one there . . .' Kirby, *Van Reenen*, p. 111.
'We found three old women who said they were sisters . . .' Ibid., p. 101.
'nothing except a few pieces of cannon . . .' Ibid., p. 104.
224 'I now wanted to take the old women with me . . .' Ibid., p. 106.
225 'It should not be dismissed as impossible . . .' *South African Magazine*, May 1906, p. 42.
'She distinctly recollected the wreck of the Grosvenor . . .' Shaw's diary, ref. SM114a, is in the history section of the Albany Museum, Grahamstown.
226 'large and beautiful gardens which they had planted . . .' Kirby, *Van Reenen*, pp. 101–2.

'decided that it would be inexpedient . . .' Kirby, *True Story*, p. 142.

227 'of an extraordinary people, far to the north . . .' Lichtenstein, vol. 1, pp. 368–9.
'. . . the wreck of the Grosvenor East Indiaman . . .' Farewell's memoir was in his *Account of Chaka*, published as an appendix to the 1833 edition of Owen's *Narrative of a Voyage*.

228 'Men went to gather mussels and found a white girl . . .' Stuart, vol. 2, p. 115.

229 '. . . a very old white woman living exactly as a native . . .' Stuart, vol. 1, p. 62.
There is a protean quality to the legend of the women, which seems to hold up a mirror to prevailing values: initial horror at the notion of sexual captivity at the hands of 'savages' giving way to racist pathology over black–white union, followed by revisionisms of various sorts. I am conscious of having come to the subject at a time when assimilation has acquired a more romantic hue, but the evidence for it is none the less persuasive for that.

19 Gquma's Tribe

231 Linda Colley's *Captives* casts a refreshing and vivid light on captivity narratives.

233 Chase's execrable verse is contained in his scrapbook held at the Brenthurst Library in Johannesburg.

234 '. . . there is now residing a Caffre with a numerous family . . .' Wesleyan Methodist Missionary Society Annual Reports, 1827, p. 43, SOAS.
'It will really be a most surprising occurrence . . .' WMMS correspondence, 31 August 1827, SOAS.
[evidence] 'of the *Grosvenor* and its unfortunate crew'. WMMS correspondence, 30 September 1827, SOAS.
'Deep ravines, the sea . . .' Kay, p. 355.

235 'He is nearly seventy years of age . . .' WMMS correspondence, 30 September 1827, SOAS.
'Of the Christian religion he seems never to have heard a word . . .' Ibid.

236 'Praise the Lord! . . .' WMMS correspondence, 31 March 1829, SOAS.
'Qanda urges: "Your mother was married to my brother" . . .' WMMS Annual Reports 1828, p. 67, SOAS.
'It is truly affecting to see so many . . .' WMMS correspondence, 30 June 1829, SOAS.

237 'was more than ordinarily attached to her . . .' and 'When our eyes saw Gquma . . .' Kay, p. 357.
'She used to dress in native costume . . .' Fynn, p. 112.

238 [She] 'lived to a good old age and went down to the grave full of days'. Kay, p. 358.
Van Reenen related his meeting with Gquma to Lady Anne Barnard, wife to the Secretary at the Cape Colony, in 1798. Far from being horrified, the spirited Lady Anne wrote to a friend: 'She still lives and proposes coming to the Cape. I wish she would make her words good while I am here; I should be very glad to give old Caffraria an apartment in the Castle [the official residence].' See Robinson, pp. 131–2.

'Two seem either to have married persons of inferior rank . . .' Kay, pp. 356–7.
'she distinctly recollected the wreck of the Grosvenor . . .' Autograph Journal by Shaw, dated 29 June 1828, in the Albany Museum, Grahamstown.

239 'When I directed him to pray to God for it . . .' WMMS correspondence, 31 April 1833, SOAS.
'it all appeared a mystery to him'. WMMS correspondence, 17 August 1831, SOAS.
'When I directed her to pray to God . . .' WMMS correspondence, 22 Aug 1833, SOAS.

240 What records of the *Dolphin* survive are in L/Mar/B/633C in the OIOC.
'that this must be the rock the *Dolphin* was lost upon . . .' Contained in the account of Evan Jones, chief mate of the *Dodington*, reprinted in the *Indian Antiquary*, October 1901, p. 455.

241 The practice of polygamy makes African genealogies especially awkward. The subject of Gquma's descendants is dealt with in some detail in Kirby's article in *African Studies*, vol. 13, 1954. The same article quotes the elder Xelo to establish Nosepesi's marriage to Ngangelizwe. However, Kirby's genealogical table is incorrect in indicating that Nosepesi was mother to Dalindyebo.

20 'When the Long Trick's Over'

243 The log of the *Manship* is L/Mar/B/363A in the OIOC .

244 'found that the sad impression . . .' CA, p. 126.
'not to be accounted for'. Ibid., p. 130.
'beating with such violence . . .' Ibid., p. 127.

245 Hynes is listed as a crewman on both legs of the voyage, Leary only homeward bound. Their pay is given in the *Manship*'s pay book, L/Mar/B/363H.
Details of Warmington's later life obtained from descendants; so too Habberley's. The latter's visits to Sarah Williams in Walthamstow were described in a letter from Elma Hailey dated 30 May 1961, found in the Kirby papers, HSL. I have been unable to trace the descendants of Williams and Tayor, or find the portrait of Williams 'by or after Gainsborough'.

247 'sailors' women, inured to immorality from childhood . . .' Ackroyd, p. 554.

249 'no conquests, or riches, or easy complacencies . . .' Colley, p. 2.

250 Captain Dempster's note to Lady Chambers is among the *Grosvenor* papers at MA.
The Windsor meeting with Charlotte Hosea is described in Mirza, vol. 1, pp. 223–4.

Epilogue

255 The hunt for the '*Grosvenor* treasure' is exhaustively covered in Kirby, the *True Story*, pp. 181–246.

258 Steve Valentine's account from interview with the author.

259 Further details of the *Grosvenor* salvage operation obtained in interviews with Jonathan Sharfman and John Gribble. The retrieved objects have been placed on permanent display at the East London Museum.

LIST OF ILLUSTRATIONS

The author and publishers would like to thank the following individuals and institutions for permission to reproduce illustrations. Particular thanks are due to the generosity of Museum Africa in Johannesburg for permitting reproduction of some items from its Catalogue of Prints.

Plate section: Museum Africa, Johannesburg 11, 12, 13, 14, 15; Gerald Johnson Fox 5, 9; William Fehr Collection, Cape Town 1; National Maritime Museum, London 6, 7; Derek Bayes/Aspect Picture Library, 8; Steve Valentine 16; National Museums & Galleries on Merseyside 10.

INDEX